GCSE CHINESE (9-1)

SPEAKING AND LISTENING REVISION GUIDE

中学汉语听说指南

Alice Webb

华语教学出版社 · 伦敦
Sinolingua · London

Endorsed for
**Pearson Edexcel
Qualifications**

GCSE CHINESE (9-1) SPEAKING AND LISTENING REVISION GUIDE

Written by Alice Webb

Commissioning editor: Ranran DU

Chinese editor: Ranran DU; Fenfen BAO

English proofreader: Rory Howard

Cover design: Beijing Qing Tao Han Culture Development Co., Ltd.

Layout/Illustrations: GEOMETRIC ORIGINAL ARTISTIC DESIGN Co., Ltd.

Copyright © 2022 Sinolingua London Limited

First published in Great Britain in July 2022 by Sinolingua London Limited

Unit 13 Park Royal Metro Centre

Britannia Way

London, NW10 7PA

United Kingdom

Tel: 0044(0)2089611919

Email: editor@sinolingualondon.com

Printed in China 2022

ISBN 978-1-907838-62-0

Endorsement Statement

In order to ensure that this resource offers high-quality support for the associated Pearson qualification, it has been through a review process by the awarding body. This process confirms that this resource fully covers the teaching and learning content of the specification or part of a specification at which it is aimed. It also confirms that it demonstrates an appropriate balance between the development of subject skills, knowledge and understanding, in addition to preparation for assessment.

Endorsement does not cover any guidance on assessment activities or processes (e.g. practice questions or advice on how to answer assessment questions), included in the resource nor does it prescribe any particular approach to the teaching or delivery of a related course.

While the publishers have made every attempt to ensure that advice on the qualification and its assessment is accurate, the official specification and associated assessment guidance materials are the only authoritative source of information and should always be referred to for definitive guidance.

Pearson examiners have not contributed to any sections in this resource relevant to examination papers for which they have responsibility.

Examiners will not use endorsed resources as a source of material for any assessment set by Pearson.
Endorsement of a resource does not mean that the resource is required to achieve this Pearson qualification, nor does it mean that it is the only suitable material available to support the qualification, and any resource lists produced by the awarding body shall include this and other appropriate resources.

User Guide

As the sequel to the GCSE Chinese Writing Revision Guide that I co-authored in 2017, this book makes a further attempt to give a comprehensive account of the GCSE Chinese revision process, aiming to help teachers and students in their teaching and learning of GCSE Chinese vocabulary, key grammar points, listening comprehension and spoken communicative skills. As a front-line GCSE teaching practitioner, I have gathered much feedback and valuable suggestions from teachers and students who have been using the GCSE Chinese Writing Revision Guide. This book now offers further improvements in many areas and hopefully will be one of the main teaching and learning resources in Chinese classrooms and in independent revision for achieving at GCSE level.

1. Corresponding to the GCSE Chinese Writing Revision Guide, many features in that book are retained or adapted with a shift of emphasis on helping students to develop their listening comprehension and speaking skills. This includes a range of language and grammatical structures that are more concentrated on minimum core vocabulary at GCSE level, concerning the nature and difficulty of the spoken language.

2. The six chapters cover all the GCSE themes and topics, with the contents of the first half of each chapter (Unit 1, 2, 5, 6, 9, 10, 13, 14, 17 and 20) preparing students for Foundation Tier and the second half (Unit 3, 4, 7, 8, 11, 12, 15, 16, 18, 19, 21 and 22) targeting the Higher Tier. Teachers and students do not have to teach and study every single unit and part of the book. They can certainly select the topics according to their scheme of work or revision plan, e.g. choose the unit topic where they feel that there are weaknesses they need to work upon.

3. The aim and objectives for each part of all units comprise of:
   Part 1: revision on GCSE core vocabulary and key grammar points
   Part 2: role-play / picture-based task activities with tips
   Part 3: listening comprehension exercises with tips
   Part 4: general conversation under the topic with tips
   Part 5: key question words and vocabulary list under the topic

4. Throughout the book are provided exam techniques and communicative strategies, such as Role Play Tips, Picture-based Task Tips, 12-Minute Preparation Tips, Listening Tips and Conversation Tips. Many key points are repeated, such as 12-Minute Preparation Tips, Role Play Tips and Picture-based Task Tips, so that students will not miss out the important points no matter which chapter or unit they choose to study.

5. With a key vocabulary list focused on 20 words per unit and key question words summarised at the end of each unit, it will help teachers and students conduct structured revision, such as planning for a routine weekly vocabulary test.

6. Grammar Notes boxes are retained and improved with many exercises to provide and enhance students' learning.

7. Question Words boxes are introduced to support spoken conversation. Relevant listening exercises and speaking tasks are designed to consolidate students' understanding.

8. Whilst the transcripts of all listening and speaking activities are provided, these activities can easily be adapted as reading and written exercises. Free downloadable audio recordings are provided by the QR code at the back of the book.

9. Most of the Part 3 GCSE exam style listening questions are adapted from the GCSE Chinese Writing Revision Guide with a focus on listening comprehension and approached from a listening point of view. They can be supplemented with each other or substituted for each other, such as using the listening questions as reading questions by providing the transcript to students.

10. Many Part 4 GCSE exam style conversation activities include some of the corresponding exam writing practice in GCSE Chinese Writing Revision Guide. They can be supplemented with each other or substituted for each other, such as adapting the questions in conversation as bullet points in English for writing tasks.

In conclusion I believe that this Edexcel GCSE Chinese Speaking Revision Guide will become an essential tool for both teachers and students in their quest to achieve well in Chinese Mandarin at GCSE level.

About the Author

Alice Webb is Head of Mandarin at Benenden School in Kent. She is an experienced Chinese teaching practitioner having worked extensively in both state comprehensive and grammar schools as well as schools in the private sector. She is an associate lecturer in Chinese for the Open University and also Chief Examiner in Chinese for a leading UK examining board including developing GCSE examination specifications and writing GCSE papers, together with conducting teacher-training sessions commissioned by the exam board.

CHAPTER ONE

My Life and My Friends
我的生活和朋友

Unit 1 My Family

第一单元 我的家庭

 Part One Warming Up

1.1 Listen to Track 1.1.1 and match these words or phrases with their English translations. Put the correct number into the second column.

A. family members	
B. birthday party	
C. child/children	
D. family	
E. friend(s)	
F. married	
G. years old	

1.2 Listen to Track 1.1.2 and sort these words or phrases into the categories below. Put each number next to an appropriate category.

A. family members

_____

B. profession

_____

C. things you do with family

_____

GRAMMAR NOTES: FUTURE EVENTS

You may consider using one of the following structures to talk about a future event.

(1) Use a verb, such as 要 / 想 / 会 / 打算 / 计划 / 希望 + another verb.

我要开一个生日会。(I'm going to have a birthday party.)

(2) Use the structures that signify something will soon happen, such as 要 / 快 / 快要 + verb + 了.

姐姐要结婚了。(My elder sister is getting married.)

(3) Use a time expression, such as 明年 (next year), 下个月 (next month), 一个星期以后 (in a week's time), etc. These time phrases should always be placed at the beginning of the sentence or before the verbs they modify.

下个月，我爷爷奶奶要来看我们。(Next month, my grandpa and grandma are coming to visit us.)

1.3 Listen to Track 1.1.3 and translate these questions about birthdays into English.

1. _____

2. _____

3. _____

4. _____

GRAMMAR NOTES: PAST EVENTS

Completed actions are expressed by adding a past time expression, such as 上个月, 昨天, at the head of the sentence or before the verb, and then the past-time aspect marker 了 placed after the action verb.

昨天我打了网球。(Yesterday I played tennis.)

To express an action carried out over a period of time in the past, you only need to use a time expression. There is no need to add 了.

三岁的时候，我和爷爷奶奶一起住。(I lived with my grandparents when I was three.)

1.4 Listen to Track 1.1.4, the questions in the previous exercise. Answer each question in Chinese. The first question has been answered for you as an example.

EXAMPLE 》》》 (You hear) 1. 你的生日是几月几日？
(You answer) 我的生日是十月二十六日。

2. _____

3. _____

4. _____

● **QUESTION WORDS: 怎么样**

When asking for someone's opinion about something, the useful pattern to use is: 觉得 + something / somebody + 怎么样

你觉得伦敦怎么样？ (What do you think of London?)

Or you can make a statement or a suggestion first, and then ask for the other person's opinion.

我们给奶奶开一个生日会，你觉得怎么样？ (Let's have a birthday party for Grandma. What do you think?)

1.5 Read the Question Words box on 怎么样 and ask the following questions in Chinese, using 怎么样.

1. How is your school?

2. How is the weather in Beijing?

3. What do you think of Chinese food?

4. I like American films. What do you think?

1.6 Listen to Track 1.1.6 and give each statement a question, using the question words provided in the brackets.

EXAMPLE 》》》

(You hear) 小明昨天参加了朋友的生日会。
(You hear) Ask when.
(You answer) 小明什么时候参加了朋友的生日会？

1. (What date — 几月几日)

_____

2. (Where — 哪儿)

_____

3. (When — 什么时候)

_____

4. (Whom — 谁)

_____

2 Part Two Role Play

Your grandparent comes to visit your new house. You two are having a chat. Your teacher or your classmate will play the role of your grandparent; or you may use the recorded questions (Track 1.2.1).

Use appropriate language for an informal conversation.
You will talk to the teacher or your classmate using the five prompts below.
- When you see – ? – you must ask a question.
- When you see – ! – you must respond to something you have not prepared.

> ### Task
> **Your grandparent comes to visit your new house. You two have a chat.**
> 1. Say your age.
> 2. Give your opinion of your new house.
> 3. !
> 4. Tell him/her when you are going to visit him/her.
> 5. ? Ask your grandparent if he/she likes shopping.

These questions have been recorded for you. Listen to Track 1.2.1, pause after each question and speak in the gaps. Track 1.2.2 provides example answers.

ROLE PLAY TIPS

There are three purposes of role play:
(1) Do you understand the questions?
(2) Can you answer the questions?
(3) Can you ask a question?
So, once you have fully answered the question using appropriate language, you don't need to say more. Wait for the next one.

3 Part Three Listening Comprehension

Matthew has sent four voice messages to his teacher Mrs Ma about his exchange visit to Beijing. Listen to Track 1.3 and put a cross ✕ in the correct box for each question.

1. How long has Matthew been in Beijing?

   ☐ A. a day   ☐ B. a week   ☐ C. a month

2. Who does Matthew's Chinese friend, Li Xiaoshan, live with?

   ☐ A. his mum   ☐ B. his mum and dad   ☐ C. his mum, dad and siblings

3. What does Matthew say about Peking duck?

   ☐ A. He heard it is delicious.   ☐ B. It is the best in the world.

   ☐ C. It is better than the roast duck in the UK.

4. Why is Matthew not interested in Peking opera?

   ☐ A. It's too long.   ☐ B. It's too noisy.   ☐ C. He prefers Italian opera.

LISTENING TIPS

You must read the questions carefully as they often provide essential information for you to understand the context or scenario.

In the first question, the question suggests you focus on the length of time that Matthew has been in Beijing. You should first recall your understanding of this type of sentence structure in Chinese when talking about the duration of an action. The length of time would normally come after the verb. You may then expect the answer will come at a later part of the sentence according to the word order.

4 Part Four Conversation

Answer the following questions. These questions have been recorded for you in Track 1.4.1. Listen to that track, pause after each question and speak in the gaps. Track 1.4.2 provides example answers.

1. 说说你自己，好吗？

2. 你们家有几口人？

3. 你喜欢宠物吗？为什么？

4. 去年夏天，你和家人去了哪儿？

5. 这个周末，你想和家人一起做什么？

CONVERSATION TIPS

The following provides some tips and suggested content for you to consider.

1. You could introduce your name, your age and what you do.

2. You could say the number of people in your family and who they are. You may also introduce their hobbies and jobs.

3. You could give your opinion about whether you like or dislike pets. If you like pets you may also say if you have any. Remember to justify your opinion by giving a reason or two using 因为 .

4. You could say where you went and what you did with one or more of your family members last summer, and how you felt about it.

5. You could say some simple and familiar things that you often do with your family, such as having dinner, watching TV or going shopping together. You may consider using the sequence words 先……再……然后…… to link these activities up.

5 Part Five Wrapping Up

5.1 Key question words and phrases covered in this unit

1	吗	ma	(a question particle used at the end of a sentence to turn a statement into a yes-no question)
2	好吗	hǎo ma	okay?
3	几	jǐ	how many
4	哪儿	nǎ er	where
5	什么	shén me	what
6	什么时候	shén me shí hou	when
7	为什么	wèi shén me	why
8	谁	shuí	who
9	多大	duō dà	how old
10	怎么样 ★	zěn me yang	how about (see "Question Words" box in Part One)

5.2 Key words and expressions covered in this unit

1	爸爸	bà ba	dad
2	妈妈	mā ma	mum
3	哥哥	gē ge	elder brother
4	姐姐	jiě jie	elder sister
5	弟弟	dì di	younger brother
6	妹妹	mèi mei	younger sister
7	爷爷	yé ye	granddad
8	奶奶	nǎi nai	grandma
9	家人	jiā rén	family (member)
10	朋友	péng you	friend
11	宠物	chǒng wù	pet
12	岁	suì	years old
13	出生	chū shēng	to be born
14	过生日	guò shēng rì	to celebrate a birthday
15	开生日会	kāi shēng rì huì	to hold a birthday party
16	结婚	jié hūn	to get married
17	离婚	lí hūn	to be divorced
18	爱	ài	love
19	看	kàn	to look at; to see; to watch; to visit (a person)
20	房间	fáng jiān	room

Unit 2 My Hobbies

第二单元 我的爱好

 Part One Warming Up

1.1 Listen to Track 2.1.1 and match the words or phrases with the right images. Each image has a letter. Put the correct letter into the second column.

1	
2	
3	
4	
5	
6	
7	
8	
9	

A. B. C.

D. E. F.

G. H. I.

1.2 Listen to Track 2.1.2 and sort these words or phrases into the categories below. Write the English translation next to an appropriate category.

看		打	1. making a phone call	玩儿	

1.3 Are there any activities in 1.1 or 1.2 that you like? If so, complete Sentence 1 with three of them. You may use different hobbies of your own choice. In Sentence 2, specify which is your favourite using the expression 我最喜欢 **.**

1. 我的爱好是 ＿＿＿＿＿＿＿＿、＿＿＿＿＿＿＿＿ 和 ＿＿＿＿＿＿＿＿。

2. 我最喜欢＿＿＿＿＿＿＿＿。

To express the meaning "apart from...also...", use the structure 除了……也 / 还…….

除了英语，他也 / 还会说法语。(Apart from English, he can also speak French.)

以外 is often attached to the end of the first part if you want to emphasise "apart from".

除了打网球以外，我弟弟还喜欢打篮球。(Apart from playing tennis, my younger brother also likes playing basketball.)

1.4 Read the Grammar Notes box about 除了 …… 也 / 还 …… **then translate phrases A - F into the spaces in the second column below. Next, listen to Track 2.1.4, which gives phrases to complete sentences A – F. Put the appropriate letter into the table alongside.**

	Translation
A. 我也爱玩电脑游戏。	A.
B. 还会下雨。	B.
C. 我们星期三也有中文课。	C. We also have a Chinese lesson on Wednesday.
D. 我也去过上海。	D.
E. 她还有中文书。	E.
F. 你们还想吃什么？	F.

1	C
2	
3	
4	
5	
6	

● **QUESTION WORDS:** 什么 (1)

When asking a "what" question, you may use 什么 .

Unlike English, in Chinese, when you ask about an object, you do not bring 什么 to the beginning of a question. Thinking in "Chinglish" (Chinese style English) is a good way to organise this type of question. For example, the question "what is..." in "Chinglish" is ……是什么 (...is what).

Using a similar concept, you may ask questions, such as 吃什么 (eat what), 做什么 (do what), etc. For example, you could ask someone to repeat by asking:

你说什么？ (What did you say?)

1.5 Read the Question Words box about the question word 什么 and ask the following questions in Chinese, using 什么 .

1. What is your friend's name?

2. What is your hobby?

3. What do you like to eat?

4. What do you do on weekends?

1.6 Extend the short sentence 我上网 into six longer sentences by adding different components to the previous sentence as directed, paying special attention to the word order. You may work with Track 2.1.6, which provides a sample answer. You could say your sentence first, play the sample sentence and then pause the recording, say your next sentence in the gap, and then play the next sentence, and so on.

1. Add an adverb to indicate you do this often, e.g. 常常 .

wǒ cháng cháng shàng wǎng

我　常　常　上　网。

———————————————————————

2. Add a time expression to Sentence 1 above to indicate when you do this often, e.g. 周末 .

———————————————————————

3. Add a verbal phrase to Sentence 2 above to indicate what you go online for, e.g. 聊天 .

———————————————————————

4. Add a noun phrase to Sentence 3 above to indicate with whom you do the activity, e.g. 和朋友 .

———————————————————————

5. Add a phrase to Sentence 4 above to indicate on which internet site you engage in this online activity, e.g. 在社交网站上 .

———————————————————————

6. Finally, add a sentence to indicate how you feel about it, e.g. "I feel happy".

———————————————————————

2 **Part Two** Picture-based Task

■ **Look at the picture and prepare statements to the following.**

1. a description of the photograph
2. your opinion on doing exercises
3. a sport you did last week
4. a new sport that you would like to do
5. who you would like to do this sport with

Questions relating to the above have been recorded for you. Listen to 2.2.1, pause after each question and speak in the gaps. Track 2.2.2 provides example answers.

PICTURE-BASED TASK TIPS

The purpose of the picture-based task is to assess communication through:
(1) expressing opinions;
(2) providing descriptions;
(3) narrating events.
So, apart from answering all the questions, you must develop your responses as well as you can by saying at least a couple more sentences.

Part Three Listening Comprehension

Lily is talking about a Chinese film she just watched. Listen to Track 2.3 and put a cross ✕ in each one of the three correct boxes.

Example	She likes learning Chinese.	✕
A	It is a famous Chinese film.	
B	The story is a bit boring.	
C	She often watches Chinese films.	
D	Her parents want her to learn Chinese.	
E	The film has English subtitles.	
F	She thinks the actress is very pretty.	
G	She wouldn't watch Chinese films anymore.	

LISTENING TIPS

Try to translate statements A-G into Chinese as much as you can and write down the key words in either Chinese characters or in pinyin. It will help you to be more focused on the key points when you listen to the recording, especially when the recording is a bit lengthy.

⬤ GRAMMAR NOTES ON 因为 AND 所以 ⬤

You may use 因为 (because) to give a reason.

(1) You can first state the result, then use 因为 to give the reason.

我爱说汉语，因为我觉得汉语很好听。(I love speaking Chinese because I think it sounds very nice.)

(2) You can also give the reason first with 因为 , and then use 所以 (therefore) to state the result.

因为作业太多，所以我不能和朋友们一起踢足球。(There is too much schoolwork, therefore I can't play football with friends.)

4 Part Four Conversation

Answer the following questions. These questions have been recorded for you in Track 2.4.1. Listen to that track, pause after each question and speak in the gaps. Track 2.4.2 provides sample answers.

1. 你的爱好是什么？

2. 你喜欢看哪国的电影？为什么？

3. 说说你最近看过的一个电影。

4. 你觉得中国音乐怎么样？

5. 你最想听谁的音乐会？

CONVERSATION TIPS

The following provides some tips and suggested content for you to consider.

1. You could use 除了……也…… to make an impressive sentence to list 2-3 of your hobbies.

2. There are two parts to this question. You should first say which country's or countries' films you like and then give your reason or reasons starting with 因为 .

3. It can be challenging to retell a story if you feel you lack the vocabulary. The best thing to do is to stick to plain and simple language, giving only a brief idea of the film rather than describing it in detail.

4. When answering a 怎么样 question, use one or two of the adjectives you have learnt so far and apply them.

5. You should never shy away from telling the truth. If you have little vocabulary to answer the question, tell your teacher in Chinese that you have not learnt this before and you want to in the future. This approach would go towards starting a good conversation. You could also take the opportunity to ask your teacher a question. In fact, demonstrating an ability to ask questions is a requirement of the GCSE Chinese syllabus. You could ask your teacher the name of a popular Chinese singer, and in this way kill two birds with one stone.

Part Five Wrapping Up

5.1 Key question words and phrases covered in this unit

1	吗	ma	(a question particle used at the end of a sentence to turn a statement into a yes-no question)
2	……是什么 ★	shì shén me	what is... (see "Question Words" box in Part One)
3	吃什么 ★	chī shén me	what to eat (see "Question Words" box in Part One)
4	做什么 ★	zuò shén me	what to do (see "Question Words" box in Part One)
5	为什么	wèi shén me	why
6	和谁	hé shuí	with whom
7	谁的	shuí de	whose
8	哪个	nǎ ge	which
9	哪国	nǎ guó	which country
10	怎么样	zěn me yang	how about

5.2 Key words and expressions covered in this unit

1	爱好	ài hào	hobby
2	最喜欢	zuì xǐ huan	like ... best
3	上网	shàng wǎng	go online
4	打网球	dǎ wǎng qiú	play tennis
5	打篮球	dǎ lán qiú	play basketball
6	打乒乓球	dǎ pīng pāng qiú	play table tennis
7	打电话	dǎ diàn huà	make a telephone call
8	踢足球	tī zú qiú	play football
9	跑步	pǎo bù	jog
10	玩电脑游戏	wán diàn nǎo yóu xì	play computer games
11	玩 (儿) 滑板	wán (er) huá bǎn	skateboard
12	滑冰	huá bīng	ice skate
13	游泳	yóu yǒng	swim
14	看书	kàn shū	read
15	看电视	kàn diàn shì	watch TV
16	看电影	kàn diàn yǐng	watch films
17	看朋友	kàn péng you	visit friends
18	唱歌	chàng gē	sing
19	做运动	zuò yùn dòng	do exercises
20	比赛	bǐ sài	competition

Unit 3 My Friends

第三单元 我的朋友

Part One Warming Up

1.1 Listen to Track 3.1.1, the different parts of the human body. Put the correct character on the line. The first one has been done for you as an example.

1. 嘴

2.

3.

4.

5.

6.

1.2 Listen to Track 3.1.2 and match the descriptions to the people. Put the correct number on each line.

_____   _____   _____   _____

(1) adjective + noun

黑头发 (dark hair), 漂亮的眼睛 (pretty eyes)

Note: when using a multi-character adjective before the noun, you must put 的 after the adjective and before the noun.

(2) noun + adjective (known as "adjective-verb")

我的手很大。(My hands are very big.)

他的个子非常高。(He is extremely tall.)

Note: there is no need to use 是 (to be) when placing the adjective after the noun. If the adjective is only one character long, you would ordinarily put an intensifier such as 很, before it.

1.3 Read the Grammar Notes above, then describe these images, using one or both of the following sentence structures.

EXAMPLE 〉〉〉 **a.** 他 (or 她) 有 adjective + noun.
b. 他 (or 她) 的 noun + 很 + adjective-verb.

  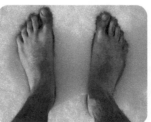 

You may first choose two or three adjective-verbs relating to the subject, then consider one of the following structures.

(1) 又……又……

她的头发又长又美丽。(Her hair is long and beautiful.)

(2) Use 也 to link two short sentences

她的头发很长，也很美丽。(Her hair is long and also beautiful.)

(3) Use 但是，可是 or 不过 to connect one positive and one negative aspect

她很漂亮，但是不太友好。(She is pretty but not very friendly.)

1.4 Think of one of your friends, say his or her name and age, then use the adjectives provided to describe him or her. Track 3.1.4 provides a sample answer.

大	dà	big
小	xiǎo	small
长	cháng	long (for length)
短	duǎn	short (for length)
高	gāo	tall (for height)
矮	ǎi	short (for height)
胖	pàng	fat
瘦	shòu	thin
黑色	hēi sè	black
白色	bái sè	white

蓝色	lán sè	blue
棕色	zōng sè	brown
金黄色	jīn huáng sè	blonde
漂亮	piào liang	pretty
帅	shuài	handsome
难看	nán kàn	ugly
聪明	cōng míng	clever
笨	bèn	stupid
友好	yǒu hǎo	friendly
亲切	qīn qiè	kind

● GRAMMAR NOTES ON 有……也有……

You are very familiar with the use of 有 when it means "to have". In other contexts, it also means "there is/are...".

我家有五口人。(There are five people in my family.)

在我的生日会上，有很多我的朋友，也有我的家人。(At my birthday party, there were many of my friends, and there were also people of my family.)

1.5 Listen to Track 3.1.5 and match the English translation below. Put the correct number into the final column.

A	I like to listen to music whilst chatting with my friend.	
B	My friend is from Beijing. He is handsome and friendly.	
C	A new classmate has arrived in our class. He is very tall and also very clever.	
D	My classmate has a pair of big hands and big feet, but her mouth is small, and her ears are also small.	
E	There are many friends and family at my birthday party.	
F	My boyfriend is one year older than me, but he is not as tall as me.	

1.6 Read the Grammar Notes box on the 是……的 structure and use it to translate the following sentences into Chinese. You can play Track 3.1.6 to check your answers.

1. It is Beijing that my friend comes from._____

2. Luke can indeed speak Mandarin._____

3. It is Tai Chi that she teaches._____

4. I do like moon cakes. _____

2 Part Two Role Play

You are talking about your best friend with a newcomer to your school. Your teacher or your classmate will play the role of the newcomer; or you may use the recorded questions (Track 3.2.1).

Use appropriate language for an informal conversation.
You will talk to the teacher or your classmate using the five prompts below.
- When you see – ? – you must ask a question.
- When you see – ! – you must respond to something you have not prepared.

> ■ Task
> You speak about your best friend with a newcomer to your school.
> 1. Describe your best friend.
> 2. !
> 3. Say what you often do with your best friend.
> 4. ? Ask the newcomer if he/she has a best friend.
> 5. ? Ask the newcomer why everyone needs friends.

Questions relating to the above have been recorded for you. Listen to 3.2.1, pause after each question and speak in the gaps. Track 3.2.2 provides example answers.

ROLE PLAY TIPS

There are three purposes of role play:
(1) Do you understand the questions?
(2) Can you answer the questions?
(3) Can you ask questions?
So, once you have fully answered the question using appropriate language, you don't need to say more. Wait for the next one.

Part Three Listening Comprehension

Gao Ming is talking about his friend. Listen to what he says in Track 3.3 and answer the following questions in English.

1. When did Gao Ming have this friend?

_____

2. What did they use to do together after school?

_____

3. Where did the friend go after secondary school?

_____

4. What does Gao Ming say about marriage?

_____

LISTENING TIPS

Sometimes you can skip irrelevant clauses or sentences in order to really focus on the key information. For example, in Question 4 above, the question is about the speaker, known as 我 (I), but the first sentence is about 他 (he), his friend, so you may ignore that sentence and pay attention only to the sentences beginning with 我.

4 Part Four Conversation

Answer the following prompts. These have been recorded for you in Track 3.4.1. Listen to that track, pause after each question and speak in the gaps. Track 3.4.2 provides sample answers.

1. 说说你的一个朋友。

2. 你参加过他 / 她的生日会吗？

3. 她家在哪儿？

4. 在她的生日会上，你们吃了什么？

5. 你的生日是几月几日？

CONVERSATION TIPS

The following provides some tips and suggested content for you to consider.

1. Use some of the expressions you have practised in Part One Warming Up to describe your friend's appearance and characteristics.

2. When a question asks you about the past, try to remember to add 了 or 过 after the action verbs.

3. Stick to something simple or something you have learned. If possible, consider using a pair of adjectives, one negative and one positive, to form a 虽然……但是…… structure.

4. Once you have an opportunity to say a list of things, consider using the 除了…… 也 / 还…… structure. Don't forget to add an opinion in order to tick that box in the marking criteria.

5. Again, consider it an opportunity to talk about a plan so you can demonstrate your ability to talk about the future, and remember to use words such as 想, 会, 打算, etc.

5 Part Five Wrapping Up

5.1 Key question words and phrases covered in this unit

1	说说······ ★	shuō shuo	talk about... (see the "SENTENCES BEGINNING WITH 说说" box in Part One)
2	吗	ma	(a question particle used at the end of a sentence to turn a statement into a yes-no question)
3	什么时候	shén me shí hou	when; what time
4	做什么	zuò shén me	do what
5	吃了什么	chī le shén me	ate what
6	为什么	wèi shén me	why
7	哪儿	nǎ er	where
8	几月几日	jǐ yuè jǐ rì	what date

5.2 Key words and expressions covered in this unit

1	大	dà	big
2	小	xiǎo	small
3	长	cháng	long (for length)
4	短	duǎn	short (for length)
5	高	gāo	tall (for height)
6	矮	ǎi	short (for height)
7	胖	pàng	fat
8	瘦	shòu	thin
9	黑色	hēi sè	black
10	白色	bái sè	white
11	蓝色	lán sè	blue
12	棕色	zōng sè	brown
13	金黄色	jīn huáng sè	blonde
14	漂亮	piào liang	pretty
15	帅	shuài	handsome
16	难看	nán kàn	ugly
17	聪明	cōng míng	clever
18	笨	bèn	stupid
19	友好	yǒu hǎo	friendly
20	亲切	qīn qiè	kind

Unit 4 My Leisure Time

第四单元 我的业余时间

1 **Part One** Warming Up

1.1 Listen to Track 4.1.1 and sort these words or phrases into the categories below. Put each number next to an appropriate category.

A. outdoor activities _____

B. food _____

C. drinks _____

D. indoor activities _____

1.2 Listen to Track 4.1.2 and match these words or phrases with their English translations. Put the correct number into the final column.

A.	get up	
B.	go home	
C.	dine out	
D.	work part-time	
E.	go to bed	
F.	go online	
G.	work out	
H.	go to school	

When making a suggestion, first write a statement about what you want to suggest and then add one of the following:

(1) 吧

我们这个星期六一起去看电影吧！ (Let's go and watch a film this Saturday!)

(2) 好吗？／好不好？

我们这个星期六一起去看电影，好吗？ (Shall we go and watch a film this Saturday?)

我们这个星期六一起去看电影，好不好？ (Shall we go and watch a film this Saturday?)

(3) 你想……吗？

我想这个星期六去看电影，你想去吗？ (I would like to go and watch a film this Saturday. Would you like to go?)

1.3 Read the Grammar Notes box about making suggestions. Work in pairs with a classmate or your teacher to suggest a leisure-time activity that you can all do together in your spare time. Alternatively, translate the following suggestions into Chinese. Listen to Track 4.1.3 to check your answers.

1. Let's listen to music!

2. Shall we watch TV for a while?

3. I want to play table tennis. Do you want to play?

4. When it's the Spring Festival, shall we go to a Chinese restaurant to have a Chinese meal?

GRAMMAR NOTES: EXPRESSING SEQUENCES

(1) 先 + action verb 1, 再 + action verb 2, 然后 + action verb 3

我们先做作业，再吃晚饭，然后一起去健身房，好吗？ (We first do schoolwork, then have dinner, after that go to the gym together, okay?)

(2) action 1 以后 , action 2

吃完晚饭以后，我们一起去健身房，好吗？ (After finishing dinner, we go to the gym together, okay?)

1.4 Read the Grammar Notes box about expressing sequences and then look at the below weekend activities. Choose two or three of them to talk about your plans.

EXAMPLE 〉〉〉 这个周末，我打算先和家人去海边，再去饭馆打工，然后和朋友一起去买东西。

这个周末，在健身房做完运动以后，我打算去博物馆。

⬤ GRAMMAR NOTES ON 得

得 is an adverbial marker. It is placed after a verb to link an adverb that modifies the degree of that verb.

她唱得很好。 (She sang/sings very well.)

In a negative sentence, 不 is placed after 得 .

她唱得不好。 (She didn't/doesn't sing well).

Some verbs are of the verb-object structure such as 跑步 (lit. run the steps), 游泳 (lit. swim a swim). When they are modified by 得 , say the full verb first and you must then repeat the first part of the verb before 得 .

Subject + full verb (verb-object structure) + first part of the verb + 得 + adverb.

他跑步跑得很快。 (He runs very fast.)

她游泳游得很慢。 (She swims very slowly.)

1.5 Read the Grammar Notes box on 得 and then translate the following sentences into Chinese. You may listen to Track 4.1.5 to check your answers.

1. I eat a lot.
2. She sleeps very late.
3. My friend speaks Chinese very well.
4. My grandma drives very slowly.

■ **Look at the picture and prepare statements to the following.**

1. a description of the photograph
2. your opinion on helping parents with the supermarket shopping
3. a recent shopping trip you went on
4. when you are going to have a meal with your family
5. !

These questions have been recorded for you. Listen to Track 4.2.1, pause after each question and speak in the gaps. Track 4.2.2 provides sample answers.

PICTURE-BASED TASK TIPS

The purpose of the picture-based task is to assess communication through:

(1) expressing opinions;

(2) providing descriptions;

(3) narrating events.

So, apart from answering all the questions, you must develop your responses as well as you can by saying at least a couple more sentences.

3 **Part Three** Listening Comprehension

Zhang Qiang is talking about his family life. Listen to what he says in Track 4.3 and answer the following questions in English.

1. For breakfast, what does each member of his family like to eat and drink?

	food	drink
Zhang Qiang		
his dad		
his mum		

2. For dinner, what do they do? Give three details.

_____   _____   _____

LISTENING TIPS

When you are asked to give details for an answer, you need to listen to the overall message and then try to divide the speech into several parts. Reading the questions carefully often gives you clues on how to make these divisions.

For Question 1, use the words 我们都 (we all), 爸爸 (dad), 妈妈 (mum) and 我 (I) to divide the speech.

For Question 2, use the time phrases 有时候 (sometimes) which is used twice, and 更多的时候 (more often) to divide the speech into three parts.

This way, finding the answers can be a lot easier.

● **GRAMMAR NOTES: VERB +** 会了 **/** 完了

Put 会了 or 完了 after the verb to indicate the successful result of an action.

我学会了开车。(I have learnt to drive.) [implication: I can drive now.]

我已经做完了数学作业。(I have already finished my maths homework.)

When an action has not been successfully completed, negate with 没 and do not use 了.

我没学会开车。(I have failed to learn how to drive.)

我还没做完数学作业。(I have not finished my maths homework yet.)

4 Part Four Conversation

Answer the following questions. These questions have been recorded for you in Track 4.4.1. Listen to that track, pause after each question and speak in the gaps. Track 4.4.2 provides sample answers.

1. 有空的时候，你看书吗？

2. 你和你的朋友们周末都做什么？

3. 你觉得学生周末打工好不好？

4. 你周末打过工吗？

5. 这个周末你想做什么？

CONVERSATION TIPS

The following provides some tips and suggested content for you to consider.

1. Of course you can either say you like reading or you don't. If you like, you may give details on the kinds of books you like to read, e.g. English books, history books or children's books; if you don't like reading, perhaps you can explain the reasons or what you prefer to do, e.g. to watch films.

2. It is a good opportunity for you to use some of the vocabulary about spare time activities that you've learnt, e.g. listening to music, playing games or sports.

3. If you are not familiar with certain words in a question, do ask your teacher to clarify. You may ask, "'打工'是什么意思?" Your teacher will probably explain, "'打工'的意思就是工作。" If you want to talk about both positive and negative aspects of students working at weekends, you may use the 虽然……但是……structure to bring out some opposing points.

4. If you find some of the questions hard, you don't have to expand your answers too much. Answer the question and perhaps give a simple opinion with a justification, and then wait for the next question.

5. When you are given an opportunity to talk about your future plans, use words such as 想, 会 or 打算. If you are confident, you can give some background about your plans, e.g. I have learnt to swim but not well enough, so I plan to swim every weekend.

Part Five Wrapping Up

5.1 Key question words and phrases covered in this unit

1	吗	ma	(a question particle used at the end of a sentence to turn a statement into a yes-no question)
2	吧 ★	ba	(a question particle used at the end of a statement to turn it into a suggestion - see "Question Words" box in Part One)
3	好吗 ★	hǎo ma	okay? (see "Question Words" box in Part One)
4	好不好 ★	hǎo bu hǎo	okay or not? (see "Question Words" box in Part One)
5	哪儿	nǎ er	where
6	什么	shén me	what
7	什么时候	shén me shí hou	when
8	为什么	wèi shén me	why

5.2 Key words and expressions covered in this unit

1	钓鱼	diào yú	fishing
2	赛车	sài chē	motor racing
3	遛狗	liù gǒu	walk the dog
4	滑雪	huá xuě	ski
5	爬山	pá shān	climb mountains
6	健身	jiàn shēn	do exercise
7	回家	huí jiā	return home
8	叫外卖	jiào wài mài	order a takeaway
9	吃饭	chī fàn	have a meal
10	做饭	zuò fàn	cook a meal
11	炒饭	chǎo fàn	fried rice
12	面包	miàn bāo	bread
13	面条	miàn tiáo	noodles
14	鸡蛋	jī dàn	egg
15	蛋糕	dàn gāo	cake
16	水果	shuǐ guǒ	fruit
17	果汁	guǒ zhī	fruit juice
18	茶	chá	tea
19	周末	zhōu mò	weekend
20	有空	yǒu kòng	having free time

CHAPTER TWO

Where I Live

我居住的地方

Unit 5　My House

第五单元　我的房子

Part One Warming Up

1.1 Listen to Track 5.1.1 and match these words or phrases with their English translations. Put the correct number into the second column.

A. small town	6
B. high rise (building)	3
C. town/city centre	2
D. city	8
E. coast/seaside	7
F. mountain area	4
G. countryside	5
H. suburb	1

1.2 Listen to Track 5.1.2 and sort these words or phrases into the categories below. Put each number next to an appropriate category.

A. furniture ___2___5___7___10,8,12___14_____

B. electronic appliances ___4___6___9___16___12___15_____

C. rooms ___1___3___8___11___13___8_____

● GRAMMAR NOTES ON 在

(1) 在 (at, in, on) + location of an action

哥哥在书房看书。 (The elder brother is/was reading in the study.)

(2) 在 (to be at, in, on) + location

我家在北京。 (My home is in Beijing.)

(3) 住在 (to live in)

我住在北京。 (I live in Beijing.)

1.3 Read the Grammar Notes box about 在 . Look at the list of people, where they are and what they do. Listen to Track 5.1.3. You will be asked to say where each person is. You will probably need to use the pause button in order to speak in the gaps. The first reply is done for you as an example.

EXAMPLE 》》》 (You hear) 1. 你在哪儿？

(You answer) 我在浴室洗手。

1. EXAMPLE	我	在浴室	洗手
2.	爸爸	坐在沙发上	看电视
3.	妈妈	在厨房	做饭
4.	姐姐	在卧室	打电话
5.	哥哥	在书房	看书
6.	妹妹	在客厅	玩游戏

● GRAMMAR NOTES ON 虽然……但是……

You can use 虽然……但是……(although..., but...) in the same sentence. If the first part of the sentence is introduced by 虽然 with a negative aspect, the second part must be introduced by 但是 with a positive aspect, or vice versa. The part after 但是 is your key message.

虽然市中心很方便，但是不干净。 (Although the city centre is very convenient, it is not clean.)

虽然房子很大，但是厨房太小。 (Although the house is big, the kitchen is too small.)

但是 can be used on its own without 虽然 . For example:

市中心很方便，但是不干净。 (The city centre is very convenient, but it is not clean.)

1.4 Read the Grammar Notes box about 虽然……但是…… **and translate the following Chinese phrases on to the lines in English. Then, listen to the first part of each sentence in Track 5.1.4. Complete the sentence using one of these phrases. Put the appropriate letter into the spaces underneath the table.**

	Translation
A. ……但是只有一个浴室。	A. But it has 1 bathroom
B. ……但是中文作业太难了。	B. But my chinese prep was too difficult
C. ……但是我不喜欢游泳。	C. but I don't like swimming.
D. ……但是风景很漂亮。	D. But the view is beautiful
E. ……但是我有两个哥哥。	E. But I have 2 older brothers
F. ……但是我不饿。	F. But I am not hungry

1. C   2. ___   3. ___   4. ___   5. ___   6. ___

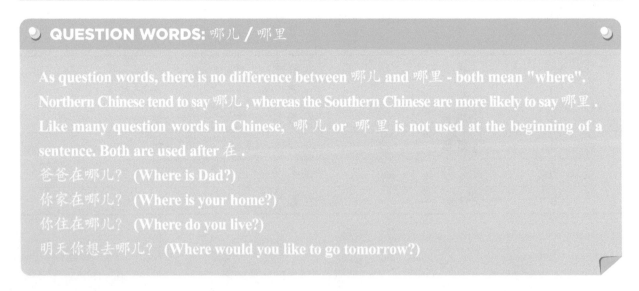

QUESTION WORDS: 哪儿 / 哪里

As question words, there is no difference between 哪儿 and 哪里 - both mean "where". Northern Chinese tend to say 哪儿 , whereas the Southern Chinese are more likely to say 哪里 . Like many question words in Chinese, 哪儿 or 哪里 is not used at the beginning of a sentence. Both are used after 在 .

爸爸在哪儿? (Where is Dad?)

你家在哪儿? (Where is your home?)

你住在哪儿? (Where do you live?)

明天你想去哪儿? (Where would you like to go tomorrow?)

1.5 Read the Question Words box about 哪儿 / 哪里 **and ask the following questions in Chinese, using** 哪儿 **or** 哪里 .

1. Where is my mobile phone?

2. Where is the city centre?

3. Where do your granddad and grandma live?

4. Where did you go last weekend?

2 **Part Two** Role Play

You are an estate agent trying to sell a property to a potential buyer from China. Your teacher or your classmate will play the role of the Chinese customer; or you may use the recorded questions (Track 5.2.1).

Use appropriate language for a formal conversation.
You will talk to the teacher or your classmate using the five prompts below.
• When you see – ? – you must ask a question.
• When you see – ! – you must respond to something you have not prepared.

■ Task

You are an estate agent trying to sell a property to a potential buyer from China.

1. Say where the house is.

2. !

3. Tell the customer when he/she can go to view the house.

4. Explain why you like the house.

5. ? Ask the customer if he/she thinks it is expensive.

Questions relating to the above have been recorded for you. Listen to 5.2.1, pause after each question and speak in the gaps. Track 5.2.2 provides example answers.

ROLE PLAY TIPS

There are three purposes of role play:
(1) Do you understand the questions?
(2) Can you answer the questions?
(3) Can you ask a question?
So, once you have fully answered the question using appropriate language, you don't need to say more. Wait for the next one.

3 Part Three Listening Comprehension

Dahai, a student from Shanghai, is talking about his home back in China. What does he say? Listen to Track 5.3 and put a cross ✕ in the correct box for each question.

1. Where does Dahai live?

☐	A in the city centre
☐	B in a small town
☐	C in the countryside

2. Do all rooms have en-suite facilities?

☐	A yes
☐	B no
☐	C not sure

3. How does Dahai describe his home area?

☐	A It's nice and not too expensive.
☐	B It's convenient and safe.
☐	C It's clean and safe.

4. When does the gate close every day?

☐	A 6:30pm
☐	B 10:30pm
☐	C 11:00pm

LISTENING TIPS

You must read the questions carefully as they often provide essential information for you to understand the context or scenario.

In the first question, the question suggests you focus on the type of residential area in which Dahai lives.

In the second question, try to spot the number of bedrooms and bathrooms in Dahai's house, as this will help you to draw a conclusion.

The structure 又 ⋯⋯ 又 ⋯⋯ is used in the third question, so you should focus on those two adjectives used after each 又 .

Time phrases in Chinese come before the action they modify, so pay attention to the number before the words "o'clock" and "close".

4 Part Four Conversation

Answer the following questions. These questions have been recorded for you in Track 5.4.1. Listen to that track, pause after each question and speak in the gaps. Track 5.4.2 provides sample answers.

1. 说说你们家，好吗？

2. 你喜欢住在大城市吗？为什么？

3. 你去过你朋友的家吗？

4. 谁常常来你家？

5. 二十五岁以后，你想住在哪儿？

CONVERSATION TIPS

The following provides some tips and suggested content for you to consider.

1. You may introduce the location and the size of your house; list a few rooms, e.g. living room, kitchen, bedrooms, bathrooms, etc.

2. You could express whether you like or dislike living in the city. If you like it, think about a couple of positive reasons, e.g. a lot of shops and cinemas; if you don't like it, you will need to focus on the disadvantages of living in the city, e.g. overpopulated, traffic jams, polluted air, etc. You may use simple language to talk about these aspects, e.g. there are many people and cars; the air is not clean.

3. Think about a relative's or a friend's house that you used to visit. You can then say one or two things that you did during your visit.

4. In a similar way to the previous question, you may choose one or two people who often come to visit your house. You can talk about the activities you do together, and it doesn't matter if you describe these activities in present time frames or as a past event.

5. This is an opportunity for you to talk about the future. One of the approaches could be to think about a job that you are going to do in the future. You can then relate this job to the place that you will live. Talking about planning to live in China is another good way to tackle this question as you will always have something to talk about regarding China, including explaining a reason or two why you wish to live there.

Part Five Wrapping Up

5.1 Key question words and phrases covered in this unit

1	吗	ma	(a question particle used at the end of a sentence to turn a statement into a yes-no question)
2	好吗	hǎo ma	okay?
3	几个	jǐ gè	how many
4	哪儿 / 哪里 ★	nǎ er / nǎ lǐ	where (see "Question Words" box in Part One)
5	住在哪儿	zhù zài nǎ er	where to live
6	什么时候	shén me shí hou	when; what time
7	为什么	wèi shén me	why
8	谁	shuí	who

5.2 Key words and expressions covered in this unit

1	城市	chéng shì	city
2	市中心	shì zhōng xīn	city centre
3	郊区	jiāo qū	suburb
4	小镇	xiǎo zhèn	small town
5	农村	nóng cūn	countryside
6	海边	hǎi biān	seaside
7	山区	shān qū	mountain area
8	客厅	kè tīng	living room
9	饭厅	fàn tīng	dining room
10	厨房	chú fáng	kitchen
11	书房	shū fáng	study
12	卧室	wò shì	bedroom
13	浴室	yù shì	bathroom
14	门	mén	door
15	灯	dēng	light
16	床	chuáng	bed
17	桌子	zhuō zi	table
18	椅子	yǐ zi	chair
19	书架	shū jià	bookshelf
20	沙发	shā fā	sofa

Unit 6
Weather, Landscape and Geography

第六单元 天气、景观和地理

1 Part One Warming Up

1.1 Listen to Track 6.1.1 and match the expressions with the right images. Each image has a letter. Put the correct letter into the second column.

A. B.

C. D.

E. F.

G. H.

1	
2	
3	
4	
5	
6	
7	
8	

1.2 Choose a few expressions provided in the box to describe each season.

很冷 有点冷	太热了 非常热	是晴天 天晴	多云 是阴天
有风 刮大风	有雨 下小雨	有雪 下大雪	有雾 有大雾

1. 春天 ＿＿＿＿＿＿＿＿。

2. 夏天 ＿＿＿＿＿＿＿＿。

3. 秋天 ＿＿＿＿＿＿＿＿。

4. 冬天 ＿＿＿＿＿＿＿＿。

天气 can mean both "weather" and "climate". To describe the temperature, use 气温 (lit. air temperature), and one of the following:

Above zero: 零上 (lit. above zero) + number + 度

Below zero: 零下 (lit. below zero) + number + 度

今天的气温（是）零下 10 度。(Today's temperature is 10 degrees below zero.)

今天最高气温 6 度，最低气温零下 1 度。(The highest temperature for today is 6 degrees, and the lowest is 1 degree below zero.)

1.3 Read the Grammar Notes box about describing the temperature. Look at the weather forecast for each city for 1st March, and listen to Track 6.1.3. Answer the questions about the weather of each city on 1st March. The first question has been done for you as an example.

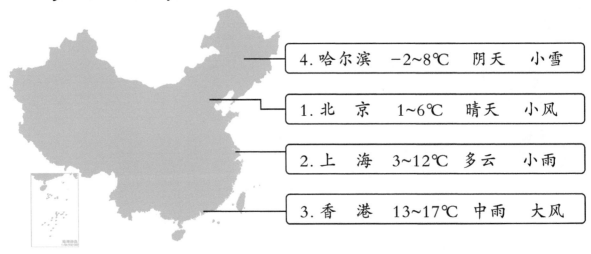

4. 哈尔滨　-2~8℃　阴天　小雪

1. 北　京　1~6℃　晴天　小风

2. 上　海　3~12℃　多云　小雨

3. 香　港　13~17℃　中雨　大风

EXAMPLE 》》》

(You hear) 1. 3 月 1 日北京的天气怎么样？

(You answer) 3 月 1 日北京是晴天，有小风，气温最低 1 度，最高 6 度。

2. 3 月 1 日上海的天气怎么样？

Answer: _____。

3. 3 月 1 日香港的天气怎么样？

Answer: _____。

4. 3 月 1 日哈尔滨的天气怎么样？

Answer: _____。

1.4 Translate the following Chinese phrases on to the lines in English. Then, listen to the first part of each sentence in Track 6.1.4. Complete the sentence using one of these phrases. Put the appropriate letter into the spaces underneath the table.

	Translation
A. 因为气温非常高。	A. _____
B. 有时候下大雪。	B. _____
C. 春夏秋冬四季很不一样。	C. The four seasons, spring, summer, autumn and winter, are very different.
D. 天气不冷也不热。	D. _____
E. 但是常常刮风。	E. _____

1. _C_   2. ____   3. ____   4. ____   5. ____

⚫ **GRAMMAR NOTES ON** 不管…… 还是…… 都……   ⚫

This structure is the Chinese equivalent of "regardless...". It shows one's determination to get something done. Introduce the sentence by using " 不管 + something positive + 还是 + negative", and then bring out the activity one is determined to carry out by putting 都 before the verb.

不管天气好还是不好，我都要去爬山。 (Regardless of good or bad weather, I will go mountain climbing.)

1.5 Read the Grammar Notes box about 不管…… 还是…… 都……**. Listen to Track 6.1.5 and complete the second part of the sentence with your own choice of activities.**

EXAMPLE 〉〉〉   (You hear) 1. 不管天气好还是不好
                       (You answer) 我都要去爬山。

2. _____ 。

3. _____ 。

4. _____ 。

1.6 Read the Question Words box about 为什么 **and ask the following questions in Chinese, using** 为什么 **.**

1. Why don't you like summer?

2. Why do you learn Chinese?

3. Why don't you want to buy a house?

4. Why do you want to do homework with me?

Part Two Picture-based Task

■ **Look at the picture and prepare statements to the following.**

1. a description of the photograph

2. who you like to go to the seaside with

3. a place you went last summer

4. what you will do this weekend if it rains

5. your opinion on your favourite season

Questions relating to the above have been recorded for you. Listen to 6.2.1, pause after each question and speak in the gaps. Track 6.2.2 provides example answers.

PICTURE-BASED TASK TIPS

The purpose of the picture-based task is to assess communication through:
(1) expressing opinions; (2) providing descriptions; (3) narrating events.
So, apart from answering all the questions, you must develop your responses as well as you can by saying at least a couple more sentences.

● GRAMMAR NOTES ON 要是 / 如果…… 就……

To introduce a conditional sentence (an 'if...' sentence), use either 要是 or 如果. Remember, 就 is often used before the verb in the second half of the conditional sentence.

如果 / 要是明天不下雪，我就开车去你家看你。(If it doesn't snow tomorrow, I will drive to your house to visit you.)

3 Part Three Listening Comprehension

You are listening to a podcast about the megacity Guangzhou in China. What does the speaker say? Listen to Track 6.3 and put a cross ✕ in each one of the three correct boxes.

Example	She likes learning Chinese.	✕
A	There is no winter in Guangzhou.	
B	There are flowers in all seasons in Guangzhou.	
C	The weather is always good in Guangzhou.	
D	The people there like to go to parks at the weekend.	
E	The park is near his home.	
F	Reading is his hobby.	
G	The restaurants there open in the morning.	

LISTENING TIPS

Besides trying to recognise key vocabulary - such as the four seasons and time expressions - listening for words that connect parts of a sentence can also be a good strategy. For example, listening for the 不管……还是…… (no matter... or...) and 要是……就…… (if... then...) structures will help you identify information that will aid you to answer the question.

4 Part Four Conversation

Answer the following questions. These questions have been recorded for you in Track 6.4.1. Listen to that track, pause after each question and speak in the gaps. Track 6.4.2 provides sample answers.

1. 在英国，一年有几个季节？

2. 春天公园里有什么？

3. 去年圣诞节，天气怎么样？

4. 如果天气好，你想做什么？

5. 你有问题吗？

CONVERSATION TIPS

The following provides some tips and suggested content for you to consider.

1. In the speaking, you should always remind yourself to provide evidence that you are capable of expressing opinions and that you can justify them. By asking follow-up questions with 为什么 , your teacher provides opportunities to give opinions. You can give reasons by using 因为 sentences.

2. Expressing "there is/are..." in Chinese is very different from English. The Chinese equivalent is "a place + 有…… ". The good news is that the sentence structure is often the same in a question and answer. So, if the teacher asks " 春天公园里有什么 ", all you need to do is use the same word order and add content with " 春天公园里有…… ".

3. When you spot a past time phrase being used in the question (for example " 去年圣诞节…… "), you should be prepared to give answers that show that you are able to talk about past events. Remember to mark the past with past time phrases (去年，上个星期，昨天 for example) or with 了 or 没 . (See Grammar Notes: Past Events in Chapter One, Unit 1)

4. When a question contains the conditional "if..." structure, it can be considered an opportunity to talk about a future event, i.e. 如果…… 我就…… (or 我想……，我会……).

5. It can be seen as slightly unusual for your teacher to ask you a vague question such as "do you have any questions". However, this provides a good opportunity to demonstrate your ability to ask questions. So, consider the conversation context and ask a question, perhaps using the formal 您 instead of 你 , to ask your teacher a related question.

5 Part Five Wrapping Up

5.1 Key question words and phrases covered in this unit

1	吗	ma	(a question particle used at the end of a sentence to turn a statement into a yes-no question)
2	什么	shén me	what
3	做什么	zuò shén me	what to do
4	有什么	yǒu shén me	what to have
5	为什么 ★	wèi shén me	why (see "Question Words" box in Part One)
6	什么季节	shén me jì jié	what season
7	几	jǐ	how many
8	谁	shuí	who
9	哪儿	nǎ er	where
10	怎么样	zěn me yang	how; how about

5.2 Key words and expressions covered in this unit

1	冷	lěng	cold
2	热	rè	hot
3	不冷（也）不热	bù lěng (yě) bú rè	neither cold nor hot
4	晴天	qíng tiān	sunny day
5	多云	duō yún	cloudy
6	有雨 / 下雨	yǒu yǔ / xià yǔ	rainy / to rain
7	有雪 / 下雪	yǒu xuě / xià xuě	snowy / to snow
8	有风 / 刮风	yǒu fēng / guā fēng	windy
9	有雾	yǒu wù	foggy
10	天气	tiān qì	weather
11	气温	qì wēn	air temperature
12	零上 / 零下	líng shàng / líng xià	above zero / below zero
13	度	dù	degree
14	春天	chūn tiān	spring
15	夏天	xià tiān	summer
16	秋天	qiū tiān	autumn
17	冬天	dōng tiān	winter
18	季节	jì jié	season
19	北方	běi fāng	north (region)
20	南方	nán fāng	south (region)

Unit 7
My Town / City
第七单元 我的城市

 Part One Warming Up

1.1 Listen to Track 7.1.1 and match the places you hear with the right image. Each image has a letter. Put the correct letter into the second row of the below grid. The first answer has been done for you as an example.

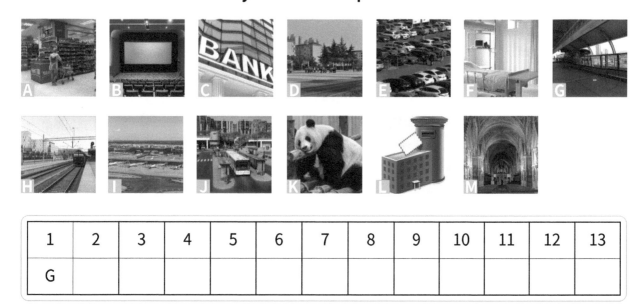

1	2	3	4	5	6	7	8	9	10	11	12	13
G												

1.2 Listen to Track 7.1.2 and match where these people are going with the right images in 1.1. Put the correct letter into the second column.

1	2	3	4	5

1.3 Add the pinyin and English translation to the following adjectives and expressions. Then use the appropriate ones to describe each of the three locations.

Adjectives and expressions	Pinyin	English translation
干净	gan jing	clean
安静	an jing	queit
热闹	re nao	lively, vibrant
风景漂亮	feng jing piao liang	pretty view
空气新鲜	kong qì xīn xiān	the air is fresh / fresh air
交通方便	jiǎo tōng fāng biàn	there is good public thransport

● GRAMMAR NOTES: DESCRIBING LOCATIONS

To describe the location of your home within a city or town, use this structure:

My home + 在 + name of the city/town + (的) + direction word + 边 / 面

我家在北京 (的) 西边。(My house is to the west of Beijing.)

You can also use a similar structure to describe the location of other places.

Place 1 + 在 + place 2 + (的) + direction word + 边 / 面

电影院在我家对面。(The cinema is opposite my house.)

1.4 Read the Grammar Notes box above and then listen to Track 7.1.4. Answer the question following the prompts. You may need to pause the recording after the prompt is given.

EXAMPLE   )))

(You hear) 1. 你家在哪儿?

(You also hear) To the east of London.

(You answer) 我家在伦敦的东边。

● QUESTION WORDS: 什么 (2)

In Chinese, to ask about things that exist or can be seen, the structure is "……有什么".

市中心有什么? (What's in the city centre?)

公园里有什么? (What's in the park?)

超市外边有什么? (What's outside the supermarket?)

To answer such a question, you should say the place first and give your answers after 有.

市中心有很多商店。(There are many shops in the city centre.)

公园里有很多游客。(There are many tourists in the park.)

超市外边有一个停车场。(There is a carpark outside the supermarket.)

As you can see, "there is/are..." sentences in Chinese are very different from English. "There is/are" is expressed in one word - 有 - in Chinese, and this goes after the location. Thankfully, the sentence structure is often given in the question. So, when a question asking " 春天公园里有什么 ", all you need to do is copy exactly the same word order and give your content by replying " 春天公园里有……".

2 **Part Two** Role Play

You are working in a tourist information office in London. Your teacher or your classmate will play the role of a Chinese tourist; or you may use the recorded questions (Track 7.2.1).

Use appropriate language for a formal conversation.
You will talk to the teacher or your classmate using the five prompts below.
- When you see - ? - you must ask a question.
- When you see - ! - you must respond to something you have not prepared.

> ■ **Task**
>
> **You are working in a tourist information office in London. You speak to a Chinese tourist.**
>
> 1. Describe what is in the city centre in London.
>
> 2. !
>
> 3. Talk about what you think of the museums in the UK.
>
> 4. ? Ask the tourist what he/she did yesterday.
>
> 5. ? Ask the tourist if he/she would like to have a meal in London.

Questions relating to the above have been recorded for you. Listen to Track 7.2.1, pause after each question and speak in the gaps. Track 7.2.2 provides sample answers.

ROLE PLAY TIPS

There are three purposes of role play:
(1) Do you understand the questions?
(2) Can you answer the questions?
(3) Can you ask questions?
So, once you have fully answered the question using appropriate language, you don't need to say more. Wait for the next one.

Part Three Listening Comprehension

You hear a radio presenter talking about her recent visit to the Chinese city, Xi'an. Listen to the radio programme on Track 7.3 and answer the following questions in English.

1. Give one reason why she likes Xi'an.

because it is old

2. Where did she visit twice?

museum

3. List three things that the locals like to eat.

noodles, dumples, beef

4. What does she recommend when travelling in Xi'an?

boat, underground station

LISTENING TIPS

You should always read the directions carefully before looking at the questions, as doing so may help you understand what you are hearing. "Xi'an" is mentioned many times in the recording, and you may find it unfamiliar. However, from the directions you can see that it is the name of a Chinese city.

In Question 2 and Question 3, there are distractors that you need to be careful of.

In Question 2, two places are mentioned, the city centre and museum. Listen again to identify where the radio presenter lives and what is next to it.

In Question 3, there was a negative comparative sentence used, in which "rice" is mentioned.

● GRAMMAR NOTES ON 而

Note that 和 (and) only links nouns and noun phrases; you need other words to join sentences together. One such word is 而 (whereas; but). It is used to link contrasting information.

爸爸妈妈的卧室很大，而我的卧室很小。(Dad and mum's bedroom is big, whereas my bedroom is small.)

我妹妹喜欢住在市中心，而我喜欢住在农村。(My younger sister likes to live in the town centre, but I like living in the country.)

4 Part Four Conversation

Answer the following questions. These questions have been recorded for you in Track 7.4.1. Listen to that track, pause after each question and speak in the gaps. Track 7.4.2 provides sample answers.

1. 伦敦有什么？

2. 你上次去伦敦是什么时候？

3. 住在大城市有什么好处？

4. 住在大城市有什么坏处？

5. 你最想去哪个城市旅游？

CONVERSATION TIPS

The following provides some tips and suggested content for you to consider.

1. Whilst you may know the names of many places in London, it is not always very easy to say them in Chinese. Be descriptive - instead of Buckingham Palace, for example, you could say 女王的家 .

2. If you have been to London, it should be straightforward to talk about your last visit. If you have not been, this is an opportunity to use 没去过 to demonstrate you can talk about past events in the negative form. You can then talk about your plans to visit London in the future.

3. When being asked to summarise advantages, you may consider using 第一 , 第二 and 第三 to give three main points. Weather, transport, shopping and going to the cinema are all good points to think about.

4. Question 4 is similar to Question 3 but asked in a slightly different way. It is wise to answer using 第一，第二，and 第三 . Think about the noise, the crowds, the traffic jams (if you don't know "traffic jam" in Chinese, you could instead say there are too many cars on the road), or indeed air pollution.

5. It is easier to pick a city that you know well, better still, a Chinese city so you can make use of all the words, i.e. the names of the places that you have learned. Beijing, Shanghai, Xi'an, Hong Kong, Taiwan or Singapore should all be more familiar cities for you to talk about.

5 Part Five Wrapping Up

5.1 Key question words and phrases covered in this unit

1	说说……	shuō shuo	talk about...
2	有什么 ★	yǒu shén me	have what (see "Question Words" box in Part One)
3	有什么好处？	yǒu shén me hǎo chu	What is/are the benefit(s)?
4	坏处是什么？	huài chu shì shén me	What is/are the disadvantage(s)?
5	做了什么	zuò le shén me	did what
6	什么时候	shén me shí hou	when; what time
7	几点	jǐ diǎn	what time
8	哪儿	nǎ er	where
9	哪个	nǎ ge	which
10	怎么样	zěn me yang	how about

5.2 Key words and expressions covered in this unit

1	市中心	shì zhōng xīn	city centre
2	商店	shāng diàn	shop
3	超市	chāo shì	supermarket
4	银行	yín háng	bank
5	邮局	yóu jú	post office
6	医院	yī yuàn	hospital
7	教堂	jiào táng	church
8	博物馆	bó wù guǎn	museum
9	动物园	dòng wù yuán	zoo
10	公园	gōng yuán	park
11	公共汽车站	gōng gòng qì chē zhàn	bus stop
12	火车站	huǒ chē zhàn	railway station
13	地铁站	dì tiě zhàn	underground station
14	飞机场	fēi jī chǎng	airport
15	停车场	tíng chē chǎng	carpark
16	伦敦	lún dūn	London
17	北京	běi jīng	Beijing
18	上海	shàng hǎi	Shanghai
19	西安	xī ān	Xi'an
20	香港	xiāng gǎng	Hong Kong

Unit 8　Festivals

第八单元　节日

Part One Warming Up

1.1 Listen to Track 8.1.1 and match the dates or approximate date with the appropriate festivals. Then translate them into English in the spaces provided.

1. 一月一日	3. 三月或四月	5. 农历八月十五日
2. 农历一月一日	4. 农历五月五日	6. 十二月二十五日

中秋节 ＿＿＿　　春 节 ＿＿＿　　端午节 ＿＿＿　　圣诞节 ＿＿＿　　新 年 ＿＿＿　　复活节 ＿＿＿

NEW WORDS　　农历 – lunar calendar

1.2 Listen to Track 8.1.2 and match each word or phrase with its associated festival. Put the number next to an associated festival. You may use the same number for more than one festival.

A. 春节 ＿＿＿＿＿＿＿　　B. 端午节 ＿＿＿＿＿＿＿　　C. 中秋节 ＿＿＿＿＿＿＿　　D. 圣诞节 ＿＿＿＿＿＿＿

NEW WORDS　团圆饭 – family reunion dinner　火鸡 – turkey　圣诞老人 – Father Christmas

CULTURE NOTE: CHINESE NEW YEAR

In Chinese-speaking countries/regions, 春节 (the Spring Festival) is a general term used to refer to the Chinese New Year festival season. The festival begins on the first day of the first month in the lunar calendar. This first day, i.e. the New Year's Day is known as 大年初一 (dà nián chū yī) or 正月初一 (zhēng yuè chū yī). The New Year's Eve is 除夕 (chú xī). A colloquial expression reserved for celebrating the Chinese New Year is 过年, the same 过 as in 过生日 (to celebrate a birthday). For example: 你们今年在哪儿过年？ (Where will you celebrate the Chinese New Year this year?)

2

Where I Live | 我居住的地方

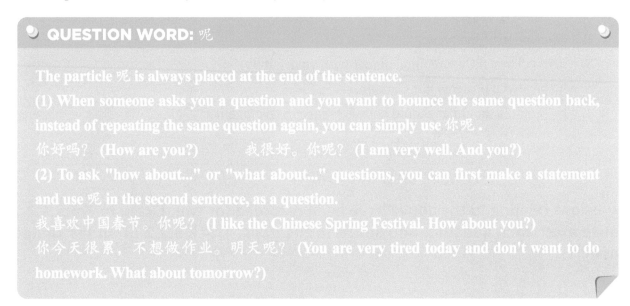

GRAMMAR NOTES ON 每······ 都······

Whenever 每 is used, whether it refers to every person (每个人), every day (每天) or every Christmas (每个圣诞节), 都 must be used before the main verb or the modal verb (i.e. can, should) in the sentence.

每 + measure word + noun + 都 + verb

我们家每个人都会说一点儿法语。 (Everyone in our family can speak a little French.)

1.3 Read the Grammar Notes box on the 每······ 都······ structure, and use it to translate the following sentences into Chinese.

1. Every weekend he goes skiing.
2. I skip breakfast every morning.
3. Grandma gives me a "red envelope" every Spring Festival.
4. During Christmas, every child is very happy.

QUESTION WORD: 呢

The particle 呢 is always placed at the end of the sentence.

(1) When someone asks you a question and you want to bounce the same question back, instead of repeating the same question again, you can simply use 你呢.

你好吗？ (How are you?)   我很好。你呢？ (I am very well. And you?)

(2) To ask "how about..." or "what about..." questions, you can first make a statement and use 呢 in the second sentence, as a question.

我喜欢中国春节。你呢？ (I like the Chinese Spring Festival. How about you?)

你今天很累，不想做作业。明天呢？ (You are very tired today and don't want to do homework. What about tomorrow?)

1.4 Read the Question Word box on 呢 and ask the following questions in Chinese, using 呢.

1. Your dad is French. What about your mum?
2. It's rainy today. How about tomorrow?
3. Chinese people eat mooncakes at the Mid-Autumn Festival. What about the Dragon Boat Festival?
4. I would like to watch the dragon boat race this Dragon Boat Festival. What about you?

Look at the picture and prepare statements to the following.

1. a description of the photograph
2. when will you have a reunion dinner with your family
3. who gave you presents last Christmas
4. why families should or should not often have meals together
5. !

Questions relating to the above have been recorded for you. Listen to Track 8.2.1, pause after each question and speak in the gaps. Track 8.2.2 provides sample answers.

PICTURE-BASED TASK TIPS

The purpose of the picture-based task is to assess communication through:
(1) expressing opinions;
(2) providing descriptions;
(3) narrating events.
So, apart from answering all the questions, you must develop your responses as well as you can by saying at least a couple more sentences.

Part Three Listening Comprehension

Chen Dong is talking about his family's Chinese New Year celebration. Listen to what he says in Track 8.3 and complete the sentences in English.

1. The children are thrilled with the activities of (1)_____,

(2) _____ , (3) _____, (4) _____ and (5) _____.

2. His sister is planning to use her New Year money to (1)_____ and

(2) _____ .

LISTENING TIPS

For Question 1, common sense and your knowledge of Chinese festival culture can help you make an educated start on answering the question; consider all the activities that you know people do during the Chinese New Year and try to spot them in the recording. The content for Question 2 is more precise, so you will need to listen carefully. As the question asks about planning, a clever approach is to listen to what the speaker says after the word 打算 and then divide the rest of the recording into two parts, looking out for the word 还 to separate them. Make sure you understand the key messages and see if they make sense.

4 Part Four Conversation

Answer the following questions. These questions have been recorded for you in Track 8.4.1. Listen to that track, pause after each question and speak in the gaps. Track 8.4.2 provides sample answers.

1. 你知道哪些中国节日？

2. 你喜欢吃中餐吗？

3. 你觉得哪个英国的节日最有意思？

4. 去年过生日，你做了什么？

5. 明年春节的时候，你希望你们学校有什么活动？

CONVERSATION TIPS

The following provides some tips and suggested content for you to consider.

1. As part of the GCSE Chinese course context, you should have learned at least three Chinese festivals: the Spring Festival, the Dragon Boat Festival and the Mid-Autumn Festival. You could use 最喜欢 to talk about which of the festivals is your favourite, and then you could say what people do or eat during the festival(s).

2. By now you should have learned a lot about Chinese food. Say a few that you like and, if possible, use the structure 除了……也/还……

3. Of the festivals celebrated in the UK, perhaps Easter and Christmas are the easiest ones to talk about. If you choose to talk about Easter, you could say when it is, e.g. 在三月或四月, and then you could talk about Easter bunnies or chocolate eggs. If talking about Christmas, you could talk about a family reunion dinner, with turkey (火鸡), Christmas carols (圣诞歌), Father Christmas (圣诞老人), and presents (礼物).

4. This question gives you the opportunity to talk about a past event. Try to recall what you did on your last birthday and remember to use a past time expression, 了 or 过.

5. Perhaps your teachers have already organised a Chinese New Year celebration in your school. You could talk about it, being sure to use the expression 明年春节的时候 and the verb 希望 from the question to express your hopes for the school's next Chinese New Year celebration.

Part Five Wrapping Up

5.1 Key question words and phrases covered in this unit

1	呢 ★	ne	how about, what about (see "Question Word" box in Part One)
2	吗	ma	(a question particle used at the end of a sentence to turn a statement into a yes-no question)
3	谁	shuí	who
4	为什么	wèi shén me	why
5	怎么	zěn me	how
6	做了什么	zuò le shén me	did what
7	有什么	yǒu shén me	what to have
8	哪个	nǎ ge	which (singular)
9	哪些	nǎ xiē	which (plural)

5.2 Key words and expressions covered in this unit

1	节日	jié rì	festival
2	新年	xīn nián	New Year
3	春节	chūn jié	Chinese New Year
4	端午节	duān wǔ jié	Dragon Boat Festival
5	中秋节	zhōng qiū jié	Mid-Autumn Festival
6	复活节	fù huó jié	Easter
7	圣诞节	shèng dàn jié	Christmas
8	团圆饭	tuán yuán fàn	family reunion dinner
9	中餐	zhōng cān	Chinese meal
10	饺子	jiǎo zi	Chinese dumpling
11	粽子	zòng zi	rice dumpling (related to the Dragon Boat Festival)
12	月饼	yuè bǐng	mooncake (related to the Mid-Autumn Festival)
13	看月亮	kàn yuè liang	moon watching
14	舞龙	wǔ lóng	dragon dance
15	舞狮	wǔ shī	lion dance
16	红包	hóng bāo	red envelope (Chinese celebratory custom)
17	放鞭炮	fàng biān pào	set off firecrackers
18	龙舟比赛	lóng zhōu bǐ sài	dragon boat race
19	礼物	lǐ wù	gift
20	庆祝会	qìng zhù huì	celebratory party

CHAPTER THREE
Travel and Holidays
旅行和假期

Unit 9　Transport

第九单元　交通工具

Part One Warming Up

1.1 Listen to Track 9.1.1 and match the expressions with the right images. Each image has a letter. Put the correct letter into the second column.

1	
2	
3	
4	
5	
6	
7	
8	
9	
10	

GRAMMAR NOTES: EXPRESSING MEANS OF TRANSPORT

(1) 坐 : when travelling by taxi, bus, underground train, train, boat or plane, use the verb 坐 (Lit. "to sit", but here it means "taking" or "by") and put this verbal phrase before the main verb.

我妈妈每天坐地铁去上班。(Lit. My mum everyday takes the underground train to go to work.)

(2) 骑 : for bikes and horses, the verb 骑 (to ride) is used.

他常常骑自行车去图书馆。(Lit. He often rides the bike to go to the library.)

(3) 开 : to drive a car, a taxi, a bus; to sail or steer a boat; or even drive a train or pilot a plane, use 开 .

以前，爸爸天天开车送我上学。(Lit. Before, Dad everyday drove car and sent me to go to school.)

(4) 走路 : when walking to places, use 走路 (walk, on foot).

为了健康和保护环境，我打算走路上学。(Lit. In order to keep fit and protect the environment, I plan to walk to go to school.)

1.2 Read the notes about expressing means of transport and the use of the question word 怎么 to ask how to go somewhere. Look at the drawings and listen to Track 9.1.2. Answer the questions about how these people go to work or school.

1 2 3 4

1.3 Read the Grammar Notes box about the use of 离 then listen to Track 9.1.3. You will hear questions about the distance between two places. Use one of the distance expressions in the below list to answer. You will probably need to use the pause button in order to speak in the gaps. The first reply is done for you as an example.

很远	very far
非常远	extremely far
不远	not far
不太远	not too far

很近	very close
非常近	extremely close
不近	not close
不太近	not too close

EXAMPLE >>> (You hear) 你家离学校远吗？
(You answer) 我家离学校不远。

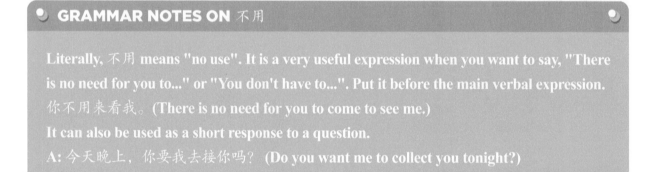

> 🔵 **GRAMMAR NOTES ON 不用**
>
> Literally, 不用 means "no use". It is a very useful expression when you want to say, "There is no need for you to..." or "You don't have to...". Put it before the main verbal expression.
> 你不用来看我。(There is no need for you to come to see me.)
> It can also be used as a short response to a question.
> A: 今天晚上，你要我去接你吗？ (Do you want me to collect you tonight?)
> B: 不用，谢谢！ (There is no need/It's not necessary. Thanks.)

1.4 Read the Grammar Notes about 不用 then translate the below phrases into the spaces in the second column. Next, listen to Track 9.1.4, which gives phrases to complete sentences A - F. Put the appropriate letter into the third column.

	Translation:
A. 不用学法语。	A. _____
B. 不用穿很多衣服。	B. _____
C. 不用买报纸。	C. _____
D. 不用开车。	D. _____
E. 不用妈妈帮她。	E. _____
F. 不用吃药。	F. No need to take medicine.

1. _F_
2. ___
3. ___
4. ___
5. ___
6. ___

2 Part Two Role Play

You are invited to take part in a street survey about using public transport. Your teacher or your classmate will play the role of the interviewer; or you may use the recorded questions (Track 9.2.1).

Use appropriate language for a formal conversation.
You will talk to the teacher or your classmate using the five prompts below.
• When you see – ? – you must ask a question.
• When you see – ! – you must respond to something you have not prepared.

> **Task**
> **You are taking part in a street survey about using public transport.**
> 1. Say where you are going.
> 2. Explain why you want to go there.
> 3. !
> 4. Say which kind of transport you prefer to take to go to school.
> 5. ? Ask the interviewer if the railway station is far from the sports centre.

These questions have been recorded for you. Listen to Track 9.2.1, pause after each question and speak in the gaps. Track 9.2.2 provides example answers.

ROLE PLAY TIPS

There are three purposes of role play:

(1) Do you understand the questions?   (2) Can you answer the questions?

(3) Can you ask a question?

So, once you have fully answered the question using appropriate language, you don't need to say more. Wait for the next one.

GRAMMAR NOTES ON 对……好 / 不好

To say "somebody / something is good / not good for...", use the structure:
A + 对 + B + 好 / 不好。A and B can be people, objects or actions.
中文老师对我很好。(The Chinese teacher is very nice to me.)
开车对环境不好。(Driving is bad for the environment.)

Peter's Chinese friend Xiaodong is coming to visit him. What do they say on the phone? Listen to Track 9.3 and complete the sentences with the phrases in the box. There are phrases that you will not use.

> new things   shopping   the railway station   not fast   cycle   walk
> good for health and environment   not far   drive   high-speed   train
> not close by   the airport

1. Peter is going to pick up Xiaodong at _____.

2. "Gaotie (高铁)" means _____.

3. According to Peter, many British people don't like _____.

4. In Xiaodong's opinion, it is fine if the UK transport is _____.

5. Peter says people in London like to _____ to work because it is

   _____.

LISTENING TIPS

When you are required to complete sentences by choosing the correct phrase from a list, you should first go through the list of phrases and try to translate as many as possible. You should then look at the half sentences provided in the questions as they offer crucial information for allocating the key sentences for answers when you start to listen. For example, in Question 1, the first half of the sentence requires you to spot a place for the two friends to meet up. You may have heard 飞机 , 火车 and 家 so perhaps you have considered the airport, the railway station or Peter's house for the answer. However, when the sentence is structured with 先……然后……, you should focus on the place they first met and treat the later places as distractors.

4. Part Four Conversation

Answer the following questions. These questions have been recorded for you in Track 9.4.1. Listen to that track, pause after each question and speak in the gaps. Track 9.4.2 provides example answers.

1. 你住的地方有什么公共交通工具？

2. 你们家离火车站近吗？

3. 你上一次坐火车是什么时候？

4. 你喜欢骑自行车吗？

5. 你想学开车吗？

CONVERSATION TIPS

The following provides some tips and suggested content for you to consider.

1. You could first introduce where you live, e.g. a small town, and give an opinion on whether it is convenient to use public transport (公共交通工具) there. You could use the 除了……也 / 还……structure to list a few kinds of public transport available where you live.

2. You could answer the question by using the same structure in the question ……离……很近 / 不很近 . You could then explain how you get to the railway station and how long it takes.

3. You should give some details about your last train trip. You could talk about where you went, what you did and who you took the train with. Remember to use 了 .

4. This question allows you to give your opinions on cycling. Consider using the structure ……对…… 好 / 有好处 , and 不但…… 而且……

5. This question allows you to talk about a possible future plan, as well as justifying it using 因为 .

5 Part Five Wrapping Up

5.1 Key question words and phrases covered in this unit

1	怎么 ★	zěn me	how (see "Question Words" box in Part One)
2	吗	ma	(a question particle used at the end of a sentence to turn a statement into a yes-no question)
3	哪儿	nǎ er	where
4	什么时候	shén me shí hou	when; what time
5	为什么	wèi shén me	why
6	有什么	yǒu shén me	what to have
7	坐什么车	zuò shén me chē	by what transport

5.2 Key words and expressions covered in this unit

1	公共交通工具	gōng gòng jiāo tōng gōng jù	public transport
2	公共汽车	gōng gòng qì chē	bus
3	火车	huǒ chē	train
4	出租车	chū zū chē	taxi
5	自行车	zì xíng chē	bicycle
6	旅游车	lǚ yóu chē	tourist coach
7	飞机	fēi jī	plane
8	地铁	dì tiě	underground
9	高铁	gāo tiě	high-speed train
10	船	chuán	ferry, boat, ship
11	走路	zǒu lù	walk
12	坐	zuò	sit
13	骑	qí	ride
14	开	kāi	drive
15	票	piào	ticket
16	离……很远	lí…hěn yuǎn	far from…
17	离……很近	lí…hěn jìn	close to…
18	只有	zhǐ yǒu	only
19	不用	bú yòng	no need
20	吃药	chī yào	take medicine

Unit 10   Hotels

第十单元 旅馆

Part One Warming Up

1.1 Listen to Track 10.1.1 and match these words or phrases with their English translations. Put the correct number into the second column.

A. double room	
B. free of charge	
C. hotel	
D. reception	
E. to have a holiday	

F. single room	
G. to book a room	
H. clean	
I. swimming pool	
J. cash	

1.2 Listen to Track 10.1.2 and decide which utterances are likely to be said by hotel staff, and which are by hotel guests. Put your chosen number next to the category "staff" or "guests".

A. staff: _____   B. guests: _____

CULTURE NOTE: NEW FORMS OF PAYMENT

(1) 微信 (wēi xìn)**: WeChat**
In major cities in China these days, 微信 payment is becoming increasingly popular. 微信 is a communication app which has a payment mechanism linked with one's bank account. So, you will hear Chinese people ask the seller in a shop: 我可以用微信付款吗？ **(May I pay by WeChat?)**
(2) 支付宝 (zhī fù bǎo)**: Alipay**
Another popular payment method is through 支付宝 which was created by Jack Ma (马云), founder of Alibaba Group. It is a third-party mobile and online payment platform.

1.3 Look at the signs that give information about the hotel facilities. Listen to Track 10.1.3 and answer the questions in Chinese.

> **GRAMMAR NOTES ON** 最
>
> In English, there are several rules for making the superlative adjective or adverb when making comparisons (e.g. the best, most beautiful, like... the most). In Chinese, however, it is simple. Just put 最 before the adjective or the verb, e.g. 最好 (best), 最漂亮 (most beautiful), 最喜欢…… (like... the most).

1.4 Read the Grammar Notes on 最 and say the following sentences in Chinese.

1. In our family, Dad is the tallest, but I am the smartest.

2. He is the best football player.

3. The oldest person lives in the UK.

4. Although I like to learn French and Spanish, I prefer Chinese.

> **QUESTION WORDS:** 有多远
>
> In Unit 9, we revised the use of 离 to ask about the distance between two places. You can use a similar structure to ask a question about the distance between two places.
> A (place) ＋ 离 ＋ B (place) ＋ 有多远？
> 上海离北京有多远？ (How far is Shanghai from Beijing?)
> There is another way to ask the same question:
> 从 A (place) ＋ 去 / 到 ＋ B (place) ＋ 有多远？
> 从你家到学校有多远？ (How far is it from your home to your school?)

2 **Part Two** Picture-based Task

■ **Look at the picture and prepare statements to the following.**

1. a description of the photo
2. your favourite hotel
3. the distance between that hotel and the city centre
4. your recent trip to a swimming pool
5. whether you plan to work in a hotel

Questions relating to the above have been recorded for you. Listen to Track 10.2.1, pause after each question and speak in the gaps. Track 10.2.2 provides example answers.

PICTURE-BASED TASK TIPS

The purpose of the picture-based task is to assess communication through:

(1) expressing opinions;

(2) providing descriptions;

(3) narrating events.

So, apart from answering all the questions, you must develop your responses as well as you can by saying at least a couple more sentences.

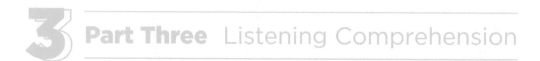

(1) 新 **as an adjective:** 新 + **noun**

新衣服 **(new clothes)**   新车 **(new car)**

(2) 新 **as an adverb:** 新 + **verb** + 的 + **noun**

新开的酒店 **(newly-opened hotel)**   新买的手机 **(recently-bought mobile phone)**

3 Part Three Listening Comprehension

Three people are giving positive feedback about a hotel. What do they say? Listen to Track 10.3 and put a cross ✕ against the feedback each guest gives.

		Guest 1	Guest 2	Guest 3
Example	It is a newly opened hotel.	✕		
A	The restaurant is very quiet.			
B	There are nice photos on display.			
C	Family rooms are available.			
D	It is located near the city centre.			
E	They guarantee a good night's sleep.			
F	You can go fishing next to the hotel.			
G	There are excellent sports facilities.			

LISTENING TIPS

Word spotting is a good strategy to get the key points for listening, but it may not always work as distracting words are sometimes added to mislead you. So, you do usually need to listen out for more details. Guest 2 mentioning 餐厅 and 鱼 doesn't guarantee Statement A with the word "restaurant" or Statement F with "fishing" are correct answers.

4 Part Four Conversation

Answer the following questions. These questions have been recorded for you in Track 10.4.1. Listen to that track, pause after each question and speak in the gaps. Track 10.4.2 provides example answers.

1. 说说你住过的一个酒店。

2. 你知道怎么上网订酒店吗？

3. 你觉得什么时候酒店最贵？

4. 酒店有没有游泳池重要吗？

5. 如果去度假，你希望住在哪儿？

CONVERSATION TIPS

The following provides some tips and suggested content for you to consider.

1. This question asks you to talk about your experiences of staying in a hotel. You could recall a hotel you stayed in with your family or on a school trip. You could then say when it was, where you went and who you went with. You could also express an opinion about this hotel, e.g. big or small, clean or quiet, etc.

2. First, directly respond to the question by giving a positive or negative answer. You may then talk about whether it is easy to book a hotel online and give a couple of tips on where to stay and whether it is expensive.

3. There is no right or wrong answer as it is about your opinion. So, you might assume hotel prices are high in summer because there are more people going on holiday and hotels can make more money.

4. It is another opportunity for you to give and justify your opinion. If you think it is important, you could explain that many guests like to swim and that children can play there. If you don't think it is important for the hotel to have a swimming pool, you could explain what you think is important, e.g. a comfortable bed or a quiet room, etc.

5. Answer the question by focusing on a future time frame. You could say where you wish to go, why and what you are going to do.

5 Part Five Wrapping Up

5.1 Key question words and phrases covered in this unit

1	有多远 ★	yǒu duō yuǎn	how far (see "Question Words" box in Part One)
2	吗	ma	(a question particle used at the end of a sentence to turn a statement into a yes-no question)
3	呢	ne	how about; what about
4	什么	shén me	what
5	什么时候	shén me shí hou	when/what time
6	几点	jǐ diǎn	what time
7	多少钱	duō shǎo qián	how much (money)
8	哪儿	nǎ er	where
9	为什么	wèi shén me	why
10	怎么	zěn me	how

5.2 Key words and expressions covered in this unit

1	饭店	fàn diàn	hotel, restaurant
2	酒店	jiǔ diàn	hotel, restaurant
3	订房间	dìng fáng jiān	book a room
4	单人房	dān rén fáng	single room
5	双人房	shuāng rén fáng	double room
6	免费	miǎn fèi	free of charge
7	现金	xiàn jīn	cash
8	信用卡	xìn yòng kǎ	credit card
9	餐厅	cān tīng	restaurant; dining hall; canteen
10	健身房	jiàn shēn fáng	gym
11	游泳池	yóu yǒng chí	swimming pool
12	服务台	fú wù tái	service desk; reception desk
13	欢迎	huān yíng	welcome
14	开门	kāi mén	open; open the door
15	关门	guān mén	close; close the door
16	干净	gān jìng	clean
17	安静	ān jìng	quiet
18	方便	fāng biàn	convenient
19	便宜	pián yi	cheap
20	贵	guì	expensive

Unit 11　Events

第十一单元　活动

Part One Warming Up

1.1 Listen to Track 11.1.1 and match the events with the right image. Put the correct letter on the answer line below.

A　　B　　C　　D　　E

1. ____　2. ____　3. ____　4. ____　5. ____

1.2 Listen to Track 11.1.2 and sort these phrases into the categories below. Write the English translation next to an appropriate category.

迷 (fan)		节 (festival)		场 (field, pitch, court)	

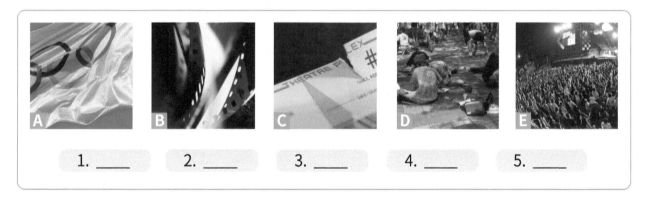

GRAMMAR NOTES ON 一……就…… (AS SOON AS / ONCE …)

To show that one action is immediately followed by another, use the sentence structure 一……就……. Put the action to be completed first after 一 and the second verbal phrase after 就.

我一放学就去踢足球。(As soon as I finish school, I go to play football.)

1.3 Read the Grammar Notes box on 一……就…… and use the structure to say the following sentences.

1. Xiaoming goes to practice singing as soon as he finishes school.

2. Mum cooked dinner as soon as she got home.

3. My elder brother watches TV after finishing his homework.

4. As soon as I finished playing football, my father bought me a hot dog.

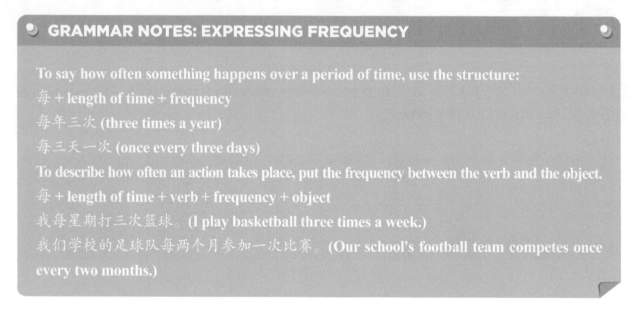

GRAMMAR NOTES: EXPRESSING FREQUENCY

To say how often something happens over a period of time, use the structure:

每 + length of time + frequency

每年三次 (three times a year)

每三天一次 (once every three days)

To describe how often an action takes place, put the frequency between the verb and the object.

每 + length of time + verb + frequency + object

我每星期打三次篮球。 (I play basketball three times a week.)

我们学校的足球队每两个月参加一次比赛。 (Our school's football team competes once every two months.)

1.4 Read the Grammar Notes box about expressing frequency and describe in Chinese how often the following event or activity takes place.

EXAMPLE 》》》

Question: Olympic Games (once every 4 years)

měisì nián yí cì
Answer: 每四年一次

1. your friend visiting his grandma (e.g. once a month)

2. you watch a show (e.g. once every morning)

3. you have Mandarin lessons (e.g. twice a week)

4. schools breaking for holidays in the UK (e.g. 6 times a year)

GRAMMAR NOTES ON 是……的 (INDICATING PAST)

When emphasising when, where or how an action took place in the past, place the time, location or phrase about how something was done between 是 and 的 .

他是昨天来的。 (He arrived yesterday.)

我是在北京学的中文。 (It was in Beijing that I learnt Chinese.)

我们是看网球比赛的时候认识的。 (We got to know each other when we were watching a tennis match.)

1.5 Read the Grammar Notes on 是……的 and then listen to Track 11.1.5 to answer the below questions in English.

1. How did they go to London?

2. Who gave him the birthday present?

3. When was the mobile phone bought?

4. Where did the new classmate come from?

QUESTION WORDS: 几次

When asking how many times or how often something happens over a period of time, use 几次 .

你每个星期去几次健身房？ (How often do you go to the gym every week?)

次 in 几次 is a measure word for frequency that can be translated into English as "time". It can be replaced by other measure words when appropriate and relating to frequency.

这本书你看过几遍？ (How many times have you read this book?)

你每天吃几顿饭？ (How many meals do you have every day?)

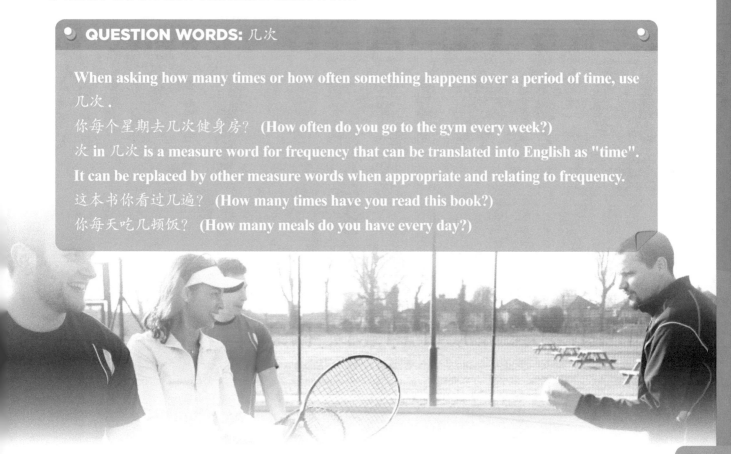

2 **Part Two** Role Play

Someone has stolen your new smartphone at a festival! You are interviewed by a police officer. Your teacher or your classmate will play the role of the police officer; or you may use the recorded questions (Track 11.2.1).

Use appropriate language for a formal conversation.
You will talk to the teacher or your classmate using the five prompts below.
• When you see – ? – you must ask a question.
• When you see – ! – you must respond to something you have not prepared.

■ **Task**

Someone has stolen your smartphone! You are interviewed by a police officer.

1. Describe the thief.
2. Say when you bought your smartphone.
3. !
4. ? Ask the name of the police officer.
5. ? Ask if the police officer can tell your parents.

These questions have been recorded for you. Listen to Track 11.2.1, pause after each question and speak in the gaps. Track 11.2.2 provides example answers.

ROLE PLAY TIPS

There are three purposes of role play:
(1) Do you understand the questions?
(2) Can you answer the questions?
(3) Can you ask questions?
So, once you have fully answered the question using appropriate language, you don't need to say more. Wait for the next one.

3

Part Three Listening Comprehension

You are hearing a culture programme on Chinese radio. What does the presenter say? Listen to Track 11.3 and put a cross X in the correct box for each question.

1. Which type of festivals are not mentioned?

☐ A. art festivals   ☐ B. book festivals   ☐ C. tourism festivals

2. According to the presenter, where are the music festivals often held?

☐ A. both indoors and outdoors   ☐ B. in the USA   ☐ C. in a field

3. Which sports event is not mentioned?

☐ A. the tennis open tournament   ☐ B. the Olympic Games

☐ C. the football World Cup

4. According to the presenter, what do Chinese fans like to do?

☐ A. travel abroad   ☐ B. go to the Bird's Nest stadium

☐ C. watch events on TV

LISTENING TIPS

Reading questions carefully is essential when answering comprehension questions. In Question 1 and 3, you are required to identify the information that is not mentioned. Not only should you note down the key words as far as you can, but you should also avoid being misled. In Question 1, art 艺术 , book 书 and tourism 旅游 are the key words for you to listen out for; similarly, in Question 3, you should focus on tennis 网球 , the Olympics 奥林匹克运动会 or 奥运会 and football 足球 . In Question 2, you may have heard 美国 , but the question is about music festivals.

4 Part Four Conversation

Answer the following questions. These questions have been recorded for you. Listen to Track 11.4.1, pause after each question and speak in the gaps. Track 11.4.2 provides sample answers.

1. 你常常参加体育比赛吗？
2. 你最喜欢看什么比赛？
3. 说说你听过的一个音乐会？
4. 你觉得电影票贵吗？
5. 你希望奥林匹克运动会在哪儿举行？

CONVERSATION TIPS

The following provides some tips and suggested content for you to consider.

1. You could think about a sport that you are good at and give a positive response. You can then talk about how good you are and how often you compete. Don't be shy if your response is negative. You can still explain why you don't take part in sports competitions often and then say what your hobbies are.

2. Again, if your answer is positive, say how often and how you watch it, e.g. by going to the stadium every month or watching it online or on TV. If your answer is negative, you could talk about why, e.g. it's too long and too boring, or you are busy so don't have time.

3. It is clearly a question that requires you to think about a particular past experience of going to a concert, who you went with, how you got there or even what you did after the concert.

4. This question is a good opportunity for you to talk about the cost of things. You may consider comparing different cinema ticket prices.

5. Listen carefully to the question as you will need to respond with the same structure, i.e. using 希望 and using a future time marker such as 会. Pick a country or continent that you think would be good at organising a future Olympic event and explain your reasoning.

5 Part Five Wrapping Up

5.1 Key question words and phrases covered in this unit

1	几次 ★	jǐ cì	how many times; how often (see "Question Words" box in Part One)
2	几遍 ★	jǐ biàn	how many times (see "Question Words" box in Part One)
3	几顿（饭）★	jǐ dùn (fàn)	how many meals (see "Question Words" box in Part One)
4	说说……	shuō shuo	talk about...
5	什么	shén me	what
6	什么时候	shén me shí hou	when; what time
7	吗	ma	(a question particle used at the end of a sentence to turn a statement into a yes-no question)
8	好吗	hǎo ma	okay?
9	哪儿	nǎ er	where

5.2 Key words and expressions covered in this unit

1	节	jié	festival
2	音乐节	yīn yuè jié	music festival
3	电影节	diàn yǐng jié	film festival
4	艺术节	yì shù jié	art festival
5	旅游节	lǚ yóu jié	tourism festival
6	世界杯	shì jiè bēi	World Cup
7	奥林匹克运动会 / 奥运会	ào lín pǐ kè yùn dòng huì / ào yùn huì	the Olympic Games
8	运动会	yùn dòng huì	sports event; sports day
9	运动场	yùn dòng chǎng	sports field
10	足球场	zú qiú chǎng	football field
11	网球场	wǎng qiú chǎng	tennis court
12	球迷	qiú mí	sports fan (for ball games)
13	影迷 / 电影迷	yǐng mí / diàn yǐng mí	film fan
14	歌迷	gē mí	music fan (for singers)
15	活动	huó dòng	activity
16	参加	cān jiā	participate
17	告诉	gào su	tell
18	乡村	xiāng cūn	rural village
19	草地	cǎo dì	grassy field, turf
20	门票	mén piào	entrance ticket

Unit 12 Holidays
第十二单元 假期

Part One Warming Up

1.1 Listen to Track 12.1.1 and match these words or phrases with their English translations. Put the correct number into the second column.

A. credit card		E. wristwatch	
B. wallet		F. mobile phone	
C. map		G. camera	
D. passport		H. flight ticket	

● GRAMMAR NOTES ON 过 (INDICATING PAST EXPERIENCE)

过 is used after an action verb to indicate that something has been experienced.

你吃过饺子吗？ (Have you ever had dumplings?)

爸爸去过好几次北京。(Dad has been to Beijing a few times.)

Place 没 or 没有 before the action verb with 过 after it to express that something has not been experienced.

她没有看过那个电影。(She hasn't seen that film.)

我从来没错过。(I have never been wrong.)

When 过 is used, a specific time in the past should not be used, but a time expression that indicates a duration in the past can be used.

我最近去过两次大英博物馆。(I've been to the British Museum twice recently.)

这两年，我妈妈只来看过我三次。(In the last two years, my mum has only been to see me three times.)

1.2 Read the Grammar Notes on 过 . Listen to Track 12.1.2 and match the questions with the images. Put the correct letter in the spaces provided and then answer each question in Chinese.

1. ____
2. ____
3. ____
4. ____

● GRAMMAR NOTES ON 越来越……

The structure " 越来越 + adjective / verb" can be used to express "more and more...".
天气越来越冷。 (The weather is getting colder and colder.)
我越来越喜欢自拍。 (I increasingly like selfies.)
A " 越来越 + adjective" phrase can also be used with 的 to modify a noun.
越来越多的中国人来英国旅游。 (More and more Chinese people come to travel in the UK.)
越来越 must be followed by either an adjective or a verb and cannot be used by itself. To describe a quantity, you can say 越来越多 (more and more) or 越来越少 (less and less).

1.3 Read the Grammar Notes on 越来越…… and use it to translate the following sentences into Chinese.

1. My younger brother is getting taller and taller.
2. I love him more and more.
3. More and more British students learn Chinese.
4. There is less and less money in my wallet.

● GRAMMAR NOTES ON 比

You can use the structure "A 比 B + adjective" to express a comparative. A and B are the two aspects for comparison.
坐飞机比坐火车快。 (Travelling by plane is faster than taking a train.)
北京的夏天比伦敦的夏天热。 (The summer in Beijing is hotter than the summer in London.)
Adverb 更 , meaning "even more", can be placed before the adjective to indicate a greater degree.
滑雪比滑冰更好玩。 (Skiing is even more fun than ice skating.)
Some fixed expressions, such as 多了 (a lot more, much more), 一点儿 (a bit, slightly), or a quantity can be added after the adjective to modify the degree or to be more specific.
中国比英国大多了。 (China is a lot bigger than Britain.)
这家饭店比那家饭店便宜一点儿。 (This hotel is a little cheaper than the other one.)
姐姐比我大四岁。 (My sister is 4 years older than me.)

1.4 Read the Grammar Notes on 比 and use the structure introduced to compare going on holiday in the UK and abroad. Some of the vocabulary is provided but you can also use an expression of your own choice.

在英国度假 vs 去国外度假	贵	累	便宜	容易	有意思	有趣	好玩	安全

● QUESTION WORDS: 还是

You can use the structure "A 还是 B" to ask a question by offering options. A and B are the two options. It is like the choice type question in English, "A or B?"
他十五岁，还是十六岁？ (Is he fifteen years old or sixteen years old?)
你喜欢在英国度假，还是去国外度假？ (Do you prefer to spend your holidays in the UK or abroad?)

Part Two Picture-based Task

■ Look at the picture and prepare statements to the following.
1. a description of the photograph
2. your preference between travelling by air or train
3. a recent train trip you had
4. your opinion on the cost of flight tickets
5. !

These questions have been recorded for you. Listen to Track 12.2.1, pause after each question and speak in the gaps. Track 12.2.2 provides sample answers.

PICTURE-BASED TASK TIPS

The purpose of the picture-based task is to assess communication through:
(1) expressing opinions;   (2) providing descriptions;   (3) narrating events.
So, apart from answering all the questions, you must develop your responses as well as you can by saying at least a couple more sentences.

● GRAMMAR NOTES ON 不但……而且……

不但……而且…… means "not only... but also...", often with an emphasis on the information after 而且.
不但 and 而且 should both be placed before the modal or main verb of each clause, and they often take the same verb.
他不但会说英语，而且会说汉语、法语和西班牙语。(He can speak not only English, but also Mandarin, French and Spanish.)
也 or 还 can be used for an added emphasis in the second clause.

GRAMMAR NOTES ON 不但…… 而且……

他不但会说英语，而且也 / 还会说汉语、法语和西班牙语。

我弟弟不但不喜欢吃青菜，而且也不喜欢吃水果。(Not only does my younger brother not like to eat vegetables, but he doesn't like fruit either.)

不但…… 而且…… can also be used with the example doesn't contain 因为 to provide two reasons.

因为我不但想去北京爬长城、吃北京烤鸭，而且还想去北京动物园看大熊猫。(Not only would I like to go to Beijing to climb the Great Wall and eat Peking Roast Duck, but I also want to visit the Beijing Zoo to see the giant pandas.)

3 Part Three Listening Comprehension

You are listening to a person speak about Chinese tourists. What does the speaker say? Listen to Track 12.3 and put a cross ✕ in each one of the four correct boxes.

A	flight	
B	sightseeing	
C	shopping	
D	restaurants	
E	travel agent	
F	destinations	
G	taking photos	
H	hotel	

LISTENING TIPS

All aspects in options A-H are travel related so you will need to listen carefully and look out for answers. You may find some answers are quite easy to spot, e.g. 买东西, 拍照片, but for the others you will need to draw conclusions, e.g. 北美洲, 澳大利亚, 欧洲.

4 Part Four Conversation

Answer the following questions. These questions have been recorded for you in Track 12.4.1. Listen to that track, pause after each question and speak in the gaps. Track 12.4.2 provides sample answers.

1. 你喜欢去度假吗？

2. 很多人喜欢去国外度假，你觉得呢？

3. 最近你去了哪儿度假？

4. 你喜欢跟家人一起度假，还是和朋友？

5. 今年暑假，你希望去哪儿度假？

CONVERSATION TIPS

The following provides some tips and suggested content for you to consider.

1. You can give a positive or a negative response. Consider giving a couple of reasons using a connecting sentence structure such as 不但……而且……(not only...but also...).

2. You could give balanced opinions by providing both sides of the argument, talking about 好处 (advantage) and 坏处 (disadvantage). You may also compare holidays abroad and in the UK.

3. Think of a past holiday about which you have more things or vocabulary to talk about, e.g. a country that you know how to say in Chinese, what you did and ate, etc. Remember to use 了, 过 or time expressions to set your answer in a past time frame.

4. You may feel you prefer spending your holidays with your family, or your friends, or both. Justify why you think that way by giving your reasons or comparing pros and cons.

5. In order to expand your answer, you might consider giving a few details about your holiday plans. For example, when you are going, who you will go with and what you are going to do. Make sure that everything you say is set under a future time frame using 希望, 想, 要, 打算, etc.

5 Part Five Wrapping Up

5.1 Key question words and phrases covered in this unit

1	A 还是 B ★	A hái shì B	A or B (see "Question Words" box in Part One)
2	什么	shén me	what
3	吗	ma	(a question particle used at the end of a sentence to turn a statement into a yes-no question)
4	呢	ne	(a question particle used at the end of a sentence to form a query)
5	什么时候	shén me shí hou	when; what time
6	贵不贵	guì bu guì	expensive or not (yes-no question type)
7	哪儿	nǎ er	where

5.2 Key words and expressions covered in this unit

1	假期	jià qī	holiday
2	度假	dù jià	spend a holiday
3	暑假	shǔ jià	summer holiday
4	旅游	lǚ yóu	travel, tourism
5	飞机票	fēi jī piào	air ticket
6	钱包	qián bāo	wallet
7	护照	hù zhào	passport
8	信用卡	xìn yòng kǎ	credit card
9	地图	dì tú	map
10	参观	cān guān	visit
11	手表	shǒu biǎo	wristwatch
12	照相机	zhào xiàng jī	camera
13	拍照片	pāi zhào piàn	take a photo
14	国外	guó wài	abroad
15	亚洲	yà zhōu	Asia
16	欧洲	ōu zhōu	Europe
17	北美洲	běi měi zhōu	North America
18	北京烤鸭	běi jīng kǎo yā	Peking roast duck
19	大熊猫	dà xióng māo	giant panda
20	长城	cháng chéng	the Great Wall

CHAPTER FOUR
School
学校

Unit 13
My School Day
第十三单元 我的学校生活

Part One Warming Up

1.1 Listen to Track 13.1.1 and match words or phrases below with their Chinese translations. Put the correct number into the second column.

A. the first lesson period		E. winter holiday	
B. summer holiday		F. school uniform	
C. subject		G. headteacher	
D. school bus		H. homework	

1.2 Look at Xiaohong's daily routine and translate it into English. Then listen to the questions in Track 13.1.2. Pause after each question and answer it with the information provided.

时间	Translation	活动	Translation
早上七点	7am	起床	get up
早上七点半		吃早饭	
早上八点		坐校车上学	
早上九点		开始上课	
中午十二点半		吃午饭	
下午三点四十五分		先参加课外活动，再做作业	
晚上六点十五分		吃晚饭	
晚上九点半		睡觉	

1.3 Read the Grammar Notes box on 要 and describe how long it takes for you to go to the following places. The first question is answered for you as an example.

EXAMPLE)))

1. from your home to your school on foot

cóng wǒ jiā dào xuéxiào zǒu lù yào bàn gè xiǎo shí

从 我 家 到 学 校 走 路 要 半 个 小 时 。

2. from your home to London by train

3. from your school to the local sports centre by bike

4. from the UK to China by air

1.4 Read the notes about asking how long it takes to travel from A to B and listen to Track 13.1.4. You will hear some answers. Ask the corresponding questions. The first question is asked for you as an example.

EXAMPLE)))

(**You hear**) 从我家到学校走路要半个小时。

(**You ask**) 从你家到学校走路要多长时间？

GRAMMAR NOTES ON ADJECTIVE + 极了

极了 is used after an adjective to show a high degree. "Adjective + 极了 " could be translated as "extremely/terribly + adjective", e.g. 好极了 (extremely good), 没意思极了 (terribly boring), or 帅极了 (extremely handsome).

It is similar to the exclamatory statement structure " 太……了 ". For example, 太好了 (brilliant), 太难学了 (so difficult to learn).

1.5 Read the Grammar Notes box on adjective + 极了 and listen to Track 13.1.5. Identify the adjective-verb in each sentence and translate it into English. Then you repeat the sentence but add 极了 to it to give the description to a higher degree. The first question is answered for you as an example.

EXAMPLE	》》》	(You hear) 从我家到学校很远。
		(You identify and translate the adjective verb) very far
		(You answer) 从我家到学校远极了！

CULTURE NOTE: CHINESE SCHOOL UNIFORM
中国校服 (zhōng guó xiào fú)

Almost all students in primary schools (小学) and secondary schools (中学) in China wear school uniforms (校服). You could be in for a shock when you first see your Chinese counterparts' uniforms.

Unlike school uniforms in the UK, which are normally formal, Chinese school uniforms are literally tracksuits (运动服)! Some may feel it is too casual or even outrageous, others think they are in fact very practical and comfortable. Perhaps next time you meet students from China, you may ask some questions about their feelings towards their uniforms.

你穿什么颜色的校服？ (What colour uniform do you wear?)

你觉得你们的校服好看吗？ (Do you think your school uniform looks good?)

为什么你们的校服和运动服一样？ (Why is your school uniform the same as a tracksuit?)

2 **Part Two** Role Play

You are greeted at the school gate in the morning by your headteacher. Your teacher or your classmate will play the role of your headteacher; or you may use the recorded questions (Track 13.2.1).

Use appropriate language for an informal conversation.
You will talk to the teacher or your classmate using the five prompts below.
• When you see – ? – you must ask a question.
• When you see – ! – you must respond to something you have not prepared.

■ **Task**

You are chatting with your headteacher about your school day.

1. Say how you go to school every morning.
2. Say what time you get up.
3. !
4. Give your opinion of your school.
5. ? Ask your headteacher if he/she likes your school uniform.

These questions have been recorded for you. Listen to Track 13.2.1, pause after each question and speak in the gaps. Track 13.2.2 provides sample answers.

ROLE PLAY TIPS

There are three purposes of role play:
(1) Do you understand the questions?
(2) Can you answer the questions?
(3) Can you ask a question?
So, once you have fully answered the question using appropriate language, you don't need to say more. Wait for the next one.

3 Part Three Listening Comprehension

You are listening to a school's advertisement about their open day. Listen to Track 13.3 and put a cross × to indicate the statement as True or False. Correct any false statements in English.

Statement	True	False	False correction
1. This school is in the city centre.			
2. There are more than 500 students.			
3. The school gate remains open after 3.30pm.			
4. The football matches are played at the city stadium every Friday.			

LISTENING TIPS

Listening comprehension requires not only understanding the words but also the grammatical structures. For example, in Question 1, although 市中心 is heard, the structure 离……不远 would be the key for the answer; in Question 3, 三点半放学 is indeed mentioned, but the time phrase 放学后 is crucial for the answer. In Question 2, two numbers are said but focus on the one relating to the students. In Question 4, focus on the location phrase which according to the word order in Chinese, is placed before the verb it modifies.

4 Part Four Conversation

Answer the following questions. These questions have been recorded for you. Listen to Track 13.4.1, pause after each question and speak in the gaps. Track 13.4.2 provides sample answers.

1. 请说说你们学校，好吗？

2. 你喜欢你们的学校吗？为什么？

3. 今天早饭你吃了什么？

4. 英国的校服和中国的校服有什么不一样？

5. 今天放学以后，你想做什么？

CONVERSATION TIPS

The following provides some tips and suggested content for you to consider.

1. Questions that start with " 请说说 " allow you a great deal of freedom, as your answer can be wide ranging. You could talk about the location of the school, the number of students and teachers, how many classes you have each day, the time your lessons start and end, and many other things. You might consider describing positive and negative aspects, using the 虽然…… 但是…… structure.

2. For this question, you need to express your opinion and justify it. You may consider a few reasons why you like or dislike your school; or you could give one reason but explain in greater detail.

3. It might appear to be the case that there is little you can talk about once you have said what you ate and drank at breakfast. However, you should try to think outside the box so you can extend your answer. For example, you could say what you like and dislike to have at breakfast or whether you often skip your breakfast because you find it hard to get up early and therefore do not have time to eat.

4. Although this question does require some culture understanding and research, there is no right or wrong answer and things have been changing rapidly in both countries. So, use your general knowledge to answer the question but of course, you should take the opportunity to use clothing vocabulary such as 外衣 , 上衣 , 毛衣 , 衬衣 , 领带 , 裤子 , 裙子 , etc.

5. To talk about the thing or things you intend to do, you could talk about one activity by giving a few more details including when, where and with whom it will take place, or use the 先…… 再…… 然后…… structure to talk about a few intentional activities you are going to do after school.

Part Five Wrapping Up

5.1 Key question words and phrases covered in this unit

1	要多长时间 ★	yào duō cháng shí jiān	how long does it take (see "Question Words" box in Part One)
2	几点	jǐ diǎn	what time
3	怎么	zěn me	how
4	怎么样	zěn me yang	how about
5	吃什么	chī shén me	what to eat
6	做什么	zuò shén me	what to do
7	为什么	wèi shén me	why
8	吗	ma	(a question particle used at the end of a sentence to turn a statement into a yes-no question)
9	好吗	hǎo ma	okay?
10	有什么不一样	yǒu shén me bù yí yàng	what is/are the difference(s)

5.2 Key words and expressions covered in this unit

1	起床	qǐ chuáng	get up
2	吃早饭	chī zǎo fàn	have breakfast
3	穿校服	chuān xiào fú	wear uniform
4	坐校车	zuò xiào chē	take the school bus
5	上学	shàng xué	go to school
6	上课	shàng kè	go to lessons
7	吃午饭	chī wǔ fàn	have lunch
8	下课	xià kè	finish lessons
9	放学	fàng xué	finish school
10	参加课外活动	cān jiā kè wài huó dòng	participate in extra-curricular activities
11	做作业	zuò zuò yè	do homework
12	吃晚饭	chī wǎn fàn	have dinner
13	睡觉	shuì jiào	go to bed
14	暑假	shǔ jià	summer holiday
15	寒假	hán jià	winter holiday
16	学生	xué sheng	student
17	老师	lǎo shī	teacher
18	校长	xiào zhǎng	headteacher
19	科目	kē mù	subject
20	节	jié	(measure word for school lessons)

Unit 14
In the Classroom
第十四单元 在教室

Part One Warming Up

1.1 Look at the school timetable below and translate the subjects into English. Then, listen to Track 14.1.1 and answer the questions.

时间 / 星期	星期一	星期二	星期三	星期四	星期五
9.00-9.50am	中文 Chinese	地理 ___	英文 ___	地理 ___	生物 ___
9.55-10.45am	数学 ___	物理 ___	中文 ___	西班牙文 ___	电脑 ___
10.45-11.00am	休息 break				
11.00-11.50am	电脑 ___	化学 ___	历史 ___	生物 ___	英文 ___
11.55-12.45pm	午饭 lunch				
12.50-1.40pm	历史 ___	西班牙文 ___	数学 ___	物理 ___	化学 ___
1.45-2.35pm	体育 ___	公民 citizenship	自习 self-study	体育 ___	公民 citizenship
2.40-3.30pm		自习 self-study	体育 ___	自习 self-study	

> ### GRAMMAR NOTES: MULTIPLE MEANINGS OF 上 AND 下
>
> 上 is one of those words in Chinese that has many different meanings. As a verb, it means "to go to", "to attend", "to board", "to climb".
> 上学 : to go to school (to study)   上大学 : to study in a university 上课 : to attend a lesson
> 上图书馆 : to go to the library   上校车 : to get on the school bus 上班 : to go to work
> 上山 : to climb the mountain
> Although not applied to all of the above phrases, 下 can be used to express the opposite action of some of them. As a verb, 下 means "to finish", "to get off", "to go down".
> 下课 : to finish lesson   下车 : to get off transport   下班 : to finish work
> 下山 : to go down the mountain

1.2 Read the Grammar Notes about 上 and 下 . Listen to Track 14.1.2 and complete the translation in English.

1. I _____ at nine o'clock in the morning and _____ at twelve o'clock.

2. He _____ at the city centre station and _____ at the sports stadium.

3. What time does your dad _____? What time does he _____?

4. The classmates _____ in the afternoon on the first day and _____ in the morning on the second day.

> ● **GRAMMAR NOTES: EXPRESSING "NOT VERY" WITH 不太**
>
> You can use 不太 (not very, not quite) before an adjective or some modal or psychological verbs, such as 会，想，喜欢，懂, to help make a negative expression sound less blunt, much like saying "not too..." in English.
> 我们学校不太远。(Our school is not very far.)
> 我不太会说汉语。(I don't know much Chinese.)
> 我的同学都不太喜欢上数学课。(My classmates don't like maths lessons very much.)
> Note that in this type of sentence with 不太，了 should not be used at the end.

1.3 Read the Grammar Notes about 不太 and listen to Track 14.1.3. Translate each word into English and then say the opposite expression using 不太 …… and adding the translation.

EXAMPLE 》》》	(You hear) 1. 好
	(You translate) good
	(You then say) 不太好
	(You then add translation) not so good

1. 好	good	1. 不太好	not so good
2. 友好			
3. 难			
4. 容易			
5. 对			
6. 严厉			
7. 喜欢			
8. 明白			

GRAMMAR NOTES: 但是 , 可是 AND 不过 (BUT, HOWEVER)

In English, "but" or "however" is used to introduce a phrase or clause contrasting with what has already been mentioned. It is similar in Chinese but there are a few words for "but" or "however" in Chinese that you can use. The three common ones are 但是 , 可是 and 不过 . They are largely the same although 但是 is slightly formal, and using 不过 is usually colloquial and soft in tone.

1.4 Read the Grammar Notes box about 但是 , 可是 and 不过 . Listen to Track 14.1.4 and combine the two contrasting sentences.

EXAMPLE   >>>   (You hear) 1. 美术课很有意思。美术考试很难。
(You answer) 美术课很有意思 , 但是 / 可是 / 不过美术考试很难。

QUESTION WORDS: 几月几日 , 星期几 AND 几点

In Chinese, when making a request for information about time, day of the week and date, 几 is usually used.

今天是几月几日？ (What is the date today?)

你星期几有中文课？ (On what day do you have a Chinese lesson?)

你几点放学？ (What time do you finish school?)

2 Part Two Picture-based Task

■ **Look at the picture and prepare statements to the following.**

1. a description of the photo
2. your opinion of learning Chinese
3. on what days of the week you have Chinese lessons
4. what homework you did last week
5. whether or not you wish to go to China to learn Chinese

Questions relating to the above have been recorded for you. Listen to Track 14.2.1, pause after each question and speak in the gaps. Track 14.2.2 provides sample answers.

PICTURE-BASED TASK TIPS

The purpose of the picture-based task is to assess communication through:

(1) expressing opinions;

(2) providing descriptions;

(3) narrating events.

So, apart from answering all the questions, you must develop your responses as well as you can by saying at least a couple more sentences.

3 Part Three Listening Comprehension

You are listening to some students talking about their school subjects. Is each of their opinion positive, negative or both positive and negative? Listen to Track 14.3 and put a cross ✕ in each one of the four correct boxes.

	Positive	Negative	Both positive and negative
1			
2			
3			
4			

LISTENING TIPS

In order to identify whether a spoken opinion is positive, negative, or both positive and negative, you should focus on the types of words often used for expressing opinions, such as the key verb and adjective. You could make a list to revise these words. Here are some examples:

Positive words – 喜欢 , 爱 , 希望 , 有意思 , 有趣 , 好看 , 好吃 , 好听 , 好玩 , 可爱 , 亲切 .

Negative words – 不喜欢 , 不爱 , 不希望 , 没意思 , 难看 , 难吃 , 难听 , 严厉 .

For opinions that are positive and negative, listen out for sentence structures that mark contrast, such as 虽然…… 但是 / 可是 / 不过…… .

4 Part Four Conversation

Answer the following questions. These questions have been recorded for you in Track 14.4.1. Listen to that track, pause after each question and speak in the gaps. Track 14.4.2 provides sample answers.

1. 你在学校学哪些科目？

2. 学什么最重要？为什么？

3. 你昨天上了什么课？

4. 说说你最喜欢的一位老师。

5. 如果上大学，你希望学什么？

CONVERSATION TIPS

The following provides some tips and suggested content for you to consider.

1. This is a straightforward question. Say what GCSEs you are studying. You need not list every subject, so you are free to leave out those that you don't know how to say in Chinese. Do, however, highlight which subject(s) you like and which you don't.

2. You could mention the subject most important to you, but you could also talk about more than one subject if you feel some are equally important. Choose words and phrases that support positive opinions, such as useful, interesting, makes me smarter, etc.

3. Recall what lessons you had yesterday morning. Note 了 should not be added to 有 as it is not an action verb. So, if you are trying to say, "yesterday morning, I had...", just say the time phrase first and the rest of the sentence in the present time frame. However, if you use 上……课, you should add 了, e.g. 上了英文课, as 上 is an action verb.

4. You only need to mention one of your favourite teachers. Give your reasons by using positive adjectives, e.g. 亲切 or 有趣. Of course you may consider using 虽然……但是…… to express contrasted things about the teacher, e.g. "although he is extremely strict, his lesson is fun."

5. Say what subject(s) you wish to study if you are going to university. You could use a phrase such as 我想做…… to talk about your future career choice; in this way, you can expand your answer.

Part Five   Wrapping Up

5.1 Key question words and phrases covered in this unit

1	几月几日 ★	jǐ yuè jǐ rì	what is the date (see "Question Words" box in Part One)
2	星期几 ★	xīng qī jǐ	on what day of the week (see "Question Words" box in Part One)
3	几点 ★	jǐ diǎn	what time (see "Question Words" box in Part One)
4	吗	ma	(a question particle used at the end of a sentence to turn a statement into a yes-no question)
5	什么	shén me	what
6	什么课	shén me kè	what lesson(s)
7	为什么	wèi shén me	why
8	怎么样	zěn me yang	how about; how is it
9	哪些	nǎ xiē	which (plural)
10	说说……	shuō shuo......	talk about...

5.2 Key words and expressions covered in this unit

1	中文 / 汉语	zhōng wén / hàn yǔ	Chinese
2	法文	fǎ wén	French
3	西班牙文	xī bān yá wén	Spanish
4	英文	yīng wén	English
5	数学	shù xué	mathematics
6	科学	kē xué	science
7	化学	huà xué	chemistry
8	物理	wù lǐ	physics
9	生物	shēng wù	biology
10	历史	lì shǐ	history
11	地理	dì lǐ	geography
12	美术	měi shù	art
13	电脑	diàn nǎo	computing, computer
14	考试	kǎo shì	exam
15	友好	yǒu hǎo	friendly
16	严厉	yán lì	strict
17	容易	róng yì	easy
18	难	nán	difficult
19	有趣	yǒu qù	fun, interesting
20	明白 / 懂	míng bai / dǒng	understand

Unit 15
My School

第十五单元 我的学校

Part One Warming Up

1.1 Listen to Track 15.1.1 and sort these places into the categories below. Write the English translation next to an appropriate category.

堂		馆	
室	1. office	场	

> **GRAMMAR NOTES ON** 花
>
> 花 has many meanings in Chinese.
> (1) As a noun, it means "flower".
> 鲜花 (fresh flowers)　　　花园 (garden)　　　花瓶 (vase)　　　花店 (florist's)
> (2) As an adjective, it means "floral" or "multi-patterned".
> 花裙子 (flower-patterned skirt)　　　花样游泳 (synchronised swimming)
> (3) As a verb, 花 can mean "spend", as in "spend time" or "spend money".
> 我每天花两个小时做作业。(I spend two hours every day doing my homework.)
> 哥哥花了一百元给爸爸买生日礼物。(My brother spent 100 yuan buying a birthday present for Dad.)

1.2 Read the Grammar Notes box on 花 **and use the word to say the following sentences.**

1. There are many flowers in the garden.

2. There are many vases in the florist's.

3. I spent one hour per week chatting with my Chinese friend online.

4. She spent 300 kuai and bought a second-hand (二手) mobile phone.

GRAMMAR NOTES ON 为了

为了 , meaning "in order to" or "for the purpose of ", can be used to indicate the purpose of an action or an aim that someone tries to achieve.

为了上最好的大学，她每天晚上都去图书馆学习。 (For the sake of going to the best university, she goes to the library to study every evening.)

他每天走路上学是为了减肥。 (He walks to school every day to lose weight).

1.3 Read the Grammar Notes on 为了 and listen to Track 15.1.3. Give the reason for each action.

1. I want to take part in the China summer camp in order to _____.

2. He did not go on holiday with his family in order to _____.

3. She works part-time on Saturday in order to _____.

4. We must drive less and walk more in order to _____.

GRAMMAR NOTES ON 多 AND 少

In English, you say "do something more" or "do something less". "more" or "less" is placed after the verb, for example, "exercise more", "drink less". However, in Chinese, the word 多 (more) or 少 (less) always comes before the verb.

你应该多运动，少看电视。(You should exercise more and watch less TV.)

1.4 Read the Grammar Notes on 多 and 少 , and give the following advice in Chinese.

EXAMPLE 》》 **1. Say less and listen more!**
(Your answer) 少说，多听！

2. Drive less and cycle more!

3. Eat less meat and eat more vegetables!

4. Play less computer games and read more books!

QUESTION WORDS: 几 AND 多少

When asking about quantity, like "how many" or "how much", use the question words 几 or 多少 .

A measure word must be used with 几 .

你有几个哥哥？ (How many elder brothers do you have?)

你爸爸每天工作几个小时？ (How many hours does your father work every day?)

When assuming the number is larger than ten, it is more appropriate to use 多少 rather than 几 .

你们学校有多少学生？ (How many students are there in your school?)

你坐过多少次飞机？ (How many times have you travelled by plane?)

When asking about price, you should say 多少钱 .

这本书多少钱？ (How much is this book?)

在学校吃午饭要多少钱？ (How much does it cost to have lunch at school?)

② **Part Two** Role Play

You are a Chinese visitor to your school's PE department and welcomed by a PE teacher. Your teacher or your classmate will play the role of the PE teacher; or you may use the recorded questions (Track 15.2.1).

Use appropriate language for a formal conversation.
You will talk to the teacher or your classmate using the five prompts below.
• When you see – ? – you must ask a question.
• When you see – ! – you must respond to something you have not prepared.

> ■ **Task**
> **You are a Chinese visitor to your school's PE department and you are talking to a PE teacher.**
> 1. Say how long you spent travelling to the school by train.
> 2. !
> 3. Say what you usually do in order to keep fit.
> 4. ? Ask how many sports fields there are in the school.
> 5. ? Ask how many students there are in the school.

These questions have been recorded for you. Listen to Track 15.2.1, pause after each question and speak in the gaps. Track 15.2.2 provides sample answers.

ROLE PLAY TIPS

There are three purposes of role play:
(1) Do you understand the questions?
(2) Can you answer the questions?
(3) Can you ask questions?
So, once you have fully answered the question using appropriate language, you don't need to say more. Wait for the next one.

The structure "A 没有 B + adjective" can be used to make a negative comparison and express that something or someone has not reached a standard. The English equivalent is "A is not as... as B".

我没有我的朋友小红聪明。(I am not as smart as my friend Xiaohong.)

羽毛球没有网球好玩。(Badminton is not as fun as tennis.)

Part Three Listening Comprehension

Yufei, an international student in the UK, is voice messaging her mother in China. Listen to Track 15.3 and answer the following questions in English.

1. What does Yufei not like about her school in the UK?

2. What does her mum ask her to do but is hard to achieve?

3. What things are available during the school breaks?

4. What is she going to do every day?

LISTENING TIPS

It is important to read the questions carefully, especially when the question is asked in a slightly unusual way. For example, Question 1 asks what the speaker doesn't like rather than what she likes.

When distracting information is given, you should focus on the key items that the questions are asking. For example, in Question 2, you may hear 青菜, 面包, 鸡蛋 and 肉, but you should pay attention to what the speaker's mum advised her to eat. In Question 4, a few activities are said relating to the time expressions 每天, 每个星期五 and 周末, but you should only concentrate on the one that will be done every day.

4 Part Four Conversation

Answer the following questions. These questions have been recorded for you in Track 15.4.1. Listen to that track, pause after each question and speak in the gaps. Track 15.4.2 provides sample answers.

1. 你在学校有什么压力？

2. 你们的校长知道你有压力吗？

3. 如果有压力，你会找谁一起谈谈？

4. 你觉得考试的好处是什么？坏处是什么？

5. 为了让自己快乐，你做过什么？

CONVERSATION TIPS

The following provides some tips and suggested content for you to consider.

1. You should first directly answer the question by saying whether you feel pressure in school or not. If you answer "yes", give details of the pressure you are facing. Alternatively you could explain why you don't feel pressure.

2. Assuming most headteachers know very well about the stress and anxiety that their students experience, you may respond with 我相信校长知道…… (I believe the headteacher knows...). You could quote what your headteacher advises about school pressure. You could also express how you feel about it or compare the pressure you feel with what you expect a sixth form student might feel.

3. 谁 (who) is the key question so you should think of one or more people that you normally go to talk to when you are under pressure, e.g. a friend, your parents, or your teachers. Give a bit more detail about when, where, and how these talks are carried out.

4. You could begin your answer using the structure 有…… 也有……(there are both... and...) to say that exams have good and bad points. Or you could use 只有 …… 没有 ……(there are only... but not...) to express your opinion of there being only advantages without any disadvantages, or vice versa.

5. Of course this question can be answered by giving examples of what you usually do to relax and ease your pressure. For example, you might say you listen to music, read, or watch films. However, to address the past-tense aspect of the question, you should also talk about a recent activity you did. You could, for example, say what you did after a recent exam that you felt was difficult.

5 Part Five Wrapping Up

5.1 Key question words and phrases covered in this unit

1	几 ★	jǐ	how many (re. less than ten) (see "Question Words" box in Part One)
2	多少 ★	duō shǎo	how many (re. more than ten) (see "Question Words" box in Part One)
3	多少钱 ★	duō shǎo qián	how much (re. asking about price) (see "Question Words" box in Part One)
4	多长时间	duō cháng shí jiān	how long (re. asking about length of time)
5	怎么样	zěn me yang	how about
6	谁	shuí	who
7	吗	ma	(a question particle used at the end of a sentence to turn a statement into a yes-no question)
8	做什么	zuò shén me	do what
9	有什么	yǒu shén me	what to have
10	.……是什么	shì shén me	what is...

5.2 Key words and expressions covered in this unit

1	教室	jiào shì	classroom
2	办公室	bàn gōng shì	office
3	图书馆	tú shū guǎn	library
4	体育馆	tǐ yù guǎn	stadium
5	运动场	yùn dòng chǎng	sports field
6	足球场	zú qiú chǎng	football pitch
7	健身房	jiàn shēn fáng	gym
8	礼堂	lǐ táng	assembly hall
9	食堂	shí táng	canteen
10	餐厅	cān tīng	canteen, restaurant
11	饭厅	fàn tīng	canteen, dining room
12	卫生间	wèi shēng jiān	bathroom
13	洗手间	xǐ shǒu jiān	restroom
14	厕所	cè suǒ	toilet
15	压力	yā lì	pressure
16	快乐	kuài lè	happy
17	好处	hǎo chu	advantage, benefit
18	坏处	huài chu	disadvantage, harm
19	谈谈	tán tan	talk about; talk
20	让	ràng	let, allow

Unit 16
Extra-curricular Activities

第十六单元 课外活动

1 Part One Warming Up

1.1 Listen to Track 16.1.1 and match these after-school activities with their English translations. Put the correct number into the second column.

A. taking part in the football team games	
B. learning Tai Chi	
C. going to the gym	
D. practising gymnastics	
E. attending calligraphy class	
F. singing Beijing opera	
G. joining school band activities	
H. playing the piano	

GRAMMAR NOTES: MAKING COMPARISONS WITH 一样

In addition to using 比 and 没有 to make positive and negative comparisons, 一样 can be used to compare two things or two people that are the same.

Use "A 和 / 跟 B 一样 " to say that two things are identical.

她的自行车和我的 (自行车) 一样。(Her bike is identical to mine.)

To say that two things are identical in some way, build on the structure with an adjective or verb phrase: A 和 / 跟 B 一样 + adjective / verb phrase.

今天跟昨天一样冷。(Today is as cold as yesterday.)

我弟弟跟我一样喜欢运动。(My brother likes sports, just like me.)

1.2 Read the Grammar Notes box about making comparisons with 一样. Listen to Track 16.1.2 and combine the sentences into one.

EXAMPLE 》》》 (You hear) 1. 我朋友的运动鞋很舒服，我的运动鞋也很舒服。
(You answer) 我朋友的运动鞋跟我的（运动鞋）一样舒服。

> **● GRAMMAR NOTES: GIVING A LIST OF EXAMPLES WITH 比如 AND 等等 ●**
>
> 比如 is the same as in English when we say "for example". You can use 比如 to give an example or a list of examples. When giving a list of items, you may place 等等 or just 等 at the end of the list. It is just like saying "and so on" or "etcetera" at the end of a list in English.
> 我喜欢室外的课外活动，比如跑步、骑自行车、滑雪等等。(I like outdoor extra-curriculum activities, for example, jogging, cycling, skiing, etc.)

1.3 Read the Grammar Notes box about giving a list of examples with 比如 and 等等, then use the structure to talk about the sports and extra-curricular activities that you like.

1. 我非常喜欢运动，比如_____、_____、_____等等。

2. 我喜欢很多课外活动，比如_____、_____、_____等等。

GRAMMAR NOTES ON 不仅……而且……

Using connective words appropriately is very important, as it makes your writing coherent. The structure 不仅…… 而且…… is one such set of connective words, which means the same as 不但…… 而且…… (not only... but also..., introduced in Unit 12). Another similar set of connective words is 除了……(以外)……也 / 还…… (apart from... also..., introduced in Unit 2).

在北京，我不仅参观了有名的长城，而且在中国朋友家吃了饺子。(In Beijing, I not only visited the famous Great Wall but also ate dumplings at my Chinese friend's home.)

In spoken Chinese, 而且 is often replaced by the adverb 也 or 还 , or can even be omitted.

他不仅汉语说得好，汉字也写得漂亮。(He not only speaks Mandarin very well, but he writes characters very beautifully too.)

1.4 Translate the following phrases into English on the lines provided and read the Grammar Notes on 不仅 / 不但…… 而且 / 也 / 还…… and 除了…… (以外)…… 也 / 还……. Then, use one of the structures to describe activities that these students do after school, starting with 放学以后……

名字 Name	活动一 Activity 1	活动二 Activity 2	活动三 Activity 3
小红 Xiaohong	打太极拳 ――――	弹钢琴 ――――	学外语 ――――
小蓝 ――――	打网球 ――――	唱歌 ――――	参观博物馆 ――――
小黑 ――――	踢足球 ――――	玩儿乐队 ――――	学书法 ――――
小白 ――――	骑马 ――――	唱京剧 ――――	学画画 ――――

QUESTION WORDS: 哪些

哪 means "which" and 些 means "some", so when an interrogative sentence contains the question words 哪些 , "which ones", you are expected to give more than one answer.

放学以后，你都参加哪些课外活动？ (What extra-curricular activities do you participate in after school?)

哪些同学想学太极拳？请举手。(Which students want to learn Tai Chi? Please raise your hand.)

■ **Look at the picture and prepare statements to the following.**

1. a description of the photograph

2. explain why you like or dislike cooking

3. a recent Chinese takeaway order you made

4. the Chinese dishes that you like

5. !

Questions relating to the above have been recorded for you. Listen to Track 16.2.1, pause after each question and speak in the gaps. Track 16.2.2 provides sample answers.

PICTURE-BASED TASK TIPS

The purpose of the picture-based task is to assess communication through:

(1) expressing opinions;

(2) providing descriptions;

(3) narrating events.

So, apart from answering all the questions, you must develop your responses as well as you can by saying at least a couple more sentences.

3 Part Three Listening Comprehension

You are listening to a UK student talking about her trip to China. What does she say? Listen to Track 16.3 and put a cross ✕ in each one of the four correct boxes.

A	I went to China three weeks' ago.	
B	It was a summer camp in China.	
C	We visited some unknown places.	
D	The food was nice and fresh.	
E	I met a friend on top of the Great Wall.	
F	My friend first visited the Great Wall when he was just over ten years old.	
G	My friend said the Great Wall looked longer than he thought.	
H	My friend talked about the history.	

LISTENING TIPS

All statements in options A-H seem possible and consistent. The spoken text is quite long so students must not only try to understand the overall messages, but also pay attention to all the key points delivered through a range of complex language. You may need to listen to the recording several times. Put a cross ✕ in those statements that you are confident that are correct. Draw a question mark next to the statements that you are not certain of. Listen to the recording again and focus on those that relate to the statements that you have doubts about and try to take in as much detail as you can.

4 Part Four Conversation

Answer the following questions. These questions have been recorded for you in Track 16.4.1. Listen to that track, pause after each question and speak in the gaps. Track 16.4.2 provides sample answers.

1. 放学以后，你一般都参加哪些课外活动？

2. 参加课外活动的好处是什么？

3. 上个周末，你做了什么？

4. 做运动和学习，哪个更重要？

5. 如果能参加奥运会，你想参加什么比赛？

CONVERSATION TIPS

The following provides some tips and suggested content for you to consider.

1. Take the opportunity to use 比如 and 等等 (see Part One) to give a list of extra-curricular activities that you participate in at school.

2. Consider using connective words, such as 不仅 / 不但…… 而且 / 还 / 也…… or 除了……(以外)…… 还 / 也…… to talk about the benefits of extra-curricular activities in a structured way. Read the Grammar Notes in Part One.

3. Think about what you did last weekend, but you don't have to give an account of everything. You could use the 先…… 再…… 然后…… structure to highlight a few things you did. Remember you need to put the events in past time frames, such as providing a time phrase (e.g. 上个周末), and adding 了 after the action verbs.

4. When you are asked to compare two aspects, such as 做运动 and 学习 , consider answering the question by using comparative sentence structures such as "A 比 B + adjective", "A 没有 B + adjective", "A 跟 / 和 B 一样 + adjective", etc.

5. Of course, this question may sound fanciful but who knows. You could give it a go by saying what sport you would like to take part in and then saying how you would prepare for the competition.

5 Part Five Wrapping Up

5.1 Key question words and phrases covered in this unit

1	哪些 ★	nǎ xiē	which (plural) (see "Question Words" box in Part One)
2	哪个	nǎ ge	which (singular)
3	吗	ma	(a question particle used at the end of a sentence to turn a statement into a yes-no question)
4	什么	shén me	what
5	有什么	yǒu shén me	what to have
6	……是什么	shì shén me	what is...
7	做了什么	zuò le shén me	what have done
8	为什么	wèi shén me	why
9	什么时候	shén me shí hou	when; what time
10	谁	shuí	who

5.2 Key words and expressions covered in this unit

1	课外活动	kè wài huó dòng	extra-curricular activities
2	参加足球队比赛	cān jiā zú qiú duì bǐ sài	participate in football team games
3	学打太极拳	xué dǎ tài jí quán	learn Tai Chi
4	去健身房	qù jiàn shēn fáng	go to the gym
5	练体操	liàn tǐ cāo	practise gymnastics
6	骑马	qí mǎ	horse riding
7	参观博物馆	cān guān bó wù guǎn	visit the museum
8	上书法课	shàng shū fǎ kè	attend a calligraphy class
9	学画画	xué huà huà	learn to draw
10	参加学校乐队活动	cān jiā xué xiào yuè duì huó dòng	participate in school band activities
11	参加合唱团	cān jiā hé chàng tuán	join the choir
12	玩儿乐队	wán er yuè duì	play in a band
13	弹钢琴	tán gāng qín	play the piano
14	唱歌	chàng gē	sing
15	唱京剧	chàng jīng jù	sing Beijing opera
16	做中餐	zuò zhōng cān	cook Chinese food
17	学外语	xué wài yǔ	learn foreign languages
18	室外	shì wài	outdoor
19	中餐外卖	zhōng cān wài mài	Chinese takeaway
20	夏令营	xià lìng yíng	summer camp

CHAPTER FIVE

Future Plans

未来计划

Unit 17 Gap Year and Work Experience

第十七单元 空档年和工作经验

Part One Warming Up

1.1 Listen to Track 17.1.1 and match these places for school work experience with their English translations. Put the correct number into the second column.

A. exhibition hall		E. shopping centre	
B. media company		F. nursery	
C. bookstore		G. hospital	
D. café		H. police station	

1.2 Look at these speech bubbles and make up four sentences.

很想 最想 有点儿想 不太想 不想	去图书馆 去幼儿园 去老人院 去快餐店 去超市	做实习生 做老师 做义工 做服务员 打工	因为……

EXAMPLE 》》》

wǒ hěnxiǎng qù tú shūguǎnzuò shí xí shēng   yīn wéi wǒ duì shū yǒuxìng qù
我很想去图书馆做实习生，因为我对书有兴趣。

(I really want to go to the library for an internship because I am interested in books.)

NEW WORDS

实习 shí xí: to do work experience; to do an apprenticeship; to do an internship
实习生 shí xí shēng: trainee; apprentice; intern

GRAMMAR NOTES ON 请

请 is often translated into English as "please", but its meaning is much broader in Chinese.

(1) please

请坐！ (Please sit down!)

请问…… (Please, may I ask...)

(2) ask or invite someone to do something

我想请朋友们来我家玩。 (I want to invite my friends to come to my house to play.)

(3) invite someone to do something at your expense

我想请你吃中餐。 (I'd like to take you out for a Chinese meal.)

(4) two more useful expressions with 请

老师，我可以请假吗？ (Teacher, may I ask for leave?)

你想喝什么？我请客。 (What would you like to drink? My treat.)

1.3 Read the Grammar Notes box on 请 and listen to Track 17.1.3. Put a cross ✕ in the box for the correct translation.

1		A. I would like to treat her to a film this weekend.
		B. She invited me to a film this weekend.

2		A. We are taking him for an Italian seafood meal today.
		B. We are going to eat Italian seafood today. He is treating us.

3		A. Mum invited me to visit her office.
		B. Mum asked for a day off from work for me.

4		A. Dad took me out ice skating yesterday.
		B. Dad took sick leave yesterday and did not go to work.

These three modal verbs, which must be followed by an action verb, translate as "can" or "be able to". Their meanings overlap in some contexts.

(1) 能 is about ability and permission.

你喝酒了，不能开车。(You have drunk alcohol so cannot drive. Implication: it is not permitted for you to drive.)

(2) 可以 has more to do with permission and is more commonly used in this sense.

十六岁可以去酒吧吗？ (May a 16-year-old go to the bar?)

It sometimes overlaps with 能 to mean "to be able to".

打工不但能 / 可以赚钱，也能 / 可以认识很多朋友。(Doing part-time work not only can earn some money but can also make many friends.)

(3) 会 is close in meaning to "to know how to".

我会说三门外语。(I can speak three foreign languages. Implication: I know how to speak three foreign languages.)

1.4 Read the Grammar Notes about the differences between 能，可以 **and** 会**, and then translate the following sentences into Chinese. You can listen to Track 17.1.4 to check your answers.**

1. Sir, may I go to the toilet?

2. Good music can help me to relax.

3. I feel unwell so can't go to work today.

4. I want to do work experience in a Chinese company because I can speak Chinese.

GRAMMAR NOTES: 为 / 给 **+ SOMEBODY + DO SOMETHING**

When you want to express "to do something for somebody", use the structure below.

为 / 给 + somebody + do something

大学毕业以后，我想为中国公司工作。(After graduating from university, I want to work for Chinese companies.)

请你给我买一瓶水，好吗？ (Could you please buy a bottle of water for me, okay?)

● QUESTION WORDS: 什么时候

什么时候 is a general question phrase used to ask "when".

请问，我什么时候可以开始工作？ (May I ask when I can start working?)

When asking for a specific time, however, 几点 is normally used.

老板，我明天早上几点要来上班？ (Boss, what time shall I come to work tomorrow morning?)

什么时候 can also be used to ask for a specific time in context. Note the differences in the following questions.

你这个星期什么时候有空？ (When are you free this week? It could be answered by a general time or day such as tomorrow, Monday, this weekend.)

你今天什么时候有空？ (When are you free today? It could be answered by a period of time such as morning, lunchtime, afternoon, evening.)

你今天上午什么时候有空？ (When are you free this morning? It could be answered by a more specific time such as 10 o'clock, before lunch.)

2 **Part Two** Role Play

You are speaking to the manager of a café about the possible opportunity for you to gain some work experience there. Your teacher or your classmate will play the role of the manager; or you may use the recorded questions (Track 17.2.1).

Use appropriate language for a formal conversation.
You will talk to the teacher or your classmate using the five prompts below.
- When you see – ? – you must ask a question.
- When you see – ! – you must respond to something you have not prepared.

> ### ▮ Task
> You are talking with a café manager about the possibility of doing work experience there.
> 1. Say what year in school you are in.
> 2. Say why you want to work in a café.
> 3. !
> 4. Say which day you want to work on.
> 5. ? Ask the manager when you can start working.

These questions have been recorded for you. Listen to Track 17.2.1, pause after each question and speak in the gaps. Track 17.2.2 provides sample answers.

ROLE PLAY TIPS

There are three purposes of role play:
(1) Do you understand the questions?
(2) Can you answer the questions?
(3) Can you ask a question?
So, once you have fully answered the question using appropriate language, you don't need to say more. Wait for the next one.

3 **Part Three** Listening Comprehension

Some students are talking about their school work experience. Where do they do their work experience? Listen to Track 17.3 and put a cross ✕ next to each one of the six correct places.

	Where they do work experience	Speaker 1	Speaker 2	Speaker 3	Speaker 4	Speaker 5	Speaker 6
EXAMPLE	hospital	✕					
A	supermarket						
B	café						
C	bakery						
D	university						
E	Chinese takeaway						
F	online advertising company						
G	library						

LISTENING TIPS

When the listening exercise is about places, you should take note of the following:

1) The location expression in a Chinese sentence is not necessarily being said at the end of the sentence as in English. It is often said before the action verb, and in many cases, it is led by 在 .

2) If the location words are unfamiliar to you, you should listen out for other related words for clues. For example, in Question 2, you hear 面包 and 做面包 .

3) The location words may not always be mentioned. If that's the case, you should try to understand the content of what is being said and identify the related wording. For example, in Question 1, "hospital" is not mentioned by Speaker 1, but it is about a nursing apprentice helping sick people, and it includes the key words 护士 and 生病 .

4) Be aware of the "distractors" when more than one workplace is mentioned. For example, in Question 3, you hear 大学 and 图书馆 ; in Question 4, 咖啡馆 and 广告公司 are both said.

4 Part Four   Conversation

Answer the following questions. These questions have been recorded for you in Track 17.4.1. Listen to that track, pause after each question and speak in the gaps. Track 17.4.2 provides sample answers.

1. 你参加过学校的社会实践活动吗？

2. 中学生参加社会实践活动的好处是什么？

3. 中学生做什么兼职能赚很多钱？

4. 你会用做兼职赚的钱买什么？

5. 你最想去哪儿做实习生？

CONVERSATION TIPS

The following provides some tips and suggested content for you to consider.

1. Say if you have or have not yet taken part in your school work experience activities. If you have, give some details about where you went and what you did; if not, explain why.

2. There are many benefits to gaining work experience: it can provide students with an opportunity to apply what they learn in school to real-life, workplace experiences; and it gives students an insight into the workplace, thereby preparing them to join the workforce. However, if you do not have the vocabulary, try give simpler reasons such as making money, getting to make new friends, or perhaps being an apprentice is more interesting than being a student. Put these ideas together by using complex sentence structures with connective words, e.g. 除了……还……，or 不但……而且…….

3. Think about the part-time jobs that students your age can do to make money. For example, delivering newspapers or working in a cafe. Give a couple of examples and say what you would or would not do.

4. There are many things you can do with the money you make. Use the same sentence structure as the question 我会用做兼职赚的钱买 …… to say what you would buy. You could give a few more details of how you would spend the money, e.g. by dining in a restaurant, going on holiday, or attending music festivals with friends.

5. Say what kind of workplace you wish to do your work experience in and explain why, focusing on applying the vocabulary and language that you can manage at this stage. For example, you can talk about going to a Chinese company for work experience because you wish to take a look at (看看) what the differences (有什么不一样) are between Chinese companies and British companies.

5 Part Five Wrapping Up

5.1 Key question words and phrases covered in this unit

1	什么时候 ★	shén me shí hou	when (see "Question Words" box in Part One)
2	几年级	jǐ nián jí	what year (in school)
3	星期几	xīng qī jǐ	which day (of the week)
4	为什么	wèi shén me	why
5	……是什么	… shì shén me	what is…
6	做什么兼职	zuò shén me jiān zhí	what part-time work to do
7	吗	ma	(a question particle used at the end of a sentence to turn a statement into a yes-no question)
8	哪儿	nǎ er	where

5.2 Key words and expressions covered in this unit

1	学校社会实践	xué xiào shè huì shí jiàn	school work experience
2	书店	shū diàn	bookstore
3	咖啡馆 / 咖啡厅 / 咖啡店	kā fēi guǎn / kā fēi tīng / kā fēi diàn	café; coffee shop
4	中餐店	zhōng cān diàn	Chinese restaurant
5	快餐店	kuài cān diàn	fast food restaurant
6	超市	chāo shì	supermarket
7	展览馆	zhǎn lǎn guǎn	exhibition hall
8	幼儿园	yòu ér yuán	nursery
9	警察局	jǐng chá jú	police station
10	媒体公司	méi tǐ gōng sī	media company
11	广告公司	guǎng gào gōng sī	advertising company
12	实习	shí xí	do work experience; do an apprenticeship; do an internship
13	实习生	shí xí shēng	trainee; apprentice; intern
14	做服务员	zuò fú wù yuán	be a waiter
15	做护士	zuò hù shi	be a nurse
16	不舒服	bù shū fu	unwell; uncomfortable
17	生病	shēng bìng	get ill
18	送外卖	sòng wài mài	deliver takeaway
19	送报纸	sòng bào zhǐ	deliver newspapers
20	赚钱	zhuàn qián	earn money

Unit 18
Life after Secondary School

第十八单元 中学毕业后

Part One Warming Up

1.1 Listen to Track 18.1.1 and match these activities that students might do after school with their English translations. Put the correct number into the second column.

A. go to university	
B. find a job	
C. volunteer	
D. work in a restaurant	
E. start your own company and do business	
F. do work experience in a factory	
G. travel to Asia	
H. take a gap year	

● GRAMMAR NOTES ON 正在

You may know how to make a sentence with the past time frame (by adding 了 or 过 after an action verb, e.g. 吃了, 去过, etc.) or a future time frame (by having 想, 要, 打算, etc. in front of a verb, e.g. 想看, 要喝, 打算做, etc.), but you may be less familiar with describing an action that is in progress. In fact, it is very easy to do so. All you need to do is add 正在 or simply 在 or 正 in front of the verb.

现在是上午十点，学生们正在上课。 (It is 10 o'clock in the morning and the students are in class.)

昨天晚上我给他打电话的时候，他在看电视。 (When I called him last night, he was watching TV.)

To ask about action in progress, use the structure: 在 + verb + 什么

你在做什么？ (What are you doing?)

他在吃什么？ (What is he eating?)

1.2 Read the Grammar Notes box on 正在 **and the Question Phrase box about** 在 **+ verb +** 什么 **. Listen to Track 18.1.2 and answer questions according to the pictures.**

In Unit 13, you practised using 从⋯⋯ 到⋯⋯ (from... to...) to describe how long in time it takes to get from one place to another.

从我家到学校走路要半个小时。 (It takes half an hour to walk from my house to my school.)

从北京到西安坐高铁只要4个半小时。 (From Beijing to Xi'an, it takes only four and a half hours by high-speed train.)

从⋯⋯ 到⋯⋯can also be used to talk about a period of time, from its beginning to its end.

从4岁到18岁，我一直在学校上学。 (From 4 to 18 years of age, I have been continuously studying in school.)

我做兼职的时间是从早上9点到中午12点。 (The working hours of my part-time job are from 9am to 12pm.)

1.3 Read the Grammar Notes on 从……到…… **and listen to Track 18.1.3. Fill in the below table with the education background and work history for the speaker.**

from	to	place	occupation
11 years old	18 years old	Town Secondary School	student

> **GRAMMAR NOTES ON** 了
>
> Let's summarise a few common usages of 了.
> (1) verb + 了 : to indicate a completed action
> 我喝了一杯牛奶。(I drank a glass of milk.)
> (2) sentence + 了 : to emphasise a change of situation
> 我十五岁了。(I am now 15.)
> (3) adjective + 极了 : to intensify the meaning
> 那个电影好看极了！(That film is fantastic!)
> (4) 快要 / 就要 / 快 / 要 + verb/verb phrase + 了 : to say that something will happen (soon) in the near future
> 我快要毕业了。(I'm soon to graduate.)

1.4 Read the Grammar Notes on 了 **and listen to Track 18.1.4. Put a cross × in the box for the correct translation.**

1		A. The concert has already started.
		B. The concert is about to start.

2		A. My classmate has already started to work in a hotel.
		B. My classmate used to work in a hotel.

3		A. After a whole day of sleep, I still feel very tired.
		B. I am going to sleep a whole day since I am so tired.

4		A. He is almost twenty so has been able to drink alcohol for some time.
		B. He is over twenty and has been drinking for some time.

2 **Part Two** Picture-based Task

■ **Look at the picture and prepare statements to the following.**

1. a description of the photograph
2. explain why you will or will not learn to drive
3. a recent driving trip you went on with your family
4. the benefits of being able to drive
5. !

Questions relating to the above have been recorded for you. Listen to Track 18.2.1, pause after each question and speak in the gaps. Track 18.2.2 provides sample answers.

PICTURE-BASED TASK TIPS

The purpose of the picture-based task is to assess communication through:

(1) expressing opinions;

(2) providing descriptions;

(3) narrating events.

So, apart from answering all the questions, you must develop your responses as well as you can by saying at least a couple more sentences.

● MORE GRAMMAR NOTES ON 如果⋯⋯ 就⋯⋯

In Unit 6, Part 2 you came across this sentence structure. Let us see two more examples.

(1) In the second half of the sentence, when 要 follows 就 , it means one must do something.

如果你想上大学，你就要参加高考。 (If you want to go to university, then you must take part in the Gaokao.)

(2) When 可以 follows 就 , it means "may / might".

在伦敦，如果到了 60 岁，你就可以免费坐地铁和公共汽车。 (In London, if you have reached 60 years of age, you may travel for free on the underground and buses.)

CULTURE NOTE: THE NATIONAL COLLEGE ENTRANCE EXAMINATION
高考 (gāo kǎo)

The National College Entrance Examination (NCEE) in China is commonly known as "Gaokao" (高考 , gāo kǎo), literally, 'high exam'. It is ranked as one of the most difficult exams in the world. Every June, secondary school students who wish to continue their education at university will need to take a series of exams over two or three days.

Traditionally, all candidates are required to take three compulsory exams, i.e. Chinese literature (语文), mathematics (数学) and one foreign language with English (英文) as the choice of most candidates. In addition, students who wish to study liberal arts (文科学生) will need to take politics (政治), history (历史) and geography (地理); whereas students who choose natural science (理科学生) will be tested in physics (物理), chemistry (化学) and biology (生物).

During the Gaokao season, it is often a major topic of conversation amongst Chinese people, with conversation often starting with:

"今年高考分数线是多少？" (What is the scoring boundary for this year's Gaokao?)

"今年的高考状元是谁？" (Who is the champion of this year's Gaokao?)

3 **Part Three** Listening Comprehension

Toby, a gap year student from the UK, is talking about his experience in China. Listen to Track 18.3 and complete the sentences by choosing a word or words from the box. There are words that you will not use.

China	Britain	~~London~~	Beijing
Hong Kong	Chinese	languages	history
classmates	colleagues		

EXAMPLE: Toby is a gap year student from ___London___.

1. Toby is doing work experience for a company in _____.

2. Toby's friend Xiaowei is studying _____ in the university.

3. Toby's _____ told him that he can apply for a course in the university.

4. Toby and Xiaowei could be _____ in the future.

LISTENING TIPS

This type of listening is rather lengthy with quite a lot of information. However, you do have the question wording to help you so make sure you read the questions carefully and write some notes, such as language you might expect to hear, before playing the audio. Remember the questions and answers are normally in chronological order so later parts of the recording will not refer to earlier questions. You may wish to write the Chinese characters or pinyin next to each word in the box to help you work out the answers. As the audio clips are repeated in the actual GCSE listening exams, you may play back the recording if you can't get all the answers the first time.

4 Part Four Conversation

Answer the following questions. These questions have been recorded for you in Track 18.4.1. Listen to that track, pause after each question and speak in the gaps. Track 18.4.2 provides sample answers.

1. 中学毕业以后，你打算做什么？

2. 我觉得每个学生都应该上大学，你同意吗？

3. 你做过什么工作？

4. 休学一年的好处是什么？

5. 休学一年有没有坏处？

CONVERSATION TIPS

The following provides some tips and suggested content for you to consider.

1. Think about what you plan to do after you graduate from secondary school. For example, if you plan to go to university, you could say what you want to study and what career choice you have in mind; if you plan to go to work, you could explain why and what you wish to do.

2. You can agree or disagree with your interviewer's opinion by using 我同意你的看法 or 我不太同意你的看法. Whatever your stance is, try to justify it by giving your reasons (因为……) or examples (比如……).

3. You should have some work experience available to answer this question with past time frames. This might include taking part in your school's work experience activities, doing a part-time job at the weekend or charity work in school or within your local community.

4. You may know a lot about the advantages of taking a gap year but if you are not totally confident with expressing them in Chinese, simplify your thoughts by sharing what you can talk about. For example, you might express something like "we have been studying for many years and everyone feels very tired, so a gap year could be good for your health (对健康有好处)".

5. Again, you don't need to try to translate everything you have to say on the matter - try to keep your answers simple. Breaking your ideas down to a few shorter sentences is a good way to deliver your thoughts and at the same time you are less likely to make grammatical mistakes.

5 Part Five Wrapping Up

5.1 Key question words and phrases covered in this unit

1	在 + verb + 什么 ★	zài + verb + shén me	(a question structure to ask about action in progress — see "Question Phrase" box in Part One)
2	哪儿	nǎ er	where
3	吗	ma	(a question particle used at the end of a sentence to turn a statement into a yes-no question)
4	你同意吗?	nǐ tóng yì ma	Do you agree?
5	什么	shén me	what
6	什么颜色	shén me yán sè	what colour
7	为什么	wèi shén me	why
8	做什么	zuò shén me	do what
9	有什么	yǒu shén me	what to have
10	有没有	yǒu mei yǒu	have or not

5.2 Key words and expressions covered in this unit

1	中学毕业以后	zhōng xué bì yè yǐ hòu	after graduating from secondary school
2	去亚洲旅行	qù yà zhōu lǚ xíng	travel to Asia
3	在餐厅打工	zài cān tīng dǎ gōng	work in a restaurant
4	上大学	shàng dà xué	go to university
5	在工厂实习	zài gōng chǎng shí xí	do work experience in a factory
6	找工作	zhǎo gōng zuò	find a job
7	休学一年	xiū xué yì nián	take a gap year
8	自己开公司	zì jǐ kāi gōng sī	start your own company
9	做生意	zuò shēng yi	do business
10	学开车	xué kāi chē	learn to drive
11	高考	gāo kǎo	National College Entrance Examination
12	同学	tóng xué	classmate
13	同事	tóng shì	colleague
14	申请	shēn qǐng	apply; application
15	成功	chéng gōng	success; successful
16	颜色	yán sè	colour
17	正在 + verb	zhèng zài	(a sentence structure to indicate an action in progress)
18	从……到……	cóng... dào...	from... to...
19	快要 / 就要……了	kuài yào / jiù yào... le	(a sentence structure to indicate events or actions that will take place very soon)
20	……极了	...jí le	extremely ...

Unit 19
Job and Career Choices

第十九单元 工作和职业选择

Part One Warming Up

1.1 Listen to Track 19.1.1 and match the words you hear with their English translations. Put the correct number into the second column.

A. actor		K. journalist	
B. artist (general)		L. lawyer	
C. artist (painter)		M. nurse	
D. chef		N. policeman	
E. dentist		O. scientist	
F. driver		P. shop assistant	
G. doctor		Q. sportsman	
H. engineer		R. teacher	
I. factory worker		S. waiter	
J. housewife		T. writer	

QUESTION WORDS: 谁 AND 谁的

(1) 谁 is used to ask a "who" question. Unlike English, it does not need to be rearranged and placed at the beginning of the sentence. You simply place it as a subject or an object in the question, to align with the word order of the sentence that answers it.

他是谁？ (Who is he? Literally, "He is who?") 他是我爸爸。 (He is my dad.)

我爸爸 is the object in the answer, so in the question, 谁 is also placed as an object.

谁会开车？ (Who can drive?) 我会开车。 (I can drive.)

我 is the subject in the answer, so in the question, 谁 is also placed as a subject.

(2) 谁的 , meaning "whose", can be used to ask about a possessive.

这是谁的书？ (Whose book is this?)

1.2 Read the Question Words box on 谁 and 谁的 . Listen to Track 19.1.2 and answer each question in Chinese.

EXAMPLE 〉〉〉 (You hear) 1. 谁的工作是教课？
(You answer) 教师的工作是教课。

○ GRAMMAR NOTES ON 就

As an adverb, 就 is another quite tricky word that you often see in Chinese sentences but rarely need to translate, such as in 一……就…… (see the Grammar Words box in Unit 11), 就要……了 (see the Grammar Words box in Unit 18). Let us see two more examples.
(1) 就 is used in front of the verb to add emphasis.
她就是我的中文老师。(She is my Chinese teacher.)
我三岁就想做数学家。(I wanted to be a mathematician when I was three years old.)
(2) When you want to explain the meaning of a word, saying or a situation, you can use the structure below.
A 就是 B 的意思。(The meaning of A is B. / A precisely means B.)
"便宜" 就是不贵的意思。("Cheap" means not expensive.)
他不来参加我的生日会，就是不想和我交朋友的意思。(He did not come to my birthday party. It means he does not want to make friends with me.)

1.3 Read the Grammar Notes box on 就 (1) and translate the following sentences by using 就 .

1. My home is right next to my school.

2. Okay, I am going to make the phone call right now.

3. My dream is to be a happy and useful person.

4. If I could go to university in the US, I would be very happy.

1.4 Read the Grammar Notes on 就 (2) and use A 就是 B 的意思 to give the definition of the following words.

EXAMPLE 〉〉〉 1. 难吃就是很不好吃的意思。

word	definition
1. 难吃	很不好吃
2. 好得不得了	非常好
3. 对健康有害	对身体很不好
4. 增加	在大小、数量上越来越多

2 Part Two Role Play

You are attending a job interview for a job as a graphic artist at an advertising company. Your teacher or your classmate will play the role of the interviewer; or you may use the recorded questions (Track 19.2.1).

Use appropriate language for a formal conversation.
You will talk to the teacher or your classmate using the five prompts below.
- When you see – ? – you must ask a question.
- When you see – ! – you must respond to something you have not prepared.

> ### Task
> **You are being interviewed for a job as a graphic artist at an advertising company.**
> 1. Describe yourself as an artist.
> 2. !
> 3. Talk about how you handle work pressure.
> 4. ? Ask who you would work with.
> 5. ? Ask how much your salary would be.

These questions have been recorded for you. Listen to Track 19.2.1, pause after each question and speak in the gaps. Track 19.2.2 provides example answers.

ROLE PLAY TIPS

There are three purposes of role play:
(1) Do you understand the questions?
(2) Can you answer the questions?
(3) Can you ask questions?
So, once you have fully answered the question using appropriate language, you don't need to say more. Wait for the next one.

3 Part Three Listening Comprehension

You are listening to a radio documentary about a Chinese personality, Yang Jiang (杨绛). What does the presenter say? Listen to Track 19.3 and put a cross × in the correct box for each question. Answer both parts for each question.

1(a). Yang Jiang was a...

☐ A. scientist ☐ B. housewife ☐ C. writer

1(b). When she was young, Yang Jiang went to Britain to...

☐ A. go to university ☐ B. work ☐ C. get married

2(a). The Chinese word "sā" (仨) means...

☐ A. three years old ☐ B. three people ☐ C. three daughters

2(b). Yang Jiang and her husband were married...

☐ A. until 2004 ☐ B. for over 60 years ☐ C. with daughters

LISTENING TIPS

When there is more than one part of the question to answer at the same time, you should read all parts of the questions carefully first before listening to the audio clip. When many details relating to the multiple choices are mentioned, it is unlikely you can simply rely on word-spotting to guess the answer. For example, in Question 2(b), 2004 年, 六十多年 and 女儿 are all mentioned by the presenter. You do need to understand the overall narrative in order to find out about the marriage of the Chinese personality, Yang Jiang.

4 Part Four Conversation

Answer the following questions. These questions have been recorded for you in Track 19.4.1. Listen to that track, pause after each question and speak in the gaps. Track 19.4.2 provides sample answers.

1. 二十五岁以后，你想做什么工作？

2. 你小时候的工作理想是什么？

3. 你认为赚钱重要吗？

4. 在英国找工作难不难？

5. 我很喜欢去外国工作，你呢？

CONVERSATION TIPS

The following provides some tips and suggested content for you to consider.

1. This question is about your future, so talk about your plans in a future time frame such as 我想做……. You could expand your answer by saying how you are going to prepare for that career path. For example, do you have a hobby related to your career choice, is it related to your favourite subject at school, or will you study for such a career at university?

2. Although you answer this question by talking about your childhood, it is not always the case that you need to add 了 in your sentences. Remember there is no such thing as tense (such as past tense, present tense or future tense) in Chinese grammar. 了 is an aspect which is only used to describe an action that is completed in a certain time frame but is not used with habitual or continuous actions, e.g. 我小时候喜欢画画。(I liked painting when I was young.) However, you can use 过 in some cases, e.g. 我小时候去过很多国家。(I had been to many countries when I was young.)

3. You should say what you think. What you say does not have to be agreeable to everyone. You could say that you think making money is very important so you can buy whatever you like, or that you'd no longer need to live with your parents (不再和父母一起住) and are able to live by yourself (自己生活). Of course, you could also use a comparative to say that, in life (生活中), happiness is more important than making money.

4. It can be quite a challenging question in terms of expanding your answer. You could give a positive answer and explain it, i.e. unemployment (失业) is a huge problem; it is harder for young people (年轻人) to find jobs. You could also give suggestions saying that society should give more work opportunities to young people and then give an example or two.

5. If you do not like the idea of working abroad, give your reasons. For example, you love Britain, and you prefer being with family and friends. But if you do like the idea of working abroad, take the opportunity to talk about China, and say what it is about China that interests you, where in China you wish to go, etc.

Part Five Wrapping Up

5.1 Key question words and phrases covered in this unit

1	谁 ★	shuí	who (see "Question Words" box in Part One)
2	谁的 ★	shuí de	whose (see "Question Words" box in Part One)
3	说说	shuō shuo	talk about...
4	什么	shén me	what
5	怎么做	zěn me zuò	how to do; what to do
6	……是多少	shì duō shǎo	how much is...
7	难不难	nàn bu nán	difficult or not (yes-no question type)
8	吗	ma	(a question particle used at the end of a sentence to turn a statement into a yes-no question)
9	好吗	hǎo ma	okay?
10	你呢	nǐ ne	what about you

5.2 Key words and expressions covered in this unit

1	科学家	kē xué jiā	scientist
2	作家	zuò jiā	writer
3	艺术家	yì shù jiā	artist (general)
4	画家	huà jiā	artist (painter)
5	教师	jiào shī	teacher
6	工程师	gōng chéng shī	engineer
7	律师	lǜ shī	lawyer
8	厨师	chú shī	chef
9	演员	yǎn yuán	actor
10	运动员	yùn dòng yuán	sportsperson
11	服务员	fú wù yuán	waiter
12	售货员	shòu huò yuán	shop assistant
13	医生	yī shēng	doctor
14	牙医	yá yī	dentist
15	护士	hù shi	nurse
16	记者	jì zhě	journalist
17	警察	jǐng chá	policeman
18	工厂工人	gōng chǎng gōng rén	factory worker
19	司机	sī jī	driver
20	家庭主妇	jiā tíng zhǔ fù	housewife

CHAPTER SIX
Technology and Global Issues
科技和全球问题

Unit 20　Internet, Mobile Technology and Social Media

第二十单元 互联网、移动技术和社交媒体

Part One Warming Up

1.1 Listen to Track 20.1.1 and match the words or phrases you hear with their English translations. Put the correct number into the second column.

A. computer	3	E. email	8
B. download	6	F. e-book; e-reader	4
C. mobile phone	7	G. blog	1
D. text message	5	H. social media	2

> ● **GRAMMAR NOTES ON** 一点儿也不 / 没　　　　　　●
>
> To say "not at all" in Chinese, you can use the structure below.
> 一点儿也不 / 没 + verb / adjective-verb
> 我妈妈一点儿也不喜欢微信。(My mum doesn't like WeChat at all.)
> 这个电子游戏一点儿也不好玩。(This electronic game is not fun at all.)

1.2 Read the Grammar Notes on 一点儿也不 / 没 **. Listen to Track 20.1.2 and rephrase each sentence with the structure** 一点儿也不 / 没 **+ verb/adjective-verb.**

EXAMPLE >>>　　(You hear) 1. 我非常不喜欢脸书。
　　　　　　　　　　(You answer) 我一点儿也不喜欢脸书。

> ● **GRAMMAR NOTES: DESCRIBING THE DURATION OF AN ACTION**　　●
>
> When describing the length of time you spend on doing something, if the verb takes an object, e.g. 玩电子游戏 or 打网球 , the duration phrase must be placed right after the verb and before the verb's object.
> 我昨天和哥哥打了两个小时网球。(I played tennis with my elder brother for two hours yesterday.)
> 我父母只让我每天玩一个小时电子游戏。(My parents only let me play computer games for one hour a day.)

In Unit 13, we revised using 从 A 到 B 要多长时间 to ask how long it takes to travel from A to B. Similarly, asking how long it takes to do something, you can also use 多长时间 .

你每个星期做多长时间运动？ (How long do you do exercise for every week?)

你每天看多长时间电视？ (How long do you watch TV for every day?)

You can use 多长时间 + 一次 to ask a "how often" question in Chinese.

你多长时间踢一次足球？ (How often do you play football?)

你多长时间给妈妈打一次电话？ (How often do you call your mum?)

1.3 Read the Grammar Notes box about describing the duration of an action and the notes about the question words 多长时间 . Listen to Track 20.1.3 and answer these survey questions in Chinese.

● GRAMMAR NOTES: CONTINUATION OF AN ACTION UNTIL A POINT

To indicate that you did something continuously until a specific time, use the below sentence structure:

verb + 到 + specific time

周末我常常睡到中午才起床。(At the weekend, I often sleep until midday and only then do I get up.)

我今天早上上网和朋友聊天聊到九点半。(I chatted with my friends online this morning until 9:30.)

When using it to describe a verb + object phrase, e.g. 做作业 or 玩手机 , the structure to use is:

verb + object + the same verb + 到 + specific time

昨天晚上我做作业做到十二点。(I did my homework till 12 o'clock last night.)

我妹妹每天晚上玩手机玩到很晚。(My younger sister plays on her mobile phone late every night.)

1.4 Read the Grammar Notes on the continuation of an action to a point using 到 , and say these sentences in Chinese.

1. He swims until five o'clock every Saturday afternoon.

2. Dad chats with friends late on social media every day.

3. I play computer games after school until my mum comes home from work.

4. After doing her homework, she listens to music until she goes to sleep.

CULTURE NOTES: POPULAR TECHNOLOGY AND SOCIAL MEDIA BRANDS IN CHINESE

苹果	píng guǒ	Apple
三星	sān xīng	Samsung
微软	wēi ruǎn	Microsoft
谷歌	gǔ gē	Google
脸书	liǎn shū	Facebook
亚马逊	yà mǎ xùn	Amazon
推特	tuī tè	Twitter
油管	yóu guǎn	YouTube
抖音	dǒu yīn	TikTok
微信	wēi xìn	WeChat (Chinese Instagram, WhatsApp, online payments... all in one)
微博	wēi bó	Weibo (Facebook of China)
华为	huá wéi	Huawei (Chinese international technology company)

2 **Part Two** Picture-based Task

◼ **Look at the picture and prepare statements to the following.**

1. a description of the photo

2. what you often use your mobile phone for

3. length of time you spend on playing games on your mobile phone per week

4. who you called today on your mobile phone

5. whether or not you wish to buy a new mobile phone

Questions relating to the above have been recorded for you. Listen to Track 20.2.1, pause after each question and speak in the gaps. Track 20.2.2 provides sample answers.

PICTURE-BASED TASK TIPS

The purpose of the picture-based task is to assess communication through:

(1) expressing opinions;

(2) providing descriptions;

(3) narrating events.

So, apart from answering all the questions, you must develop your responses as well as you can by saying at least a couple more sentences.

3 Part Three Listening Comprehension

You are listening to two friends talking about the advantages and disadvantages of social media. Listen to Track 20.3 and give one advantage and one disadvantage for each speaker.

	advantage	disadvantage
1		
2		

LISTENING TIPS

It is no doubt challenging to listen to not only what people say but at the same time also sort out the information you understand into the categories of advantage and disadvantage. Usually this type of question provides more than one answer for each category, and although not always the case, these pieces of information are often related. So, you should try to identify as much meaning as you can but you certainly do not have to understand everything to get all the marks. Trying to recognise the key adjectives or adjective-verbs is a great strategy to spot the answer — can you hear 方便 or 没意思 in this exercise?

4. Part Four Conversation

Answer the following questions. These questions have been recorded for you in Track 20.4.1. Listen to that track, pause after each question and speak in the gaps. Track 20.4.2 provides sample answers.

1. 你喜欢玩电子游戏吗？

2. 你上一次玩电子游戏是什么时候？

3. 你用社交媒体做什么？

4. 你每天都上社交媒体吗？

5. 如果让你给一个人发电子邮件，你会发给谁？

CONVERSATION TIPS

The following provides some tips and suggested content for you to consider.

1. It is a straightforward question, so say you like to play computer games, or you don't, whichever is the case. Give a reason or two to explain why or why not. Of course, you can mention your favourite game. If it is difficult to translate the name of the game in Chinese, you may say the name of the game in English and explain it, e.g. by generalising it as, a sport game or a music game, etc.

2. Think about a recent time that you played a computer game, be that on your computer, phone or gaming console. You could say what game you played, and when. Use 了 after the main action verb, e.g. 玩了. You could also expand your answer by saying how long you played and how you felt (but don't add 了 to 觉得 as it is not an action verb).

3. You might find it helpful to listen to Part Three Listening Comprehension or read its transcript to borrow some ideas about the benefits of using social media. Of course, you can also "show off" your knowledge of Chinese social media, e.g. say you use WeChat (微信) to text (发短信) your Chinese friends.

4. You could give further details of how often and the total length of time you spend on social media every day. Remember, both frequency (e.g. three times 三次 , several times 几次) and total length of time (e.g. over an hour 一个多小时 , a long time 很长时间) will need to be placed directly after the verb, and before the verb's object if there is one, in these sentences, e.g. 上三次社交媒体 , 花一个多小时 .

5. Consider this question an opportunity to talk about future events. You could talk about a family member or friend who you wish to send an email to, using the structure 给…… (someone) 发电子邮件 . Give some detail about this email, e.g. you wish to visit this person this summer holiday.

Part Five Wrapping Up

5.1 Key question words and phrases covered in this unit

1	多长时间 ★	duō cháng shí jiān	how long does it take (see "Question Words" box in Part One)
2	多长时间 …… 一次 ★	duō cháng shí jiān… yí cì	how often (see "Question Words" box in Part One)
3	什么时候	shén me shí hou	when; what time
4	有什么	yǒu shén me	what to have
5	做什么	zuò shén me	do what
6	为什么	wèi shén me	why
7	给谁	gěi shuí	to whom
8	吗	ma	(a question particle used at the end of a sentence to turn a statement into a yes-no question)

5.2 Key words and expressions covered in this unit

1	科技	kē jì	technology
2	社交媒体	shè jiāo méi tǐ	social media
3	手机	shǒu jī	mobile phone
4	电脑	diàn nǎo	computer
5	电子游戏	diàn zǐ yóu xì	computer games
6	电子邮件	diàn zǐ yóu jiàn	email
7	电子书	diàn zǐ shū	e-book
8	脸书	liǎn shū	Facebook
9	微信	wēi xìn	WeChat
10	短信	duǎn xìn	text message
11	博客	bó kè	blog
12	网站	wǎng zhàn	website
13	上网	shàng wǎng	go online
14	下载	xià zài	download
15	聊天	liáo tiān	chat
16	打电话	dǎ diàn huà	make a phone call
17	看新闻	kàn xīn wén	read/watch the news
18	学外语	xué wài yǔ	learn foreign languages
19	发	fā	send (e.g. send text, send email)
20	浪费时间	làng fèi shí jiān	waste time

Unit 21   Weather and Environmental Issues

第二十一单元 气候和环境问题

Part One Warming Up

1.1 Listen to Track 21.1.1 about things that people do in their daily life, and sort them into the categories below. Put each number next to an appropriate category.

A. 对环境好 (good for the environment) _____

B. 对环境不好 (bad for the environment) _____

● GRAMMAR NOTES: VERB + ADJECTIVE

In Chapter 1, Unit 4, you revised putting 会了 or 完了 after the verb to indicate the successful result of an action. There are also a few adjectives that can follow immediately after a verb to express the result of an action. Here are a few common ones:

(1) 对 (right) 你说对了。(You said it right.)

(2) 错 (wrong)

我写错了。(I wrote it incorrectly.)

(3) 干净 (clean)

衣服洗干净了。(The clothes have been washed clean.)

(4) 漂亮 (pretty)

她长漂亮了。(She is growing prettier.)

To negate such phrases, place 没 (有) before the verb and do not use 了.

你没说对。(You didn't say it right.)

我没写错。(I didn't write it incorrectly.)

1.2 Read the Grammar Notes box above on verb + adjective and also review the Grammar Notes verb + 会 了 / 完 了 in Chapter 1, Unit 4. Try to use the suggested phrases to say the following sentences.

1. I learned to swim last week. (学会了)

2. She finished. Do you want to speak? (说完了)

3. You are so smart; you answered it correctly. (答对了)

4. This book is really boring. I didn't finish it. (没看完)

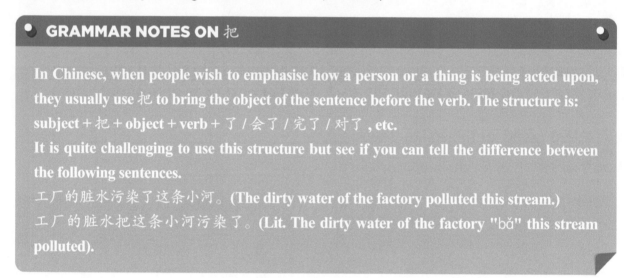

GRAMMAR NOTES ON 把

In Chinese, when people wish to emphasise how a person or a thing is being acted upon, they usually use 把 to bring the object of the sentence before the verb. The structure is:

subject + 把 + object + verb + 了 / 会了 / 完了 / 对了 , etc.

It is quite challenging to use this structure but see if you can tell the difference between the following sentences.

工厂的脏水污染了这条小河。(The dirty water of the factory polluted this stream.)

工厂的脏水把这条小河污染了。(Lit. The dirty water of the factory "bǎ" this stream polluted).

1.3 Read the Grammar Notes on 把 and listen to Track 21.1.3. Rephrase each sentence in the gaps using the structure subject + 把 + object + verb + 了 / 会了 / 完 了 / 对了 , etc. You may need to pause the recording after each sentence is said and speak. The correct answers are provided after each gap.

EXAMPLE 》》》

(You hear) 1. 我做了晚饭。
(You answer) 我把晚饭做了。
(You hear) 我把晚饭做了。

QUESTION WORDS: 哪 + MEASURE WORD

哪 means "which", but when being used in a question, it is usually followed by a measure.

你在哪个学校上学？ (Which school do you go to?)

哪条河里有污染？ (Which river is polluted?)

When assuming the answer is plural, 哪些 could be used.

哪些垃圾可以回收？ [Lit. Which (plural, meaning what kinds of) rubbish can be recycled?]

Read more about 哪些 in Chapter 4, Unit 16.

1.4 Read the Question Words box on 哪 then listen to Track 21.1.4. You will hear some answers followed by a question word. Ask the corresponding question by using the given question word.

EXAMPLE 》》》 (You hear) 1. 这位老师是校长。哪位？
(You answer) 哪位老师是校长？

CULTURE NOTE: ROAD SPACE RATIONING POLICY IN BEIJING

In order to improve air quality and reduce traffic in the city, the even-odd license plate road space rationing policy 单双号车辆限行 (dān shuāng hào chē liàng xiàn xíng) was first introduced in Beijing during the 2008 Summer Olympic Games. The policy permits private cars with license plates ending in an odd number (单号) to drive on city roads one day, whilst cars with an even-numbered (双号) license plate are allowed to go on city roads the next day. After the successful results of this policy in terms of reducing vehicle emissions and increasing road space availability, Beijing authorities have implemented a series of further road-space rationing policies. Do you want to drive in Beijing? You had better check whether your number plate is allowed to be on the road first. You may ask:

什么尾号的车今天可以上路？ (What number plates are allowed to be on the road today?)

我的车尾号是3，今天我能开出去吗？ (The last digit of my car license plate is 3. Can I drive out today?)

2 **Part Two** Role Play

You are the head of the household (家长) and have a pile of rubbish in your front garden. The environmental officer from your local council knocks on your door and speaks to you. Your teacher or your classmate will play the role of the council officer; or you may use the recorded questions (Track 21.2.1).

Use appropriate language for a formal conversation.
You will talk to the teacher or your classmate using the five prompts below.
• When you see – ? – you must ask a question.
• When you see – ! – you must respond to something you have not prepared.

> ■ **Task**
>
> **You are a home owner talking to your local council environmental officer.**
> 1. Say who the head of the household is.
> 2. Say why you have rubbish in front of your house.
> 3. !
> 4. ? Ask where the recycling centre is.
> 5. ? Ask what kinds of rubbish can be recycled.

These questions have been recorded for you. Listen to Track 21.2.1, pause after each question and speak in the gaps. Track 21.2.2 provides sample answers.

ROLE PLAY TIPS

There are three purposes of role play:
(1) Do you understand the questions?
(2) Can you answer the questions?
(3) Can you ask questions?
So, once you have fully answered the question using appropriate language, you don't need to say more. Wait for the next one.

3 **Part Three** Listening Comprehension

You are listening to a radio programme about William Lindesay OBE, a British geographer. Listen to Track 21.3 and put a cross ✕ to indicate the statement as True or False. Correct any false statements in English.

Statement	True	False	False correction
1(a). William Lindesay has been climbing the Great Wall since he was a child.			
1(b). He is the author of several books about the Great Wall.			
2(a). He suggested not to put bins on the Great Wall because they spoil the view.			
2(b). He picks up litter on the Great Wall every year.			

LISTENING TIPS

True or false questions can be tricky sometimes. You could first consider what would be said if a statement were true. For example, look at statement 1(a) and think about how you would translate "he has been climbing the Great Wall since he was a child". You could then listen to the recording and see if it uses your translation or something similar.

True statements may not always be a direct translation of what is said in the recording. Make sure you consider other ways of expressing the statements. For example, a statement might contain an occupation but the recording instead describes what someone in that line of work does.

When all else fails, guess the answer and don't leave blanks. You won't be penalised for giving a wrong answer so there's nothing to lose if you don't know the answer, and you might get lucky!

4 Part Four Conversation

Answer the following questions. These questions have been recorded for you in Track 21.4.1. Listen to that track, pause after each question and speak in the gaps. Track 21.4.2 provides example answers.

1. 你喜欢买新衣服吗?

2. 你用过什么旧东西?

3. 坐飞机去国外旅行有什么坏处?

4. 你经常骑自行车上学吗?

5. 为了保护环境,你打算做些什么?

CONVERSATION TIPS

The following provides some tips and suggested content for you to consider.

1. Of course, there is nothing wrong with buying new things. However, if you consider the question is about environmental issues, you may want to mention some negative impacts of buying too many new things, e.g. there will be more and more (越来越多) factories and rubbish.

2. Think about an old object that you have used and talk about this experience. For example, an old book given by your grandparent, a trip to or online shopping at a vintage clothes shop. Remember to include sentences with verbs in the past time frame, e.g. 用过,去过,买了.

3. Again, no doubt it is amazing to be able to travel abroad. Concerning the environmental impact though, this question requests you to focus on the disadvantages. If you find it difficult to talk in Chinese about air travel, try to imagine that you are a five-year-old or you are explaining your reasons to a five-year-old. This may help you come out with some simple but clear expressions, e.g. 污染很大,空气对身体不好.

4. By now you should be pretty good with answering this kind of question. If you do often cycle to school, give details, e.g. say when you leave home, how long it takes for you to cycle to school (从 A 到 B 要……); if you don't cycle to school, you could say your house is too far from school or that the morning traffic (早上车很多) makes it unsafe to cycle (骑车不太安全).

5. As the question is asking 做些什么, you do need to give more than one detail about what you plan to do to protect the environment. You could use 第一,第二,第三 to give a more structured response. Take a look at the key words and expressions listed in Part Five to give you some ideas.

5 Part Five Wrapping Up

5.1 Key question words and phrases covered in this unit

1	哪 ★	nǎ	which (see "Question Words" box in Part One)
2	哪个 ★	nǎ ge	which one (see "Question Words" box in Part One)
3	哪些 ★	nǎ xiē	which ones (see "Question Words" box in Part One)
4	……在哪儿	...zài nǎ er	where is...
5	多长时间	duō cháng shí jiān	how long (length of time)
6	为什么	wèi shén me	why
7	用过什么	yòng guo shén me	what has been used
8	有什么坏处	yǒu shén me huài chu	what are the disadvantages
9	做些什么	zuò xiē shén me	do what (plural)
10	吗	ma	(a question particle used at the end of a sentence to turn a statement into a yes-no question)

5.2 Key words and expressions covered in this unit

1	少开车	shǎo kāi chē	drive less
2	少用电	shǎo yòng diàn	use less electricity
3	多骑自行车	duō qí zì xíng chē	cycle more
4	多种树	duō zhòng shù	plant more trees
5	二十四小时开空调	èr shí sì xiǎo shí kāi kōng tiáo	24 hours with air conditioning on
6	经常换手机	jīng cháng huàn shǒu jī	frequently change mobile phones
7	在花园用雨水浇花	zài huā yuán yòng yǔ shuǐ jiāo huā	water flowers in the garden with rain water
8	在咖啡店用自己的杯子喝咖啡	zài kā fēi diàn yòng zì jǐ de bēi zi hē kā fēi	drink coffee with your own cup in a coffee shop
9	干净	gān jing	clean
10	脏水	zāng shuǐ	dirty water
11	河水	hé shuǐ	river water
12	污染	wū rǎn	pollution
13	垃圾	lā jī	rubbish
14	垃圾桶	lā jī tǒng	rubbish bin
15	捡垃圾	jiǎn lā jī	pick up rubbish
16	回收	huí shōu	recycle
17	保护环境 / 环保	bǎo hù huán jìng / huán bǎo	protect the environment / environmental protection
18	空瓶子	kōng píng zi	empty bottle
19	旧报纸	jiù bào zhǐ	old newspaper
20	旧东西	jiù dōng xi	old things

Unit 22
Public Welfare and Volunteer Work
第二十二单元 公益和志愿工作

 Part One Warming Up

1.1 Listen to Track 22.1.1 and match these voluntary work-related words with their English translations. Put the correct number into the second column.

A. be a volunteer		E. protect animals	
B. charity shop		F. donate money	
C. elderly people's home		G. experience	
D. help poor people		H. CV	

> **GRAMMAR NOTES ON A** 对 **B** 有 / 没 (有) + 好处 / 坏处
>
> To express that something or someone is good or bad for something or someone else, use the structure: A 对 B 有 + 好处 / 坏处 .
> 电动汽车对环境有好处。 (Electric cars are good for the environment.)
> 抽烟对健康有坏处。 (Smoking is bad for your health.)
> You can also use 没 (有) to say something or someone is not good or not harmful:
> A 对 B 没 (有) + 好处 / 坏处
> 喝酒对你没好处。 (Drinking is not good for you.)

1.2 Read the Grammar Notes on A 对 B 有 / 没 (有) + 好处 / 坏处 . Listen to Track 22.1.2 and answer the questions in Chinese according to your opinion.

> **GRAMMAR NOTES ON** 一边…… 一边……
>
> When you give a spoken or written narrative of events or stories, you can use 一边…… 一边…… to talk about two things that are being done at the same time.
> 每天晚上，我一边做作业，一边听音乐。 (Every evening, I listen to music whilst doing homework.)
> 他一边上学，一边做义工。 (He does voluntary work while going to school.)
> You may have noticed that there is a difference between Chinese and English expressions on this. In English, you say the main action after "while" or "whilst", but in Chinese, the main action would normally come first.

1.3 Read the Grammar Notes on 一边······ 一边······ **and use the structure to say the following sentences.**

1. My family like to watch TV while having dinner.
2. Please don't make phone calls whilst driving.
3. Grandpas and grandmas dance happily while singing.
4. I often chat with the children while cooking for them.

> **● GRAMMAR NOTES ON** ······以前 / 以后 / 的时候（时）
>
> To use a time phrase to talk about an event that happened before, after or during a particular time, you can use 以前 (before), 以后 (after) or 的时候 (during, at). However, in Chinese, these words must be placed after the time expression, rather than in front like in English.
> 在上中学以前，我已经参加了很多小学的慈善活动。(Before going to my secondary school, I had already participated in many charity activities in my primary school.)
> 天晴的时候（天晴时），我常常和老人院的老人们一起去海边散步。(When it's sunny, I often go for a walk along the beach with the elderly people from the nursing home.)
> 大学毕业以后，我打算去非洲帮助那里的穷人。(After graduating from university, I plan to go to Africa to help the poor there.)

1.4 Read the Grammar Notes on ······以前 / 以后 / 的时候（时）. **Listen to Track 22.1.4 and answer the questions according to Ranran's routine on Tuesday.**

get up → 7am → go to lessons → lunch → work in the charity shop → dinner → read → sleep

> **● QUESTION WORDS: 吧**
>
> If you have come this far in this book, congratulations! You have nearly mastered all the question words needed for Chinese at GCSE level! There is only one more minor word to add to your collection: 吧 .
> 吧 is surely not a new word to you as you have revised it in Chapter 1, Unit 4 when using it to make a suggestion.
> 我们去帮助他们吧！ (Let's go to help them!)
> 吧 can also be used as a question particle, similar to 吗 , by placing it at the end of the sentence. However, when you use 吧 to ask a question, you are almost certain that what you are saying is true. In a way, you are merely seeking confirmation from the person or people you are speaking to.
> 您是老师吧? (You must be the teacher, right?)
> 一天都没吃饭，你们很饿吧? (You haven't eaten all day. You must be hungry, mustn't you?)

2 **Part Two** Picture-based Task

■ **Look at the picture and prepare statements to the following.**

1. a description of the photograph
2. whether you have been to an elderly people's home
3. your opinion on elderly people learning to use the computer
4. how to make elderly people happy
5. !

These questions have been recorded for you. Listen to Track 22.2.1, pause after each question and speak in the gaps. Track 22.2.2 provides sample answers.

PICTURE-BASED TASK TIPS

The purpose of the picture-based task is to assess communication through:

(1) expressing opinions;

(2) providing descriptions;

(3) narrating events.

So, apart from answering all the questions, you must develop your responses as well as you can by saying at least a couple more sentences.

3 **Part Three** Listening Comprehension

You are listening to a charity event advertisement. Listen to Track 22.3, the advertisement, and answer the following questions in English. Answer both parts for each question.

1(a). Where is the charity event?

1(b). How much is the ticket?

2(a). Which charity is the fund raising for?

2(b). Who else can attend the event with you?

LISTENING TIPS

Always read the questions before you listen to the recording, so you know exactly what you are listening out for. For example, in Question 1(a), think about the word order of a Chinese sentence and when the location expressions are normally said. Could the answer be led by 在 (in, at, on), or verb 去 (go to) or 来 (come to)?

Be careful of Chinese words that are pronounced the same but in different tones, e.g. 是 (to be) and 十 (ten). Think about how a possible answer would be said before listening to the recording and use the context to help you. For example, in Question 1(b), make out a price and say "the ticket is..." in Chinese beforehand. Like saying your age, think carefully if you need 是 (to be) to describe prices.

Last but not least, relax! Don't panic if you don't get it. Use your instinct to guess the answer and then move on. Don't leave blanks. It is okay if you don't understand everything. There will still be plenty you can do!

4 Part Four Conversation

Answer the following questions. These questions have been recorded for you in Track 22.4.1. Listen to that track, pause after each question and speak in the gaps. Track 22.4.2 provides example answers.

1. 你做过义工吧?

2. 你认为上大学应该免费吗?

3. 在医院工作的好处是什么?

4. 富人可以帮助穷人做什么?

5. 如果捐钱，你最想把钱捐给谁?

CONVERSATION TIPS

The following provides some tips and suggested content for you to consider.
1. Surely, we have all done some form of charity work, no matter how big or small. You could choose a couple of experiences to talk about or focus just on one. To answer the question positively, replace 你 with 我 and drop the question particle 吗, then give some detail about what you did, when, and for how long.
2. There is no right or wrong answer to an opinion question as long as you can justify it by giving your reason or reasons. Being able to communicate your points using simple language is a skill that you can learn. For example, it might be too ambitious to say in Chinese that for many low-income students, college has become the unattainable, but you may simplify the point by saying 如果爸爸妈妈没有钱, 孩子就不能上大学.
3. Helping patients, highly-paid doctors, friendly working environment... there are many merits to working in a hospital that you can talk about confidently with the vocabulary that you know. To make a contrast, you could use the structure 虽然……但是…… to bring out some disadvantages, such as long hours, dirty and tiring work, etc.
4. You may not always have a lot to say with some of the questions. It doesn't matter at all. Don't forget you can be creative and use your imagination. Say as much as you can, but if it becomes impossible, move on to the next question. It doesn't have to be a balanced answer to all the questions. Some questions may suit you better, and you can always say more in answer to these.
5. Take full advantage of Chinese questions. The question words are not placed at the beginning of the questions as in English but the word order in a question is usually exactly the same as how you answer it. So, listen carefully to the question. If necessary, ask your teacher to repeat it, identify the question word and give your answer in a sentence with the same word order by replacing the question word with your answer. Therefore, it is important that you learn the question words. There is a list of the key question words at the end of each unit, and a general question list at the back of this book. Spend some time to revise them and best of luck with your speaking exams! You can do it!

5 Part Five Wrapping Up

5.1 Key question words and phrases covered in this unit

1	对什么有好处	duì shén me yǒu hǎo chu	be good for something
2	对什么没有好处	duì shén me méi yǒu hǎo chu	be not good for something
3	对谁有好处	duì shuí yǒu hǎo chu	be good for somebody
4	对谁有坏处	duì shuí yǒu huài chu	be bad for somebody
5	做什么	zuò shén me	what to do
6	有什么	yǒu shén me	what to have
7	……是什么	...shì shén me	what is...
8	怎么	zěn me	how
9	谁	shuí	who
10	吧 ★	ba	(a question particle used at the end of a sentence to turn a statement into a yes-no question for confirmation — see "Question Word" box in Part One)

5.2 Key words and expressions covered in this unit

1	做义工	zuò yì gōng	be a volunteer
2	慈善商店	cí shàn shāng diàn	charity shop
3	老人院	lǎo rén yuàn	elderly people's home
4	富人	fù rén	the rich
5	帮助穷人	bāng zhù qióng rén	help the poor
6	病人	bìng rén	patient
7	人口	rén kǒu	population
8	保护动物	bǎo hù dòng wù	animal protection
9	保护中心	bǎo hù zhōng xīn	protection centre
10	捐钱	juān qián	donate money
11	经验	jīng yàn	experience
12	个人简历	gè rén jiǎn lì	resume
13	抽烟	chōu yān	smoke
14	喝酒	hē jiǔ	drink alcohol
15	健康	jiàn kāng	health; healthy
16	全球变暖	quán qiú biàn nuǎn	global warming
17	机会	jī huì	opportunity
18	晚会	wǎn huì	evening party
19	热闹	rè nao	lively
20	应该	yīng gāi	should

Keys to the Exercises
练习题参考答案

Listening Transcript
听力文本

Key Question Words
疑问词总表

Key Grammar List
语法总表

Glossary
总词汇表

Keys to the Exercises
练习题参考答案

CHAPTER ONE My Life and My Friends

Unit 1 My Family

■ Part One Warming Up

1.1   A. 5 B. 6 C. 2 D. 1 E. 4 F. 3 G. 7

1.2   A. family members: 1, 3, 5, 8, 11, 12
       B. profession: 2, 9
       C. things you do with family: 4, 6, 7, 10

1.3   1. What date is your birthday?
       2. Where will you hold your birthday party?
       3. What did you do last year for your birthday?
       4. Do you like celebrating birthdays? Why?

1.4   Sample answer for reference only
       1. 我的生日是十月二十六日。
       　　wǒ de shēng rì shì shí yuè èr shí liù rì
       2. 我想在家开生日会。
       　　wǒ xiǎng zài jiā kāi shēng rì huì
       3. 去年生日，我看了电影。
       　　qù nián shēng rì　wǒ kàn le diàn yǐng
       4. 我喜欢过生日，因为我爱吃生日蛋糕。
       　　wǒ xǐ huan guò shēng rì　yīn wèi wǒ ài chī shēng rì dàn gāo

1.5   Sample answer for reference only
       1. 你们学校怎么样？
       　　nǐ men xué xiào zěn me yàng
       2. 北京的天气怎么样？
       　　běi jīng de tiān qì zěn me yàng
       3. 你觉得中国菜怎么样？
       　　nǐ jué de zhōng guó cài zěn me yàng
       4. 我喜欢美国电影。你觉得怎么样？
       　　wǒ xǐ huan měi guó diàn yǐng　nǐ jué de zěn me yàng

1.6　　1. 小红的生日是几月几日？
xiǎo hóng de shēng rì shì jǐ yuè jǐ rì

2. 小红在哪儿出生？
xiǎo hóng zài nǎ er chū shēng

3. 妈妈和爸爸什么时候去看奶奶？
mā ma hé bà ba shén me shí hou qù kàn nǎi nai

4. 飞飞跟谁一起去游泳？
fēi fei gēn shuí yì qǐ qù yóu yǒng

■ Part Two Role Play

Sample answer for reference only

1. 我十五岁了。
wǒ shí wǔ suì le

2. 我觉得我的新家很漂亮。
wǒ jué de wǒ de xīn jiā hěn piào liang

3. 我的房间里有床和电脑。
wǒ de fáng jiān lǐ yǒu chuáng hé diàn nǎo

4. 我下个月去你家看你。
wǒ xià ge yuè qù nǐ jiā kàn nǐ

5. 您喜欢买东西吗？
nín xǐ huan mǎi dōng xi ma

■ Part Three Listening Comprehension

1. B　　　　2. A　　　　3. C　　　　4. B

■ Part Four Conversation

Sample answer for reference only

1. 好！我叫丽丽，我十五岁，我是一个中学生。我喜欢学
hǎo　　wǒ jiào lì li　　wǒ shí wǔ suì　　wǒ shì yí gè zhōng xué shēng　　wǒ xǐ huan xué
中文，不喜欢学数学。
zhōng wén　　bù xǐ huan xué shù xué

2. 我们家有五口人，我有爸爸、妈妈、一个哥哥和一个妹妹，
wǒ men jiā yǒu wǔ kǒu rén　　wǒ yǒu bà ba　　mā ma　　yí gè gē ge hé yí gè mèi mei
我的爸爸是工人，妈妈在商店工作，我哥哥十八岁，妹妹九岁。
wǒ de bà ba shì gōng rén　　mā ma zài shāng diàn gōng zuò　　wǒ gē ge shí bā suì　　mèi mei jiǔ suì

3. 我喜欢宠物，因为宠物是我的好朋友。我有一只狗，我
wǒ xǐ huan chǒng wù　　yīn wèi chǒng wù shì wǒ de hǎo péng you　　wǒ yǒu yì zhī gǒu　　wǒ
的狗叫飞飞，它很友好。
de gǒu jiào fēi fei　　tā hěn yǒu hǎo

4. 去年夏天，我和家人去了法国。法国很热，我们天天都游
qù nián xià tiān　　wǒ hé jiā rén qù le fǎ guó　　fǎ guó hěn rè　　wǒ men tiān tiān dōu yóu
泳，也吃冰淇淋。
yǒng　　yě chī bīng qí lín

5. 这个周末，我想先和哥哥一起踢足球，再和家人一起吃晚
zhè ge zhōu mò　　wǒ xiǎng xiān hé gē ge yì qǐ tī zú qiú　　zài hé jiā rén yì qǐ chī wǎn
饭，然后和妹妹一起看电视。
fàn　　rán hòu hé mèi mei yì qǐ kàn diàn shì

Unit 2 My Hobbies

■ Part One Warming Up

1.1   1. H 2. E 3. F 4. C 5. B 6. I 7. D 8. A 9. G

1.2

看 kàn	2. reading	打 dǎ	1. making a phone call	玩 wán 儿 er	4. skateboarding
	5. watching films		3. playing basketball		7. playing computer games
	8. watching television		6. playing table tennis		
	10. visiting friends		9. playing tennis		

1.3   Sample answer for reference only

wǒ de ài hào shì kàn diàn yǐng   dǎ lán qiú hé wán er diàn zǐ yóu xì
1. 我的爱好是看电影、打篮球和玩儿电子游戏。

wǒ zuì xǐ huan wán er diàn zǐ yóu xì
2. 我最喜欢玩儿电子游戏。

1.4   1. C 2. E 3. F 4. A 5. D 6. B

1.5   Sample answer for reference only

nǐ de péng you jiào shén me
1. 你的朋友叫什么？

nǐ de ài hào shì shén me
2. 你的爱好是什么？

nǐ xǐ huan chī shén me
3. 你喜欢吃什么？

nǐ zhōu mò zuò shén me
4. 你周末做什么？

1.6   Sample answer for reference only

wǒ chángcháng shàngwǎng
1. 我常常上网。

zhōu mò wǒ chángcháng shàngwǎng
2. 周末我常常上网。

zhōu mò wǒ chángcháng shàngwǎng liáo tiān
3. 周末我常常上网聊天。

zhōu mò wǒ chángcháng shàngwǎng hé péng you liáo tiān
4. 周末我常常上网和朋友聊天。

zhōu mò wǒ chángcháng shàngwǎng zài shè jiāo wǎngzhànshang hé péng you liáo tiān
5. 周末我常常上网在社交网站上和朋友聊天。

zhōu mò wǒ chángcháng shàngwǎng zài shè jiāo wǎngzhànshang hé péng you liáo tiān   wǒ jué de hěn kuài lè
6. 周末我常常上网在社交网站上和朋友聊天。我觉得很快乐。

■ Part Two Picture-based Task

2.2　Sample answer for reference only

zhào piàn lǐ yǒu sān gè xué sheng　　tā men zài gōngyuán lǐ pǎo bù　　tā men hěn xǐ huan yùn dòng
1. 照片里有三个学生，他们在公园里跑步。他们很喜欢运动。

wǒ fēi cháng xǐ huan yùn dòng　　yùn dòng duì shēn tǐ hǎo　　rú guǒ bú yùn dòng　　nǐ jiù huì hěn pàng
2. 我非常喜欢运动。运动对身体好。如果不运动，你就会很胖。

shàng ge xīng qī wǒ cān jiā le lán qiú bǐ sài　　wǒ men zuò huǒ chē qù lún dūn de lán qiú guǎn
3. 上个星期我参加了篮球比赛。我们坐火车去伦敦的篮球馆
bǐ sài　　lún dūn de lán qiú guǎn yòu dà yòu piào liang
比赛。伦敦的篮球馆又大又漂亮。

suī rán wǒ huì dǎ lán qiú　　dàn shì wǒ bú huì yóu yǒng　　wǒ xiǎng qù yùn dòngzhōng xīn xué
4. 虽然我会打篮球，但是我不会游泳。我想去运动中心学
yóu yǒng　　yùn dòngzhōng xīn zài wǒ jiā páng biān
游泳。运动中心在我家旁边。

wǒ xiǎng hé mèi mei yì qǐ yóu yǒng　　yīn wèi wǒ hěn ài wǒ de mèi mei　　zhōu mò wǒ xǐ huan
5. 我想和妹妹一起游泳，因为我很爱我的妹妹，周末我喜欢
hé tā yì qǐ zuò yùn dòng
和她一起做运动。

■ Part Three Listening Comprehension

A C F

■ Part Four Conversation

Sample answer for reference only

wǒ yǒu hěn duō ài hào　　wǒ chú le xǐ huan tīng yīn yuè　　kàn diàn yǐng　　wǒ yě xǐ huan mǎi
1. 我有很多爱好。我除了喜欢听音乐、看电影，我也喜欢买
dōng xi　　zhōu mò de shí hou　　wǒ chángchángshàngwǎng mǎi dōng xi
东西。周末的时候，我常常上网买东西。

wǒ xǐ huan kàn hěn duō guó jiā de diàn yǐng　　bǐ rú　　yīng guó de　　zhōng guó de　　dàn shì
2. 我喜欢看很多国家的电影，比如，英国的，中国的，但是
wǒ zuì xǐ huan kàn měi guó de diàn yǐng　　yīn wèi měi guó diàn yǐng bǐ yīng guó diàn yǐng hǎo kàn
我最喜欢看美国的电影，因为美国电影比英国电影好看。

zuì jìn wǒ kàn le yí gè měi guó diàn yǐng　　diàn yǐng lǐ yǒu hěn duō zhōng xué sheng　　nán xué
3. 最近我看了一个美国电影，电影里有很多中学生，男学
sheng dōu hěn shuài　　nǚ xué sheng yě hěn piào liang
生都很帅，女学生也很漂亮。

wǒ méi yǒu tīng guò hěn duō zhōng guó yīn yuè　　wǒ tīng guò yì diǎn er zhōng guó liú xíng yīn
4. 我没有听过很多中国音乐。我听过一点儿中国流行音
yuè　　wǒ jué de zhōng guó yīn yuè yì bān dōu hěn màn　　dàn shì hěn hǎo tīng
乐，我觉得中国音乐一般都很慢。但是很好听。

yīn wèi wǒ méi yǒu tīng guò hěn duō zhōng guó de yīn yuè　　suǒ yǐ wǒ xiǎng tīng yí gè zhōng guó
5. 因为我没有听过很多中国的音乐，所以我想听一个中国
de yīn yuè huì　　lǎo shī　　qǐng wèn nǐ xǐ huan nǎ ge zhōng guó gē shǒu　　zhōu jié lún　　hǎo　　wǒ
的音乐会。老师，请问你喜欢哪个中国歌手？周杰伦？好，我
zuì xiǎng tīng zhōu jié lún de yīn yuè huì
最想听周杰伦的音乐会。

Part One Warming Up

1.1

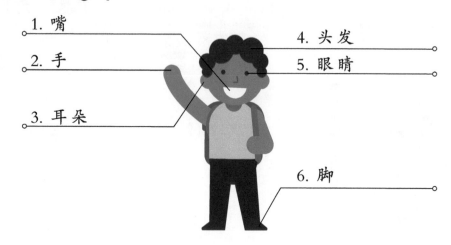

1. 嘴
2. 手
3. 耳朵
4. 头发
5. 眼睛
6. 脚

1.2   4, 1, 3, 2

1.3
tā yǒu yì shuāng lán yǎn jing   tā de yǎn jing hěn lán
1. 他 有 一 双 蓝 眼睛。 / 他 的 眼睛 很 蓝。
tā yǒu yí gè xiǎo zuǐ   tā de zuǐ hěn xiǎo
2. 她 有 一 个 小 嘴。 / 她 的 嘴 很 小。
tā yǒu yì shuāng dà jiǎo   tā de jiǎo hěn dà
3. 他 有 一 双 大 脚。 / 他 的 脚 很 大。
tā yǒu yì tóu cháng tóu fa   tā de tóu fa hěn cháng
4. 她 有 一 头 长 头 发。 / 她 的 头 发 很 长。

1.4   Sample answer for reference only

wǒ de péng you jiào lì li   tā shí wǔ suì   tā yǒu yì shuāng lán sè de yǎn jing hé jīn huáng
我 的 朋 友 叫 丽 丽 ， 她 十 五 岁。 她 有 一 双 蓝 色 的 眼 睛 和 金 黄
sè de tóu fa   tā yòu piào liang yòu cōng míng   yě hěn qīn qiè   dàn shì tā bù xǐ huan shàng xué
色 的 头 发。 她 又 漂 亮 又 聪 明 ， 也 很 亲 切 ， 但 是 她 不 喜 欢 上 学。

1.5   A. 3 B. 5 C. 1 D. 6 E. 4 F. 2

1.6
wǒ de péng you shì cóng běi jīng lái de
1. 我 的 朋 友 是 从 北 京 来 的。
shì huì shuō hàn yǔ de
2. Luke 是 会 说 汉 语 的。
tā shì jiāo tài jí quán de
3. 她 是 教 太 极 拳 的。
wǒ shì xǐ huan chī yuè bing de
4. 我 是 喜 欢 吃 月 饼 的。

■ Part Two Role Play

Sample answer for reference only

1. 我的朋友叫大海，他十五岁。他又高又帅，也很可爱。

2. 五年前上中学的时候，我在学校认识了他。

3. 我们常常在一起听音乐、做作业和玩游戏。

4. 你有最好的朋友吗？

5. 为什么每个人都要有朋友？

■ Part Three Listening Comprehension

1. (When he was) in secondary school.

2. (They used to) chat and listen to music (together).

3. (He went to) the U.S.A. (to attend university).

4. (He is) not interested (in marriage) / (He) doesn't want to get married.

■ Part Four Conversation

Sample answer for reference only

1. 我的朋友叫小红，她是我最好的朋友，她有又长又黑的头发，她非常可爱。

2. 我参加过她的生日会。上个星期六晚上，我去了她家，参加了她十五岁的生日会。我的爸爸、妈妈也去了，因为他们和小红的父母也是好朋友。

3. 她家在市中心。虽然她家不大，但是花园很漂亮，她的生日会是在花园里开的。

4. 我们吃了很多好吃的东西，除了饺子和牛肉面条，我们还吃了生日蛋糕。大家都高兴极了。

5. 我的生日是十月二十六日。我也打算在家里开生日会，请朋友们参加，我们会一边听音乐，一边吃比萨饼。

Unit 4 My Leisure Time

■ Part One Warming Up

1.1　A. 1, 3, 4, 5, 12, 14, 15

　　　B. 8, 10, 11, 13, 16

　　　C. 2, 6

　　　D. 7, 9

1.2　A. 3　B. 2　C. 1　D. 4　E. 7　F. 5　G. 8　H. 6

1.3　1. wǒ men tīng yīn yuè ba
　　　我们听音乐吧！
　　　2. wǒ men kàn yí huì er diàn shì　hǎo ma
　　　我们看一会儿电视，好吗？
　　　3. wǒ xiǎng dǎ pīng pāng qiú　nǐ xiǎng dǎ ma
　　　我想打乒乓球，你想打吗？
　　　4. chūn jié de shí hou　wǒ men qù zhōng guó fàn guǎn chī zhōng guó cài　hǎo bu hǎo
　　　春节的时候，我们去中国饭馆吃中国菜，好不好？

1.5　1. wǒ chī de hěn duō
　　　我吃得很多。
　　　2. tā shuì de hěn wǎn　　tā shuì jiào shuì de hěn wǎn
　　　她睡得很晚。/ 她睡觉睡得很晚。
　　　3. wǒ de péng you shuō hàn yǔ shuō de hěn hǎo
　　　我的朋友说汉语说得很好。
　　　4. wǒ nǎi nai kāi chē kāi de hěn màn
　　　我奶奶开车开得很慢。

■ Part Two Picture-based Task

Sample answer for reference only

1. zhào piàn lǐ yǒu yí gè mā ma hé yí gè nǚ ér　tā men zài chāo shì mǎi dōng xi　chāo shì
照片里有一个妈妈和一个女儿，她们在超市买东西。超市
lǐ de rén bù duō
里的人不多。

2. wǒ zài jiā bù bāng bà ba mā ma qù chāo shì mǎi dōng xi　yīn wèi wǒ hěn máng　wǒ chú le yǒu hěn
我在家不帮爸爸妈妈去超市买东西，因为我很忙。我除了有很
duō zuò yè　yě cháng cháng yào qù cān jiā lán qiú bǐ sài　suǒ yǐ wǒ méi yǒu shí jiān bāng bà ba mā ma
多作业，也常常要去参加篮球比赛，所以我没有时间帮爸爸妈妈。

3. wǒ shàng gè xīng qī liù qù shì zhōng xīn gěi mèi mei mǎi le yí gè shēng rì lǐ wù　wǒ de
我上个星期六去市中心给妹妹买了一个生日礼物。我的
mèi mei zhè ge xīng qī tiān guò shēng rì　wǒ gěi tā mǎi le yì tiáo qún zi
妹妹这个星期天过生日，我给她买了一条裙子。

4. wǒ zhè ge xīng qī tiān huì hé jiā rén yì qǐ qù fàn guǎn chī fàn　wǒ men huì chī yì dà lì bǐ sà
我这个星期天会和家人一起去饭馆吃饭，我们会吃意大利比萨
bǐng　hái huì qǐng mèi mei chī shēng rì dàn gāo　wǒ fēi cháng xǐ huan mèi mei　tā yòu piào liang yòu kě ài
饼，还会请妹妹吃生日蛋糕。我非常喜欢妹妹，她又漂亮又可爱。

^{duì bu qǐ} ^{suī rán wǒ hěn xǐ huan kàn zhōng guó diàn yǐng} ^{dàn shì zhè ge zhōu mò wǒ bù}
5. 对 不 起！ 虽 然 我 很 喜 欢 看 中 国 电 影， 但 是 这 个 周 末 我 不
^{xiǎng qù} ^{yīn wèi xīng qī tiān shì wǒ mèi mei de shēng rì} ^{suǒ yǐ zhè ge zhōu mò wǒ yào hé mèi mei}
想 去。 因 为 星 期 天 是 我 妹 妹 的 生 日， 所 以 这 个 周 末 我 要 和 妹 妹
^{zài yì qǐ} ^{xī wàng zhè ge diàn yǐng hěn hǎo kàn} ^{nǐ men dōu kàn de hěn gāo xìng}
在 一 起。 希 望 这 个 电 影 很 好 看， 你 们 都 看 得 很 高 兴。

■ Part Three Listening Comprehension

1.

	food	drink
Zhang Qiang	bread and fruit	fruit juice
his dad	bread and fruit	tea
his mum	bread and fruit	coffee

2. For dinner, what do they do? Give three details.

a. eat in the restaurant

b. call for a takeaway

c. cook at home

■ Part Four Conversation

Sample answer for reference only

^{yǒu kòng de shí hou} ^{wǒ chángcháng kàn shū} ^{wǒ hěn xǐ huan kàn shū} ^{wǒ zuì xǐ huan kàn}
1. 有 空 的 时 候， 我 常 常 看 书。 我 很 喜 欢 看 书， 我 最 喜 欢 看
^{lì shǐ shū} ^{yīn wèi wǒ duì lì shǐ yǒu xìng qù}
历 史 书， 因 为 我 对 历 史 有 兴 趣。
^{wǒ hé wǒ de péng you zhōu mò yì bān dōu zài shè jiāo méi tǐ shang liáo tiān} ^{wǒ men yě shàng}
2. 我 和 我 的 朋 友 周 末 一 般 都 在 社 交 媒 体 上 聊 天， 我 们 也 上
^{wǎng wán yóu xì} ^{yǒu de shí hou} ^{wǒ men yì qǐ qù hē kā fēi hé kàn diàn yǐng}
网 玩 游 戏。 有 的 时 候， 我 们 一 起 去 喝 咖 啡 和 看 电 影。
^{wǒ jué de xué sheng zhōu mò dǎ gōng hěn hǎo} ^{chú le kě yǐ zhuàn qián} ^{hái kě yǐ jiāo péng}
3. 我 觉 得 学 生 周 末 打 工 很 好， 除 了 可 以 赚 钱， 还 可 以 交 朋
^{you} ^{suī rán xué sheng zhōu mò dǎ gōng yǒu hǎo chu} ^{dàn shì yě yǒu huài chu} ^{yīn wèi dǎ wán le gōng}
友。 虽 然 学 生 周 末 打 工 有 好 处， 但 是 也 有 坏 处， 因 为 打 完 了 工
^{hěn lèi} ^{xīng qī yī jiù bù xiǎngshàng xué}
很 累， 星 期 一 就 不 想 上 学。
^{wǒ zhōu mò de shí hou sòng guò bào zhǐ} ^{wǒ bù xǐ huan sòng bào zhǐ} ^{yīn wèi sòng bào zhǐ}
4. 我 周 末 的 时 候 送 过 报 纸， 我 不 喜 欢 送 报 纸， 因 为 送 报 纸
^{yào hěn zǎo qǐ chuáng}
要 很 早 起 床。
^{zhè ge zhōu mò wǒ xiǎng qù yùn dòng zhōng xīn yóu yǒng} ^{wǒ zuì jìn xué huì le yóu yǒng} ^{bú}
5. 这 个 周 末 我 想 去 运 动 中 心 游 泳。 我 最 近 学 会 了 游 泳， 不
^{guò yóu de bù hǎo} ^{suǒ yǐ wǒ dǎ suan měi gè xīng qī dōu qù yóu yǒng}
过 游 得 不 好， 所 以 我 打 算 每 个 星 期 都 去 游 泳。

Unit 5 My House

■ Part One Warming Up

1.1   A. 6 B. 3 C. 2 D. 8 E. 7 F. 4 G. 5 H. 1

1.2   A. furniture: 5, 7, 10, 13, 14, 15

B. electronic appliances: 4, 9, 12, 16

C. rooms: 1, 2, 3, 6, 8, 11

1.3   1. 我在浴室洗手。
wǒ zài yù shì xǐ shǒu

2. 爸爸坐在沙发上看电视。
bà ba zuò zài shā fā shang kàn diàn shì

3. 妈妈在厨房做饭。
mā ma zài chú fáng zuò fàn

4. 姐姐在卧室打电话。
jiě jie zài wò shì dǎ diàn huà

5. 哥哥在书房看书。
gē ge zài shū fáng kàn shū

6. 妹妹在客厅玩游戏。
mèi mei zài kè tīng wán yóu xì

1.4   1. C 2. E 3. F 4. B 5. D 6. A

	Translation
A. ……但是只有一个浴室。	A. but there is only one bathroom.
B. ……但是中文作业太难了。	B. but the Chinese homework is too hard.
C. ……但是我不喜欢游泳。	C. but I don't like swimming.
D. ……但是风景很漂亮。	D. but the view is beautiful.
E. ……但是我有两个哥哥。	E. but I have two elder brothers.
F. ……但是我不饿。	F. but I am not hungry.

1.5   Sample answer for reference only

1. 我的手机在哪儿？
wǒ de shǒu jī zài nǎ er

2. 市中心在哪儿？
shì zhōng xīn zài nǎ er

nǐ de yé ye hé nǎi nai zhù zài nǎ er
3. 你的爷爷和奶奶住在哪儿？

shàng ge zhōu mò nǐ qù le nǎ er
4. 上个周末你去了哪儿？

■ Part Two Role Play

Sample answer for reference only

zhè ge fáng zi zài shì zhōng xīn
1. 这个房子在市中心。

zhè ge fáng zi yǒu sān gè wò shì
2. 这个房子有三个卧室。

nín jīn tiān xià wǔ kě yǐ qù kàn zhè ge fáng zi
3. 您今天下午可以去看这个房子。

wǒ hěn xǐ huan zhè ge fáng zi   yīn wèi zhù zài shì zhōng xīn hěn fāng biàn
4. 我很喜欢这个房子，因为住在市中心很方便。

nín jué de zhè ge fáng zi guì ma
5. 您觉得这个房子贵吗？

■ Part Three Listening Comprehension

1. A 2. B 3. B 4. C

■ Part Four Conversation

Sample answer for reference only

hǎo   wǒ men jiā zài yí gè xiǎo zhèn   wǒ men jiā bú dà bù xiǎo   yǒu yí gè kè tīng
1. 好！我们家在一个小镇。我们家不大不小，有一个客厅、

yí gè fàn tīng   yí gè chú fáng   liǎng gè yù shì hé sì gè wò shì   wǒ fēi cháng ài wǒ de jiā hé
一个饭厅、一个厨房、两个浴室和四个卧室。我非常爱我的家和

wǒ de jiā rén
我的家人。

wǒ bú tài xǐ huan zhù zài dà chéng shì   yīn wèi dà chéng shì lǐ yǒu hěn duō chē hé rén
2. 我不太喜欢住在大城市，因为大城市里有很多车和人，

kōng qì bù xīn xiān   suī rán wǒ bù xǐ huan zhù zài dà chéng shì   dàn shì wǒ xǐ huan qù dà chéng shì
空气不新鲜。虽然我不喜欢住在大城市，但是我喜欢去大城市

mǎi dōng xi
买东西。

wǒ yǒu yí gè péng you   tā jiào lì li   wǒ qù guò tā jiā   tā jiā lí wǒ jiā bù
3. 我有一个朋友，她叫丽丽，我去过她家。她家离我家不

yuǎn   zuó tiān wǒ qù le tā jiā   wǒ men yì qǐ wán le yí gè hǎo wán de diàn nǎo yóu xì
远。昨天我去了她家，我们一起玩了一个好玩的电脑游戏。

wǒ de péng you lì li cháng cháng lái wǒ jiā   wǒ mā ma hěn xǐ huan lì li   lì li hěn
4. 我的朋友丽丽常常来我家。我妈妈很喜欢丽丽，丽丽很

huì zuò fàn   tā cháng cháng bāng wǒ mā ma zuò wǎn fàn
会做饭，她常常帮我妈妈做晚饭。

èr shí wǔ suì yǐ hòu   wǒ xiǎng zhù zài zhōng guó   wǒ xī wàng zuò yí gè yī shēng   xué
5. 二十五岁以后，我想住在中国。我希望做一个医生，学

hǎo zhōng wén   yǐ hòu qù zhōng guó de yī yuàn gōng zuò
好中文，以后去中国的医院工作。

Unit 6 Weather, Landscape and Geography

■ Part One Warming Up

1.1　　1. C　2. A　3. D　4. F　5. B　6. E　7. G　8. H

1.2　　Sample answer for reference only

1. chūn tiān yǒu fēng　　xià xiǎo yǔ
春天有风，下小雨。

2. xià tiān tiān qíng　　tài rè le
夏天天晴，太热了。

3. qiū tiān duō yún　　yǒu wù
秋天多云，有雾。

4. dōng tiān xià dà xuě　　hěn lěng
冬天下大雪，很冷。

1.3　　Sample answer for reference only

1. 3 月 1 日北京晴天，有风，气温最低 1 度，最高 6 度。

2. 3 月 1 日上海多云，有小雨，气温最低 3 度，最高 12 度。

3. 3 月 1 日香港有大风，有雨，气温最低 13 度，最高 17 度。

4. 3 月 1 日哈尔滨阴天，有小雪，气温最低零下 2 度，最高 8 度。

1.4　　1. C　2. E　3. A　4. D　5. B

	Translation
A. 因为气温非常高。	A. because the temperature is very high.
B. 有时候下大雪。	B. sometimes it snows heavily.
C. 春夏秋冬四季很不一样。	C. The four seasons, spring, summer, autumn and winter, are very different.
D. 天气不冷也不热。	D. it is neither hot nor cold.
E. 但是常常刮风。	E. but it is often windy.

1.5　　Sample answer for reference only

1. wǒ dōu yào qù pá shān
我都要去爬山。

2. wǒ dōu huì qù pǎo bù
我都会去跑步。

3. wǒ dōu huì qù yóu yǒng
我都会去游泳。

4. wǒ dōu yào shàng xué
我都要上学。

1.6 Sample answer for reference only

wèi shén me nǐ bù xǐ huan xià tiān
1. 为什么你不喜欢夏天？

nǐ wèi shén me xué zhōng wén
2. 你为什么学中文？

nǐ bù xiǎng mǎi fáng zi wèi shén me
3. 你不想买房子，为什么？

wèi shén me nǐ yào hé wǒ yì qǐ zuò zuò yè
4. 为什么你要和我一起做作业？

Part Two Picture-based Task

Sample answer for reference only

wǒ zhào piàn lǐ yǒu sān gè nǚ hái   tā men zài hǎi biān wán   hǎi biān de fēng hěn dà
1. 我照片里有三个女孩，她们在海边玩。海边的风很大。

wǒ xǐ huan hé péng you men yì qǐ qù hǎi biān   hǎi biān yòu piào liang yòu hǎo wán   wǒ zuì
2. 我喜欢和朋友们一起去海边。海边又漂亮又好玩。我最
xǐ huan yì biān kàn hǎi   yì biān chī bīng qí lín
喜欢一边看海，一边吃冰淇淋。

qù nián xià tiān wǒ hé jiā rén yì qǐ qù le xī bān yá   xī bān yá de tiān qì hěn hǎo
3. 去年夏天我和家人一起去了西班牙。西班牙的天气很好，
měi tiān dōu shì qíng tiān   wǒ wán le hěn duō shuǐ shang yùn dòng
每天都是晴天，我玩了很多水上运动。

zhè ge zhōu mò rú guǒ xià yǔ   wǒ jiù zài jiā kàn diàn shì hé zuò zuò yè   wǒ hái huì hé
4. 这个周末如果下雨，我就在家看电视和做作业，我还会和
wǒ de péng you shàng wǎng liáo tiān   wǒ fēi cháng tǎo yàn xià yǔ
我的朋友上网聊天。我非常讨厌下雨。

wǒ zuì xǐ huan dōng tiān   yīn wèi wǒ hěn ài huá xuě   wǒ men jiā páng biān yǒu yí gè huá xuě
5. 我最喜欢冬天，因为我很爱滑雪，我们家旁边有一个滑雪
tǐ yù guǎn   zhōu mò wǒ cháng cháng qù huá xuě
体育馆，周末我常常去滑雪。

Part Three Listening Comprehension

B D G

Part Four Conversation

Sample answer for reference only

zài yīng guó   yì nián yǒu sì gè jì jié   chūn tiān   xià tiān   qiū tiān hé dōng tiān   yīng guó
1. 在英国，一年有四个季节，春天、夏天、秋天和冬天。英国
de dōng tiān hěn cháng   xià tiān bú rè   wǒ zuì xǐ huan chūn tiān   yīn wèi chūn tiān de huā zuì piào liang
的冬天很长，夏天不热，我最喜欢春天，因为春天的花最漂亮。

chūn tiān gōng yuán lǐ chú le yǒu hěn duō yóu kè   yě yǒu fēi cháng duō piào liang de huā   gōng
2. 春天公园里除了有很多游客，也有非常多漂亮的花。公
yuán lí wǒ jiā bù yuǎn   zài chūn tiān   wǒ hé jiā rén cháng cháng qù gōng yuán liù gǒu   chī wǔ fàn
园离我家不远。在春天，我和家人常常去公园遛狗、吃午饭。

qù nián shèng dàn jié   tiān qì hěn bù hǎo   suī rán bú tài lěng   yě méi xià xuě   dàn shì
3. 去年圣诞节，天气很不好。虽然不太冷，也没下雪，但是
xià le hěn duō yǔ   yǔ tiān ràng wǒ bú kuài lè jí le
下了很多雨。雨天让我不快乐极了。

rú guǒ tiān qì hǎo   wǒ jiù xiǎng hé péng you men yì qǐ qù hǎi biān   wǒ men huì xiān zài hǎi
4.如果天气好，我就想和朋友们一起去海边。我们会先在海

biān sàn bù   rán hòu qù mǎi bīng qí lín   wǒ xī wàng měi tiān dōu shì qíng tiān
边散步，然后去买冰淇淋。我希望每天都是晴天。

wǒ yǒu wèn tí   lǎo shī   wǒ zuì xǐ huan de jì jié shì chūn tiān   qǐng wèn nín zuì xǐ huan
5.我有问题。老师，我最喜欢的季节是春天。请问您最喜欢

de jì jié shì shén me   nín yě xǐ huan chūn tiān ma
的季节是什么？您也喜欢春天吗？

Unit 7 My Town/ City

Part One Warming Up

1.1   1. G 2. A 3. B 4. K 5. I 6. J 7. H 8. M 9. E 10. D 11. F 12. C 13. L

1.2   1. F 2. A 3. K 4. L 5. E

1.3   Sample answer for reference only

Adjectives and expressions	Pinyin	English translation
干净	gān jìng	clean
安静	ān jìng	quiet
热闹	rè nao	lively
风景漂亮	fēng jǐng piào liang	The view is beautiful.
空气新鲜	kōng qì xīn xiān	The air is fresh.
交通方便	jiāo tōng fāng biàn	There is good public transport.

hǎi biān fēng jǐng piào liang   yě hěn gān jìng
海边风景漂亮，也很干净。
nóng cūn kōng qì xīn xiān   yě hěn ān jìng
农村空气新鲜，也很安静。
shì zhōng xīn jiāo tōng fāng biàn   yě hěn rè nao
市中心交通方便，也很热闹。

wǒ jiā zài lún dūn de dōng bian
1.4   1.我家在伦敦的东边。
huǒ chē zhàn zài wǒ jiā duì miàn
2.火车站在我家对面。
xué xiào zài huǒ chē zhàn de zuǒ bian
3.学校在火车站的左边。
tú shū guǎn zài xué xiào lǐ miàn
4.图书馆在学校里面。

■ Part Two Role Play

Sample answer for reference only

1. lún dūn shì zhōng xīn chú le yǒu hěn duō shāng diàn　hái yǒu yǒu míng de gōngyuán
伦敦市中心除了有很多商店，还有有名的公园。

2. lún dūn de shāng diàn yǒu de jiǔ diǎn bàn kāi mén　yǒu de shí diǎn kāi mén
伦敦的商店有的九点半开门，有的十点开门。

3. yīng guó de bó wù guǎn shì quán shì jiè zuì hǎo de　yòu dà yòu gǔ lǎo
英国的博物馆是全世界最好的，又大又古老。

4. nín zuó tiān zuò le shén me
您昨天做了什么？

5. nín xiǎng zài lún dūn chī zhōng cān ma
您想在伦敦吃中餐吗？

■ Part Three Listening Comprehension

1. (Xi'an is an) ancient/old (city).

2. The museum (next to her hotel in the city centre).

3. Noodles, dumplings (jiaozi) and beef.

4. Take the underground/tube, using the mobile phone (APP) to buy tickets (any one of these).

■ Part Four Conversation

Sample answer for reference only

1. lún dūn shì gè dà chéng shì　yǒu hěn duō yǒu míng de dì fang　bǐ rú　chú le yǒu dà bèn zhōng　lún dūn yǎn　nǚ wáng de jiā　hái yǒu fēi cháng piào liang de hé　hú hé gōng yuán　wǒ jué de lún dūn shì shì jiè shang zuì bàng de chéng shì
伦敦是个大城市，有很多有名的地方，比如，除了有大笨钟、伦敦眼、女王的家，还有非常漂亮的河、湖和公园。我觉得伦敦是世界上最棒的城市。

2. wǒ shàng cì qù lún dūn shì qù nián de shǔ jià　wǒ hé wǒ de jiā rén yì qǐ zuò huǒ chē qù le lún dūn　wǒ men cān guān le lún dūn de dà yīng bó wù guǎn　rán hòu qù zhōng guó chéng chī le hǎo chī de zì zhù cān
我上次去伦敦是去年的暑假，我和我的家人一起坐火车去了伦敦。我们参观了伦敦的大英博物馆，然后去中国城吃了好吃的自助餐。

3. zhù zài dà chéng shì de hǎo chu yǒu sān gè　dì yī shì jiāo tōng hěn fāng biàn　dì èr shì rú guǒ nǐ xǐ huan gòu wù　dà chéng shì yǒu hěn duō shāng diàn　dì sān　dà chéng shì yǒu hěn duō hǎo wán er de dì fang　bǐ rú　diàn yǐng yuàn hé yùn dòng zhōng xīn　děngděng
住在大城市的好处有三个，第一是交通很方便；第二是如果你喜欢购物，大城市有很多商店；第三，大城市有很多好玩儿的地方，比如，电影院和运动中心，等等。

4. zhù zài dà chéng shì yǒu hěn duō hǎo chu　ér huài chu yě bù shǎo　dà chéng shì de rén hé chē dōu tài duō　suǒ yǐ chángcháng hěn chǎo　huán jìng bú tài hǎo　kōng qì yě bù gān jìng
住在大城市有很多好处，而坏处也不少，大城市的人和车都太多，所以常常很吵，环境不太好，空气也不干净。

5. wǒ zuì xiǎng qù běi jīng lǚ yóu　wǒ zhī dào běi jīng bǐ lún dūn hái dà　rú guǒ qù běi jīng　wǒ yào qù pá chángchéng　qù dòng wù yuán kàn dà xióng māo　wǒ hái xiǎng chī běi jīng de jiǎo zi
我最想去北京旅游。我知道北京比伦敦还大。如果去北京，我要去爬长城，去动物园看大熊猫，我还想吃北京的饺子。

■ Part One Warming Up

1.1 1. 一月一日　　　　新年　New Year
　　　yí yuè yī rì　　　　xīn nián

　　2. 农历一月一日　　春节　The Spring Festival
　　　nóng lì yí yuè yī rì　chūn jié

　　3. 三月或四月　　　复活节　Easter
　　　sān yuè huò sì yuè　fù huó jié

　　4. 农历五月五日　　端午节　The Dragon Boat Festival
　　　nóng lì wǔ yuè wǔ rì　duān wǔ jié

　　5. 农历八月十五日　　中秋节　The Mid-Autumn Festival
　　　nóng lì bā yuè shí wǔ rì　zhōng qiū jié

　　6. 十二月二十五日　　圣诞节　Christmas
　　　shí èr yuè èr shí wǔ rì　shèng dàn jié

1.2 A. 1, 2, 4, 5, 8, 9

　　B. 6, 12

　　C. 1, 3, 11

　　D. 1, 7, 10

1.3 1. 每个周末他都去滑雪。
　　　měi gè zhōu mò tā dōu qù huá xuě

　　2. 我每天早上都不吃早饭。
　　　wǒ měi tiān zǎo shang dōu bù chī zǎo fàn

　　3. 奶奶每年春节都给我红包。
　　　nǎi nai měi nián chūn jié dōu gěi wǒ hóng bāo

　　4. 圣诞节的时候，每个孩子都很快乐。
　　　shèng dàn jié de shí hou　měi gè hái zi dōu hěn kuài lè

1.4 1. 你爸爸是法国人。你妈妈呢？
　　　nǐ bà ba shì fǎ guó rén　nǐ mā ma ne

　　2. 今天下雨。明天呢？
　　　jīn tiān xià yǔ　míng tiān ne

　　3. 中秋节中国人吃月饼，端午节呢？
　　　zhōng qiū jié zhōng guó rén chī yuè bing　duān wǔ jié ne

　　4. 今年端午节我想去看龙舟比赛。你呢？
　　　jīn nián duān wǔ jié wǒ xiǎng qù kàn lóng zhōu bǐ sài　nǐ ne

■ Part Two Picture-based Task

Sample answer for reference only

1. 照片里有一家人，他们在吃团圆饭。我觉得他们在庆祝
zhào piàn lǐ yǒu yì jiā rén　tā men zài chī tuán yuán fàn　wǒ jué de tā men zài qìng zhù
中国春节，因为桌子上有很多好吃的东西。
zhōng guó chūn jié　yīn wèi zhuō zi shang yǒu hěn duō hào chī de dōng xi

2. 我过圣诞节的时候和家人一起吃饭。圣诞节是英国最重
wǒ guò shèng dàn jié de shí hou hé jiā rén yì qǐ chī fàn　shèng dàn jié shì yīng guó zuì zhòng
要的节日。圣诞节吃团圆饭的时候，家人会一边吃烤火鸡，一边
yào de jié rì　shèng dàn jié chī tuán yuán fàn de shí hou　jiā rén huì yì biān chī kǎo huǒ jī　yì biān

chàngshèng dàn gē
唱 圣 诞 歌。

qù nián shèng dàn jié wǒ de jiā rén dōu gěi le wǒ lǐ wù māma gěi le wǒ yí gè xīn
3.去年圣诞节，我的家人都给了我礼物。妈妈给了我一个新

diàn nǎo mèi mei gěi le wǒ yí jiàn yī fu bà ba de lǐ wù zuì méi yì si tā gěi le wǒ yì
电脑；妹妹给了我一件衣服；爸爸的礼物最没意思，他给了我一

běn shū
本书。

wǒ jué de jiā rén yīng gāi cháng cháng zài yì qǐ chī fàn yīn wèi wǒ men dōu ài zì jǐ de
4.我觉得家人应该常常在一起吃饭，因为我们都爱自己的

jiā rén rú guǒ měi ge rén dōu hěn máng jiù bú yòng měi tiān dōu zài yì qǐ chī fàn dàn shì yīng gāi
家人。如果每个人都很忙，就不用每天都在一起吃饭，但是应该

zài zhōu mò zhǎo yí gè shí jiān yì qǐ chī fàn
在周末找一个时间一起吃饭。

míng nián wǒ xī wàng qù zhōng guó guò shēng rì wǒ zhī dào zhōng guó rén guò shēng rì de shí
5.明年我希望去中国过生日。我知道中国人过生日的时

hou chī miàn tiáo wǒ hěn xǐ huan chī miàn tiáo wǒ yào chī hěn duō hěn duō hǎo chī de miàn tiáo
候吃面条，我很喜欢吃面条，我要吃很多很多好吃的面条。

■ Part Three Listening Comprehension

1. lion dance, dragon dance, having a family reunion dinner, setting off firecrackers, receiving red envelopes (can be in any order)

2. buy (some story) books and give them to the orphans, buy a ticket for Grandma Chen (in the care home) and take her to see Beijing opera (can be in reversed order)

■ Part Four Conversation

Sample answer for reference only

wǒ zhī dào sān gè zhōng guó jié rì tā men shì chūn jié duān wǔ jié hé zhōng qiū jié
1.我知道三个中国节日，它们是春节、端午节和中秋节。

wǒ zuì xǐ huan de zhōng guó jié rì shì duān wǔ jié yīn wèi wǒ tè bié xǐ huan lóng zhōu bǐ sài
我最喜欢的中国节日是端午节，因为我特别喜欢龙舟比赛。

wǒ fēi cháng xǐ huan chī zhōng cān wǒ de jiā rén hé wǒ yí yàng yě hěn ài chī zhōng cān
2.我非常喜欢吃中餐，我的家人和我一样也很爱吃中餐。

wǒ chú le xǐ huan chī dàn chǎo fàn hé niú ròu miàn tiáo hái xǐ huan chī běi fāng de jiǎo zi
我除了喜欢吃蛋炒饭和牛肉面条，还喜欢吃北方的饺子。

wǒ jué de shèng dàn jié shì yīng guó zuì yǒu yì si de jié rì wǒ huì chàng hěn duō shèng dàn
3.我觉得圣诞节是英国最有意思的节日。我会唱很多圣诞

gē qǔ tā men dōu hěn hǎo tīng shèng dàn jié de shí hou wǒ men jiā huì yì qǐ chī tuán yuán fàn
歌曲，它们都很好听。圣诞节的时候，我们家会一起吃团圆饭。

wǒ de shēng rì shì 2 yuè 26 rì qù nián guò shēng rì de shí hou wǒ yé ye qǐng wǒ
4.我的生日是2月26日，去年过生日的时候，我爷爷请我

qù huá le bīng rán hòu wǒ men yì qǐ zài jiǔ bā chī le xīn xiān de yú hé shǔ tiáo
去滑了冰，然后，我们一起在酒吧吃了新鲜的鱼和薯条。

míng nián chūn jié de shí hou wǒ xī wàng xué xiào kāi yí gè qìng zhù huì lǎo shī men yào
5.明年春节的时候，我希望学校开一个庆祝会，老师们要

mǎi hěn duō hǎo chī de zhōng cān hé xué sheng men yì qǐ chī rú guǒ yǒu wǔ lóng wǔ shī duì lái biǎo
买很多好吃的中餐和学生们一起吃，如果有舞龙舞狮队来表

yǎn nà jiù gèng hǎo le
演，那就更好了！

Unit 9 Transport

■ Part One Warming Up

1.1　1. D　2. G　3. C　4. E　5. F　6. H　7. B　8. A　9. J　10. I

1.2　Sample answer for reference only

1. 那个老爷爷坐公共汽车去公园。
<small>nà ge lǎo yé ye zuò gōnggòng qì chē qù gōngyuán</small>

2. 那个男孩骑自行车上学。
<small>nà ge nán hái qí zì xíng chē shàng xué</small>

3. 那个医生坐出租车上班。
<small>nà ge yī shēng zuò chū zū chē shàng bān</small>

4. 那个女孩走路去火车站。
<small>nà ge nǚ hái zǒu lù qù huǒ chē zhàn</small>

1.3　Sample answer for reference only

1. 我家离学校不远。
<small>wǒ jiā lí xué xiào bù yuǎn</small>

2. 我们学校离火车站很近。
<small>wǒ men xué xiào lí huǒ chē zhàn hěn jìn</small>

3. 火车站离市中心不太近。
<small>huǒ chē zhàn lí shì zhōng xīn bú tài jìn</small>

4. 市中心离海边非常远。
<small>shì zhōng xīn lí hǎi biān fēi cháng yuǎn</small>

1.4

	Translation
A. 不用学法语。	A. No need to learn French.
B. 不用穿很多衣服。	B. No need to wear a lot of clothes.
C. 不用买报纸。	C. No need to buy newspaper.
D. 不用开车。	D. No need to drive.
E. 不用妈妈帮她。	E. No need for mum to help her.
F. 不用吃药。	F. No need to take medicine.

1. F　2. D　3. A　4. E　5. B　6. C

■ Part Two Role Play

Sample answer for reference only

wǒ xiǎng qù chāo shì
1. 我想去超市。

wǒ xiǎng qù chāo shì   yīn wèi wǒ xiǎng mǎi dōng xī
2. 我想去超市，因为我想买东西。

wǒ zǒu lù qù nà er
3. 我走路去那儿。

wǒ zuì xǐ huan zuò huǒ chē shàng xué
4. 我最喜欢坐火车上学。

huǒ chē zhàn lí yùn dòng zhōng xīn yuǎn ma
5. 火车站离运动中心远吗？

■ Part Three Listening Comprehension

1. the airport

2. high-speed train

3. new things

4. not fast

5. cycle; good for health and environment

■ Part Four Conversation

Sample answer for reference only

wǒ zhù zài yīng guó nán fāng de yí gè xiǎo zhèn   nà li de gōng gòng jiāo tōng hěn fāng biàn
1. 我住在英国南方的一个小镇，那里的公共交通很方便。
xiǎo zhèn shang chú le yǒu gōng gòng qì chē hé huǒ chē   yě yǒu chū zū chē   dàn shì méi yǒu dì tiě
小镇上除了有公共汽车和火车，也有出租车，但是没有地铁。

wǒ jiā lí huǒ chē zhàn bù hěn jìn   rú guǒ yào qù huǒ chē zhàn   nǐ yào xiān zuò gōng gòng qì
2. 我家离火车站不很近。如果要去火车站，你要先坐公共汽
chē   cóng wǒ jiā zuò gōng gòng qì chē qù huǒ chē zhàn yào bàn gè xiǎo shí
车，从我家坐公共汽车去火车站要半个小时。

shàng ge zhōu mò   wǒ hé mèi mei yì qǐ zuò huǒ chē qù le lún dūn   wǒ men zài wǎng shang
3. 上个周末，我和妹妹一起坐火车去了伦敦。我们在网上
mǎi le pián yi de yīn yuè jù piào   lún dūn de yīn yuè jù shì quán shì jiè zuì bàng de
买了便宜的音乐剧票，伦敦的音乐剧是全世界最棒的！

wǒ fēi cháng xǐ huan qí zì xíng chē   qí zì xíng chē bú dàn shì zuò yùn dòng   ér qiě duì
4. 我非常喜欢骑自行车。骑自行车不但是做运动，而且对
huán jìng hǎo   wǒ měi tiān dōu qí zì xíng chē shàng xué
环境好。我每天都骑自行车上学。

wǒ hěn xiǎng xué kāi chē   yīn wèi huì kāi chē hěn yǒu yòng   rú guǒ yǐ hòu nǐ gōng zuò de dì
5. 我很想学开车，因为会开车很有用。如果以后你工作的地
fang méi yǒu gōng gòng jiāo tōng gōng jù   huì kāi chē jiù méi guān xi   wǒ xī wàng shí qī suì de shí hou
方没有公共交通工具，会开车就没关系。我希望十七岁的时候
jiù huì kāi chē
就会开车。

■ Part One Warming Up

1.1   A. 4 B. 8 C. 10 D. 1 E. 3 F. 7 G. 2 H. 9 I. 6 J. 5

1.2   A. staff: 2, 6

B. guest: 1, 3, 4, 5, 7

1.3
1. yóu yǒng chí zài dì xià yī céng
游 泳 池 在 地 下 一 层。
2. jiàn shēn fáng zǎo shang liù diǎn bàn kāi mén   wǎn shang shí diǎn guān mén
健 身 房 早 上 六 点 半 开 门 ， 晚 上 十 点 关 门。
3. zǎo fàn cóng qī diǎn kāi shǐ
早 饭 从 七 点 开 始。
4. wǎn fàn cóng liù diǎn kāi shǐ
晚 饭 从 六 点 开 始。

1.4   Sample answer for reference only
1. zài wǒ men jiā   bà ba zuì gāo   dàn shì wǒ zuì cōng míng
在 我 们 家 ， 爸 爸 最 高 ， 但 是 我 最 聪 明。
2. tā shì zuì hǎo de zú qiú yùn dòng yuán
他 是 最 好 的 足 球 运 动 员。
3. zuì lǎo de rén zhù zài yīng guó
最 老 的 人 住 在 英 国。
4. suī rán wǒ xǐ huan xué fǎ wén hé xī bān yá wén   dàn shì wǒ zuì xǐ huan zhōng wén
虽 然 我 喜 欢 学 法 文 和 西 班 牙 文 ， 但 是 我 最 喜 欢 中 文。

■ Part Two Picture-based Task

Sample answer for reference only
1. zhào piàn lǐ yǒu yí gè dà fàn diàn   zhè jiā fàn diàn jiào běi jīng fàn diàn   běi jīng fàn diàn hěn yǒu míng
照 片 里 有 一 个 大 饭 店 ， 这 家 饭 店 叫 北 京 饭 店 ， 北 京 饭 店 很 有 名。
2. wǒ zuì xǐ huan de fàn diàn zài xī bān yá nán bù   nà ge fàn diàn yòu dà yòu piào liang   fàn diàn lǐ de fàn yě hěn hǎo chī
我 最 喜 欢 的 饭 店 在 西 班 牙 南 部 ， 那 个 饭 店 又 大 又 漂 亮 ， 饭 店 里 的 饭 也 很 好 吃。
3. nà ge fàn diàn lí shì zhōng xīn hěn yuǎn   zuò gōng gòng qì chē yào yí gè xiǎo shí   dàn shì fàn diàn lí hǎi biān hěn jìn   zǒu lù zhǐ yào shí fēn zhōng
那 个 饭 店 离 市 中 心 很 远 ， 坐 公 共 汽 车 要 一 个 小 时 ， 但 是 饭 店 离 海 边 很 近 ， 走 路 只 要 十 分 钟。
4. wǒ shàng yí cì qù yóu yǒng chí shì zài shàng gè yuè   yóu yǒng chí zài wǒ jiā páng biān   wǒ de péng you zài nà er kāi le shēng rì huì
我 上 一 次 去 游 泳 池 是 在 上 个 月 ， 游 泳 池 在 我 家 旁 边 ， 我 的 朋 友 在 那 儿 开 了 生 日 会。

wǒ bù dǎ suan zài fàn diàn gōng zuò   yīn wèi zài fàn diàn gōng zuò tài lèi   wǒ xiǎng zài xué
5.我 不 打 算 在 饭 店 工 作 ， 因 为 在 饭 店 工 作 太 累。 我 想 在 学
xiào zuò lǎo shī
校 做 老 师。

Part Three Listening Comprehension

Guest 1: G

Guest 2: C

Guest 3: E

Part Four Conversation

Sample answer for reference only

qù nián   wǒ gēn xué xiào de lǎo shī hé tóng xué yì qǐ qù le zhōng guó shàng hǎi   wǒ men
1.去 年 ， 我 跟 学 校 的 老 师 和 同 学 一 起 去 了 中 国 上 海。 我 们
zhù zài yì jiā xīn kāi de jiǔ diàn   jiǔ diàn suī rán hěn xiǎo   dàn shì hěn gān jìng
住 在 一 家 新 开 的 酒 店。 酒 店 虽 然 很 小， 但 是 很 干 净。

wǒ zhī dào zěn me shàng wǎng dìng jiǔ diàn   shàng wǎng dìng jiǔ diàn hěn róng yì   nǐ xiān kàn kan
2.我 知 道 怎 么 上 网 订 酒 店。 上 网 订 酒 店 很 容 易， 你 先 看 看
nǐ xiǎng zhù shén me dì fang   zài kàn kan jiǔ diàn guì bu guì
你 想 住 什 么 地 方； 再 看 看 酒 店 贵 不 贵。

wǒ jué de xià tiān jiǔ diàn zuì guì   yīn wèi hěn duō rén shǔ jià de shí hou qù lǚ xíng   jiǔ
3.我 觉 得 夏 天 酒 店 最 贵， 因 为 很 多 人 暑 假 的 时 候 去 旅 行， 酒
diàn dōu xī wàng zài xià tiān zhuàn hěn duō qián
店 都 希 望 在 夏 天 赚 很 多 钱。

jiǔ diàn yǒu mei yǒu yóu yǒng chí bú tài zhòng yào   wǒ rèn wéi jiǔ diàn yǒu shū fu de chuáng zuì
4.酒 店 有 没 有 游 泳 池 不 太 重 要， 我 认 为 酒 店 有 舒 服 的 床 最
zhòng yào   yīn wèi dà jiā zhù jiǔ diàn shì xiǎng wǎn shang yǒu dì fang shuì jiào   jiǔ diàn de fàn yě yào
重 要， 因 为 大 家 住 酒 店 是 想 晚 上 有 地 方 睡 觉， 酒 店 的 饭 也 要
hǎo chī
好 吃。

rú guǒ qù dù jià   wǒ xī wàng zhù zài měi lì de hǎi biān   wǒ zuì xǐ huan hé péng you yì
5.如 果 去 度 假， 我 希 望 住 在 美 丽 的 海 边。 我 最 喜 欢 和 朋 友 一
qǐ qù dù jià   wǒ men yào měi tiān qù zuò shuǐ shàng yùn dòng hé chī bīng qí lín
起 去 度 假， 我 们 要 每 天 去 做 水 上 运 动 和 吃 冰 淇 淋。

Part One Warming Up

1.1　1. E　2. B　3. D　4. A　5. C

1.2

 mí 迷 (fan)	3. film fan	 jié 节 (festival)	2. music festival	 chǎng 场 (field, pitch, court)	1. sports field
	6. music fan		5. film festival		4. football pitch
					7. tennis court

1.3　Sample answer for reference only

xiǎo míng yí fàng xué jiù qù liàn xí chàng gē
1. 小 明 一 放 学 就 去 练 习 唱 歌。
mā ma yī huí jiā jiù zuò wǎn fàn
2. 妈 妈 一 回 家 就 做 晚 饭。
wǒ gē ge yí zuò wán zuò yè jiù kàn diàn shì
3. 我 哥 哥 一 做 完 作 业 就 看 电 视。
wǒ yì tī wán zú qiú bà ba jiù gěi wǒ mǎi rè gǒu chī
4. 我 一 踢 完 足 球 爸 爸 就 给 我 买 热 狗 吃。

1.4　Sample answer for reference only

měi gè yuè yí cì
1. 每 个 月 一 次
měi tiān zǎo shang yí cì
2. 每 天 早 上 一 次
měi gè xīng qī liǎng cì
3. 每 个 星 期 两 次
měi nián liù cì
4. 每 年 六 次

1.5　Sample answer for reference only

1. By train.

2. His younger brother.

3. Last year.

4. Hong Kong.

■ Part Two Role Play

Sample answer for reference only

1. 他个子很高，也很胖。他的头发非常短。他的眼睛又大又黑。

2. 我的手机是上个月买的，非常新。

3. 我今天用手机给爸爸妈妈打过两次电话。

4. 请问，您叫什么名字？

5. 请您告诉我的爸爸妈妈，好吗？

■ Part Three Listening Comprehension

1. B   2. C   3. A   4. A

■ Part Four Conversation

Sample answer for reference only

1. 对，我常常参加体育比赛。我打篮球打得非常好，我参加了学校的篮球队，我们每个星期五下午都有比赛。

2. 我喜欢打篮球，所以我最喜欢看篮球比赛，我是美国篮球的球迷。我天天做完作业以后都会在电视上看他们的比赛。

3. 上个月我过生日，我的好朋友请我去伦敦体育馆听了一个流行音乐会，歌手唱得非常棒。音乐会以后，我们去吃了意大利饼。

4. 我觉得电影票太贵了，3D电影票比一般的电影票更贵，所以我和朋友们不常常去电影院，放假的时候我们会在家里上网看电影。

5. 我希望奥林匹克运动会可以在非洲举行，因为非洲有很多穷人，奥运会应该帮助穷人。

■ Part One Warming Up

1.1   A. 6 B. 2 C. 8 D. 5 E. 7 F. 3 G. 4 H. 1

1.2   1. B
wǒ qù guo hǎi biān
我去过海边。

2. D
wǒ kàn guo dà xióng māo
我看过大熊猫。

3. A
wǒ méi huá guo xuě
我没滑过雪。

4. C
wǒ méi pá guo chángchéng
我没爬过长城。

1.3   1.
wǒ dì di yuè lái yuè gāo
我弟弟越来越高。

2.
wǒ yuè lái yuè ài tā
我越来越爱他。

3.
yuè lái yuè duō de yīng guó xué sheng xué zhōng wén
越来越多的英国学生学中文。

4.
wǒ qián bāo lǐ de qián yuè lái yuè shǎo
我钱包里的钱越来越少。

1.4   Sample answer for reference only

1.
zài yīng guó dù jià bǐ qù guó wài dù jià pián yi
在英国度假比去国外度假便宜。

2.
zài yīng guó dù jià bǐ qù guó wài dù jià ān quán yì diǎn
在英国度假比去国外度假安全一点。

3.
qù guó wài dù jià bǐ zài yīng guó dù jià gèng yǒu qù
去国外度假比在英国度假更有趣。

4.
qù guó wài dù jià bǐ zài yīng guó dù jià hǎo wán duō le
去国外度假比在英国度假好玩多了。

■ Part Two Picture-based Task

Sample answer for reference only

1.
zhào piàn lǐ yǒu yí gè fēi jī chǎng zhè shì yí gè zhōng guó de fēi jī chǎng fēi jī chǎng
照片里有一个飞机场。这是一个中国的飞机场。飞机场
yòu dà yòu piào liang
又大又漂亮。

2.
suī rán wǒ xǐ huan zuò fēi jī dàn shì wǒ gèng xǐ huan zuò huǒ chē yīn wèi zuò huǒ chē hěn
虽然我喜欢坐飞机，但是我更喜欢坐火车，因为坐火车很
fāng biàn huǒ chē zhàn bǐ fēi jī chǎng jìn duō le
方便，火车站比飞机场近多了。

3.上个周一，我和朋友一起坐过火车，我们坐火车去了市中心。因为是上班的时间，所以火车上的人多极了。

4.我认为，有的飞机票很贵，有的飞机票不太贵。从英国去欧洲的飞机票比火车票便宜，但是去亚洲的飞机票就越来越贵。

5.我想坐飞机去北京。我不但想去北京爬长城、吃北京烤鸭，而且我想去北京动物园看大熊猫。

Part Three Listening Comprehension

B C F G

Part Four Conversation

Sample answer for reference only

1.我非常喜欢去度假。因为度假不但可以让人放松，而且可以天天玩，不用做作业。度假的时候，我最快乐。

2.我觉得去国外度假有好处，也有坏处。好处是去国外度假比在英国度假更有意思；坏处是去国外度假比在英国度假贵多了。

3.最近我和家人去了美国。我们不但参观了很多名胜古迹，而且还去了有名的游乐场。美国的比萨饼好吃极了。

4.我喜欢和家人一起度假，但是我更喜欢和朋友一起度假，因为我的父母总是要去参观博物馆，真没意思！我更喜欢和朋友们一起逛街买东西。

5.今年暑假，我希望去香港度假。我的朋友是香港人，他请我今年暑假去香港玩，他说香港有很多商店，商店晚上也开门，非常热闹。

Unit 13 My School Day

■ Part One Warming Up

1.1   A. 8   B. 3   C. 5   D. 2   E. 6   F. 1   G. 7   H. 4

1.2

时间	Translation	活动	Translation
早上七点	7am	起床	get up
早上七点半	7.30am	吃早饭	have breakfast
早上八点	8am	坐校车上学	go to school by school bus
早上九点	9am	开始上课	start lessons
中午十二点半	12.30pm	吃午饭	have lunch
下午三点四十五分	3.45pm	先参加课外活动，再做作业	take part in after-school activities first, then do homework
晚上六点十五分	6.15pm	吃晚饭	have dinner
晚上九点半	9.30pm	睡觉	go to bed

xiǎo hóng zǎo shang qī diǎn qǐ chuáng
1. 小红早上七点起床。
xiǎo hóng zǎo shang qī diǎn bàn chī zǎo fàn
2. 小红早上七点半吃早饭。
xiǎo hóng zǎo shang bā diǎn zuò xiào chē shàng xué
3. 小红早上八点坐校车上学。
xiǎo hóng zǎo shang jiǔ diǎn kāi shǐ shàng kè
4. 小红早上九点开始上课。
xiǎo hóng zhōng wǔ shí èr diǎn bàn chī wǔ fàn
5. 小红中午十二点半吃午饭。
xiǎo hóng xià wǔ sān diǎn sì shí wǔ fēn xiān cān jiā kè wài huó dòng   zài zuò zuò yè
6. 小红下午三点四十五分先参加课外活动，再做作业。
xiǎo hóng wǎn shang liù diǎn shí wǔ fēn chī wǎn fàn
7. 小红晚上六点十五分吃晚饭。
xiǎo hóng wǎn shang jiǔ diǎn bàn shuì jiào
8. 小红晚上九点半睡觉。

1.3   Sample answer for reference only
cóng wǒ jiā dào xué xiào zǒu lù yào bàn gè xiǎo shí
1. 从我家到学校走路要半个小时。
cóng wǒ jiā dào lún dūn zuò huǒ chē yào liǎng gè xiǎo shí
2. 从我家到伦敦坐火车要两个小时。
cóng xué xiào dào yùn dòng zhōng xīn qí chē yào èr shí fēn zhōng
3. 从学校到运动中心骑车要二十分钟。
cóng yīng guó dào zhōng guó zuò fēi jī yào shí gè xiǎo shí
4. 从英国到中国坐飞机要十个小时。

1.4 Sample answer for reference only

cóng nǐ jiā dào xué xiào zǒu lù yào duō cháng shí jiān
1. 从你家到学校走路要多长时间？
cóng nǐ jiā dào lún dūn zuò huǒ chē yào duō cháng shí jiān
2. 从你家到伦敦坐火车要多长时间？
cóng xué xiào dào yùn dòng zhōng xīn qí chē yào duō cháng shí jiān
3. 从学校到运动中心骑车要多长时间？
cóng yīng guó dào zhōng guó zuò fēi jī yào duō cháng shí jiān
4. 从英国到中国坐飞机要多长时间？

1.5 Sample answer for reference only

cóng wǒ jiā dào xué xiào yuǎn jí le
1. very far / 从我家到学校远极了！
zhōng wén zuò yè róng yì jí le
2. easy / 中文作业容易极了！
wǒ men de xiào zhǎng yán lì jí le
3. strict / 我们的校长严厉极了！
wǒ men de xiào fú nán kàn jí le
4. ugly / 我们的校服难看极了！

■ Part Two Role Play

Sample answer for reference only

wǒ měi tiān zǎo shang zǒu lù shàng xué
1. 我每天早上走路上学。
wǒ qī diǎn bàn qǐ chuáng
2. 我七点半起床。
wǒ zǎo fàn chī miàn bāo
3. 我早饭吃面包。
wǒ jué de nǐ men de xué xiào hěn piào liang
4. 我觉得你们的学校很漂亮。
nǐ xǐ huan wǒ men de xiào fú ma
5. 你喜欢我们的校服吗？

■ Part Three Listening Comprehension

1. False. The school is not far from the city centre but not in it.

2. True.

3. True.

4. False. Football matches are played in the school sports field every Friday.

■ Part Four Conversation

Sample answer for reference only

hǎo wǒ de xué xiào zài yīng guó de dōng bù hǎi biān wǒ men xué xiào suī rán bú piào liang
1. 好，我的学校在英国的东部海边，我们学校虽然不漂亮，
dàn shì hěn dà wǒ men xué xiào yǒu sān qiān duō gè xué sheng hé wǔ bǎi duō wèi lǎo shī
但是很大。我们学校有三千多个学生和五百多位老师。
wǒ hěn xǐ huan wǒ men de xué xiào yīn wèi wǒ zài xué xiào lǐ yǒu hěn duō hǎo péng you
2. 我很喜欢我们的学校，因为我在学校里有很多好朋友。

wǒ men měi tiān zǎo shang yì qǐ zuò xiào chē shàng xué　　zhōng wǔ wǒ men zài xué xiào cān tīng yì biān chī wǔ
我们每天早上一起坐校车上学；中午我们在学校餐厅一边吃午
fàn　　yì biān liáo tiān
饭，一边聊天。

jīn tiān zǎo fàn wǒ chī le kǎo miàn bāo　　hē le yīng guó chá　　zǎo fàn wǒ yì bān chī de hěn
3.今天早饭我吃了烤面包，喝了英国茶。早饭我一般吃得很
shǎo　　rú guǒ qǐ chuáng tài wǎn　　méi yǒu shí jiān　　wǒ jiù bù chī zǎo fàn
少；如果起床太晚，没有时间，我就不吃早饭。

yīng guó de xiào fú hé zhōng guó de xiào fú bú tài yí yàng　　zài yīng guó　　wǒ men de xiào fú
4.英国的校服和中国的校服不太一样。在英国，我们的校服
yǒu wài yī　　chèn yī hé lǐng dài　　nán shēng chuān kù zi　　nǚ shēng chuān qún zi　　dàn shì zài zhōng
有外衣、衬衣和领带，男生穿裤子，女生穿裙子；但是在中
guó　　hěn duō xué xiào de xiào fú shì yùn dòng yī
国，很多学校的校服是运动衣。

jīn tiān fàng xué yǐ hòu　　wǒ xiǎng hé péng you men yì qǐ dǎ lán qiú　　wǒ men xué xiào yǒu hěn
5.今天放学以后，我想和朋友们一起打篮球。我们学校有很
duō kè wài huó dòng　　wǒ měi gè xīng qī sān fàng xué hòu dōu huì cān jiā xué xiào lán qiú duì de huó dòng
多课外活动，我每个星期三放学后都会参加学校篮球队的活动。

Unit 14 In the Classroom

■ Part One Warming Up

1.1

时间／星期	星期一	星期二	星期三	星期四	星期五
9.00-9.50am	中文 Chinese	地理 geography	英文 English	地理 geography	生物 biology
9.55-10.45am	数学 maths	物理 physics	中文 Chinese	西班牙文 Spanish	电脑 computing
10.45-11.00am	休息 break				
11.00-11.50am	电脑 computing	化学 chemistry	历史 history	生物 biology	英文 English
11.55-12.45pm	午饭 lunch				
12.50-1.40pm	历史 history	西班牙文 Spanish	数学 maths	物理 physics	化学 chemistry
1.45-2.35pm	体育 sports	公民 citizenship	自习 self-study	体育 sports	公民 citizenship
2.40-3.30pm		自习 self-study	体育 sports	自习 self-study	

xīng qī yī shàng wǔ shí yì diǎn yǒu diàn nǎo kè
1.星期一上午十一点有电脑课。
xīng qī èr zhōng wǔ shí èr diǎn wǔ shí fēn shì xī bān yá wén kè
2.星期二中午十二点五十分是西班牙文课。
xīng qī sān de zhōng wén kè zài shàng wǔ jiǔ diǎn wǔ shí wǔ fēn
3.星期三的中文课在上午九点五十五分。
xīng qī èr hé xīng qī sì yǒu dì lǐ kè
4.星期二和星期四有地理课。
xīng qī wǔ xià wǔ liǎng diǎn sì shí fēn méi yǒu kè
5.星期五下午两点四十分没有课。

1.2   1. start my lesson, finish

         2. got on transport, got off

         3. go to work, finish

         4. went uphill, went downhill

1.3

1. 好	good	不太好	not so good
2. 友好	friendly	不太友好	not very friendly
3. 难	difficult	不太难	not too difficult
4. 容易	easy	不太容易	not very easy
5. 对	correct	不太对	not quite right
6. 严厉	strict	不太严格	not too strict
7. 喜欢	like	不太喜欢	do not like very much
8. 明白	understand	不太明白	do not quite understand

1.4   Sample answer for reference only

1. 美术课很有意思，但是 / 可是 / 不过美术考试很难。

2. 我喜欢上科学课，但是 / 可是 / 不过我不太喜欢科学老师。

3. 我爱学中文，但是 / 可是 / 不过我不爱写汉字。

4. 今天我们没有英文作业，但是 / 可是 / 不过我们有很多数学作业。

■ Part Two Picture-based Task

Sample answer for reference only

1. 照片里有一个老师和几个学生。学生们在学中文。学生们很喜欢他们的中文老师。

2. 我觉得学中文又有意思又有用，我和我弟弟都学中文，不过，我不喜欢写汉字。

3. 我星期二和星期五有中文课。我每个星期有两节中文课。我觉得我的中文课太少了。

yīn wèi zhè ge xīng qī yào kǎo shì   shàng ge xīng qī wǒ men de zhōng wén lǎo shī méi yǒu gěi wǒ
4.因为这个星期要考试，上个星期我们的中文老师没有给我
men zuò yè   dàn shì tā ràng wǒ men kàn le yí ge zhōng wén diàn yǐng
们作业，但是他让我们看了一个中文电影。

wǒ hěn xiǎng qù zhōng guó xué zhōng wén   rú guǒ qù zhōng guó xué zhōng wén   wǒ jiù huì měi
5.我很想去中国学中文。如果去中国学中文，我就会每
tiān yòng zhōng wén hé zhōng guó rén liáo tiān
天用中文和中国人聊天。

■ Part Three Listening Comprehension

	Positive	Negative	Both positive and negative
1	✕		
2			✕
3		✕	
4	✕		

■ Part Four Conversation

Sample answer for reference only

zài xué xiào   wǒ xué yīng wén   shù xué   kē xué   diàn nǎo   fǎ wén hé zhōng wén   wǒ
1.在学校，我学英文、数学、科学、电脑、法文和中文。我
zuì ài xué yīng wén hé kē xué   wǒ bú tài ài xué shù xué   shù xué kǎo shì tài nán le
最爱学英文和科学；我不太爱学数学，数学考试太难了。

wǒ jué de xué kē xué zuì zhòng yào   yīn wèi kē xué yòu yǒu yòng yòu yǒu yì si   xué kē xué
2.我觉得学科学最重要，因为科学又有用又有意思，学科学
ràng wǒ yuè lái yuè cōng míng
让我越来越聪明。

wǒ zuó tiān shàng le yīng wén   shēng wù hé zhōng wén kè   wǒ zuò le hěn duō yīng wén hé shēng wù zuò
3.我昨天上了英文、生物和中文课。我做了很多英文和生物作
yè   zài zhōng wén kè shang   lǎo shī hé wǒ men yì qǐ shuō le hěn cháng shí jiān de hàn yǔ
业；在中文课上，老师和我们一起说了很长时间的汉语。

wǒ zuì xǐ huan wǒ men de yīng wén lǎo shī   tā shì yí ge zuò jiā   kàn guo hěn duō shū
4.我最喜欢我们的英文老师。他是一个作家，看过很多书。
suī rán tā hěn yán lì   dàn shì tā de kè fēi cháng yǒu qù
虽然他很严厉，但是他的课非常有趣。

rú guǒ shàng dà xué   wǒ xī wàng xué xí diàn nǎo   wǒ yě xiǎng xué hǎo zhōng wén   dà xué
5.如果上大学，我希望学习电脑，我也想学好中文。大学
bì yè yǐ hòu   wǒ xiǎng qù zhōng guó zuò yí ge diàn nǎo gōng chéng shī
毕业以后，我想去中国做一个电脑工程师。

Unit 15 My School

■ Part One Warming Up

1.1

堂	4. canteen	馆	2. library
	7. assembly hall		5. sports hall
室	1. office	场	3. sports field
	8. classroom		6. football pitch

1.2 Sample answer for reference only

huā yuán lǐ yǒu hěn duō xiān huā
1. 花园里有很多鲜花。
huā diàn lǐ yǒu hěn duō huā píng
2. 花店里有很多花瓶。
wǒ měi gè xīng qī huā yí gè xiǎo shí shàngwǎng gēn wǒ de zhōng guó péng you liáo tiān
3. 我每个星期花一个小时上网跟我的中国朋友聊天。
tā huā le sān bǎi kuài mǎi le yí gè èr shǒushǒu jī
4. 她花了三百块买了一个二手手机。

1.3 1. learn Chinese

2. be with his girlfriend

3. earn money

4. stay healthy

1.4 Sample answer for reference only

shǎoshuō duō tīng
1. 少说，多听！
shǎo kāi chē duō qí chē
2. 少开车，多骑车！
shǎo chī ròu duō chī cài
3. 少吃肉，多吃菜！
shǎo wán diàn nǎo yóu xì duō kàn shū
4. 少玩电脑游戏，多看书。

■ Part Two Role Play

Sample answer for reference only

wǒ huā le yí gè duō xiǎo shí zuò huǒ chē lái xué xiào
1. 我花了一个多小时坐火车来学校。
wǒ jué de nǐ men de tǐ yù guǎn yòu dà yòu piào liang
2. 我觉得你们的体育馆又大又漂亮。

3.
wǒ xǐ huan yóu yǒng   wèi le jiàn kāng   wǒ měi gè xīng qī dōu yóu liǎng cì yǒng
我喜欢游泳，为了健康，我每个星期都游两次泳。

4.
nǐ men xué xiào yǒu jǐ gè yùn dòngchǎng
你们学校有几个运动场？

5.
nǐ men xué xiào yǒu duō shǎo xué sheng
你们学校有多少学生？

■ Part Three Listening Comprehension

1. food, meals

2. eating more vegetables

3. cakes, fizzy drinks, unhealthy food

4. jogging, working out

■ Part Four Conversation

Sample answer for reference only

1.我在学校有很多压力。每天我除了要上很多课以外，还有非常多的作业，休息和午饭的时间很短，我忙极了，所以我觉得压力很大。

2.我相信校长知道我有压力，但是他认为我们的压力没有高中学生的压力大，他常常说："有压力没关系，你要放松。"

3.如果有压力，我就会找我的好朋友一起谈谈。我们会一边在公园里遛狗，一边聊天。如果我的朋友有压力，他也会来找我谈谈。

4.考试有好处，也有坏处。考试的好处是让我知道我学了什么，哪些东西我会了，哪些东西我还不明白。考试的坏处是给我非常大的压力。

5.为了让自己快乐，我一般会听音乐、看书和看电影。昨天考试以后，我回家看了一个有趣的电影，这个电影让我觉得很快乐。

Unit 16 Extra-curricular Activities

■ Part One Warming Up

1.1   A. 5 B. 1 C. 3 D. 7 E. 6 F. 4 G. 8 H. 2

1.2   Sample answer for reference only

　　　wǒ péng you de yùn dòng xié gēn wǒ de　　 yùn dòng xié 　 yí yàng shū fu
1. 我 朋 友 的 运 动 鞋 跟 我 的 （运 动 鞋） 一 样 舒 服。
　　chàng jīng jù gēn tán gāng qín yí yàng nán
2. 唱 京 剧 跟 弹 钢 琴 一 样 难。
　　lǎo shī de shū fǎ gēn nà ge huà jiā de　 shū fǎ　 yí yàng piào liang
3. 老 师 的 书 法 跟 那 个 画 家 的 （书 法） 一 样 漂 亮。
　　wǒ dì di gēn wǒ yí yàng xǐ huan dǎ tài jí quán
4. 我 弟 弟 跟 我 一 样 喜 欢 打 太 极 拳。

1.4   Sample answer for reference only

名字 Name	活动一 Activity 1	活动二 Activity 2	活动三 Activity 3
小红 Xiaohong	打太极拳 doing Tai Chi	弹钢琴 playing the piano	学外语 learning foreign languages
小蓝 Xiaolan	打网球 playing tennis	唱歌 singing	参观博物馆 visiting museums
小黑 Xiaohei	踢足球 playing football	玩儿乐队 playing in the band	学书法 learning calligraphy
小白 Xiaobai	骑马 horse riding	唱京剧 singing Beijing opera	学画画 learning painting

　　fàng xué yǐ hòu　　　xiǎo hóng bù jǐn dǎ tài jí quán　　tán gāng qín　　hái xué wài yǔ
1. 放 学 以 后， 小 红 不 仅 打 太 极 拳、 弹 钢 琴， 还 学 外 语。
　　fàng xué yǐ hòu　　　xiǎo lán bú dàn dǎ wǎng qiú　　chàng gē　　　ér qiě cān guān bó wù guǎn
2. 放 学 以 后， 小 蓝 不 但 打 网 球、 唱 歌， 而 且 参 观 博 物 馆。
　　fàng xué yǐ hòu　　　xiǎo hēi chú le tī zú qiú　　wán er yuè duì　　yě xué shū fǎ
3. 放 学 以 后， 小 黑 除 了 踢 足 球、 玩 儿 乐 队， 也 学 书 法。
　　fàng xué yǐ hòu　　　xiǎo bái bù jǐn qí mǎ　　chàng jīng jù　　ér qiě xué huà huà
4. 放 学 以 后， 小 白 不 仅 骑 马、 唱 京 剧， 而 且 学 画 画。

■ Part Two Picture-based Task

Sample answer for reference only

　　zhào piàn lǐ yǒu yí gè jiào shì　　lǎo shī shì yí gè zhōng guó chú shī　　xué sheng men zài xué
1. 照 片 里 有 一 个 教 室， 老 师 是 一 个 中 国 厨 师， 学 生 们 在 学
zuò zhōng cān
做 中 餐。
　　wǒ fēi cháng xǐ huan zuò fàn　　yīn wèi wǒ méi yǒu shén me ài hào　　bú guò wǒ tè bié ài
2. 我 非 常 喜 欢 做 饭， 因 为 我 没 有 什 么 爱 好， 不 过 我 特 别 爱

chī wǒ de lǐ xiǎng shì zuò yí gè dà fàn diàn de chú shī
吃， 我 的 理 想 是 做 一 个 大 饭 店 的 厨 师。

shàng ge yuè shí wǔ hào shì wǒ de shēng rì   nà tiān wǒ jiào le zhōng cān wài mài qǐng wǒ de
3. 上 个 月 十 五 号 是 我 的 生 日， 那 天 我 叫 了 中 餐 外 卖 请 我 的
péng you men yì qǐ chī   tā men dōu gěi le wǒ lǐ wù
朋 友 们 一 起 吃， 他 们 都 给 了 我 礼 物。

wǒ ài chī chǎo miàn   chǎo fàn hé běi jīng kǎo yā   wǒ men cūn lǐ yǒu yí gè zhōng cān wài mài
4. 我 爱 吃 炒 面、 炒 饭 和 北 京 烤 鸭。 我 们 村 里 有 一 个 中 餐 外 卖
diàn   tā men zuò de běi jīng kǎo yā hǎo chī jí le
店， 他 们 做 的 北 京 烤 鸭 好 吃 极 了。

wǒ zuì xiǎng hé wǒ de zhōng guó péng you lì li yì qǐ chī zhōng cān   yīn wèi lì li shì
5. 我 最 想 和 我 的 中 国 朋 友 丽 丽 一 起 吃 中 餐， 因 为 丽 丽 是
zhōng guó rén   suǒ yǐ tā zhī dào shén me cài zuì hǎo chī   zhè ge zhōu mò   lì li yào jiāo wǒ zuò
中 国 人， 所 以 她 知 道 什 么 菜 最 好 吃。 这 个 周 末， 丽 丽 要 教 我 做
zhōng cān
中 餐。

■ Part Three Listening Comprehension

B D E H

■ Part Four Conversation

Sample answer for reference only

fàng xué yǐ hòu   wǒ cān jiā hěn duō kè wài huó dòng   bǐ rú dǎ wǎng qiú   dǎ tài jí quán
1. 放 学 以 后， 我 参 加 很 多 课 外 活 动， 比 如 打 网 球、 打 太 极 拳
hé cān jiā xué xiào hé chàng tuán děng děng   chú le xué xiào de kè wài huó dòng   wǒ yě cháng cháng zài
和 参 加 学 校 合 唱 团 等 等。 除 了 学 校 的 课 外 活 动， 我 也 常 常 在
jiā gēn mā ma xué zuò fàn   wǒ měi tiān fàng xué yǐ hòu dōu hěn máng
家 跟 妈 妈 学 做 饭。 我 每 天 放 学 以 后 都 很 忙。

cān jiā kè wài huó dòng yǒu tài duō hǎo chu le   nǐ bú dàn kě yǐ jiāo péng you   ér qiě kě yǐ
2. 参 加 课 外 活 动 有 太 多 好 处 了， 你 不 但 可 以 交 朋 友， 而 且 可 以
xué xīn dōng xi   kè wài huó dòng hái kě yǐ gěi nǐ jī huì jì huà wèi lái de shēng huó hé gōng zuò
学 新 东 西， 课 外 活 动 还 可 以 给 你 机 会 计 划 未 来 的 生 活 和 工 作。

shàng ge zhōu mò   wǒ hé péng you men yì qǐ qù le shì zhōng xīn   wǒ men xiān qù diàn yǐng
3. 上 个 周 末， 我 和 朋 友 们 一 起 去 了 市 中 心。 我 们 先 去 电 影
yuàn kàn le yí gè měi guó diàn yǐng   rán hòu qù shū diàn mǎi le yì xiē kǎo shì fù xí yòng de shū
院 看 了 一 个 美 国 电 影， 然 后 去 书 店 买 了 一 些 考 试 复 习 用 的 书。

wǒ jué de zuò yùn dòng hé xué xí yí yàng zhòng yào   yīn wèi rú guǒ zhǐ zuò yùn dòng   bù xué
4. 我 觉 得 做 运 动 和 学 习 一 样 重 要， 因 为 如 果 只 做 运 动， 不 学
xí   nǐ jiù huì hěn bèn   kě shì rú guǒ zhǐ xué xí   bú zuò yùn dòng   nǐ de shēn tǐ jiù huì yuè
习， 你 就 会 很 笨； 可 是 如 果 只 学 习， 不 做 运 动， 你 的 身 体 就 会 越
lái yuè bú jiàn kāng
来 越 不 健 康。

rú guǒ néng cān jiā ào yùn huì   wǒ xiǎng cān jiā tài jí quán bǐ sài   dàn shì wǒ bù zhī dào
5. 如 果 能 参 加 奥 运 会， 我 想 参 加 太 极 拳 比 赛， 但 是 我 不 知 道
ào yùn huì yǒu mei yǒu tài jí quán   wǒ měi gè xīng qī shàng sān cì tài jí quán kè   wǒ xī wàng zuò
奥 运 会 有 没 有 太 极 拳。 我 每 个 星 期 上 三 次 太 极 拳 课， 我 希 望 做
yí gè tài jí quán yùn dòng yuán
一 个 太 极 拳 运 动 员。

Unit 17 Gap Year and Work Experience

Part One Warming Up

1.1　A. 7　B. 3　C. 2　D. 1　E. 8　F. 5　G. 4　H. 6

1.3　1. A　2. B　3. A　4. B

1.4　Sample answer for reference only

　　lǎo shī　　wǒ kě yǐ qù cè suǒ ma
1. 老师，我可以去厕所吗？

　　hǎo tīng de yīn yuè néng　　kě yǐ bāng zhù wǒ fàng sōng
2. 好听的音乐能 / 可以帮助我放松。

　　wǒ jué de bù shū fu　　suǒ yǐ jīn tiān bù néng qù shàng bān
3. 我觉得不舒服，所以今天不能去上班。

　　wǒ xiǎng zài yì jiā zhōng guó gōng sī shí xí　　yīn wèi wǒ huì shuō hàn yǔ
4. 我想在一家中国公司实习，因为我会说汉语。

Part Two Role Play

Sample answer for reference only

　　wǒ shì shí yī nián jí de xué sheng
1. 我是十一年级的学生。

　　wǒ xiǎng zài kā fēi tīng gōng zuò　　yīn wèi wǒ xǐ huan zuò fú wù yuán
2. 我想在咖啡厅工作，因为我喜欢做服务员。

　　wǒ de ài hào shì tīng yīn yuè　　kàn shū hé hē kā fēi
3. 我的爱好是听音乐、看书和喝咖啡。

　　wǒ xiǎng zài xīng qī liù hé xīng qī tiān gōng zuò
4. 我想在星期六和星期天工作。

　　wǒ shén me shí hou kě yǐ kāi shǐ gōng zuò
5. 我什么时候可以开始工作？

Part Three Listening Comprehension

1. Speaker 1: EXAMPLE

2. Speaker 2: C

3. Speaker 3: G

4. Speaker 4: B

5. Speaker 5: F

6. Speaker 6: E

■ Part Four Conversation

Sample answer for reference only

1.我参加过学校的社会实践活动。十年级的时候，我去一个小学参加了一个星期的社会实践活动。这个小学有很多外国学生，我教他们说英语。

2.中学生参加社会实践活动有很多好处。参加社会实践活动除了有时候可以赚钱，还可以交朋友。参加社会实践活动比在学校上课有意思。

3.中学生送报纸能赚钱，但是我不会骑自行车，所以不能去做这个工作。

4.我会用做兼职赚的钱买新衣服，也会和朋友一起去饭馆吃饭。如果能赚很多钱，我就会自己花钱去旅游，或者买票参加音乐节。

5.我最想去华为公司做实习生。在英国，大家都知道华为手机。我想看看中国公司和英国公司有什么不一样。

Unit 18 Life after Secondary School

■ Part One Warming Up

1.1　A. 3　B. 6　C. 5　D. 2　E. 8　F. 4　G. 1　H. 7

1.2　1. 他在看书。
　　　　tā zài kàn shū

　　　2. 小狗在玩球。
　　　　xiǎo gǒu zài wán qiú

　　　3. 这个女孩在想家。
　　　　zhè ge nǚ hái zài xiǎng jiā

　　　4. 他们在唱歌。
　　　　tā men zài chàng gē

1.3

from	to	place	occupation
11 years old	18 years old	town secondary school	student
19 years old	20 years old	Africa	charity worker
2017	2020	University of London	student
last year	present	Taiwan Computer Company	engineer

1.4　1. B　2. A　3. A　4. A

■ Part Two Picture-based Task

Sample answer for reference only

1. 照片里有一个学生和一个老师。学生正在学开车。教开
zhào piàn lǐ yǒu yí gè xué sheng hé yí gè lǎo shī　xué sheng zhèng zài xué kāi chē　jiào kāi
车的老师看起来非常不高兴。
chē de lǎo shī kàn qǐ lai fēi cháng bù gāo xìng

2. 我很想学开车，因为我觉得开车有意思极了。在英国，如
wǒ hěn xiǎng xué kāi chē　yīn wèi wǒ jué de kāi chē yǒu yì si jí le　zài yīng guó　rú
果你十六岁，就可以学开车。我就要十六岁了。
guǒ nǐ shí liù suì　jiù kě yǐ xué kāi chē　wǒ jiù yào shí liù suì le

3. 上个周末，我和家人开车去了海边。上个周末的天气非常
shàng ge zhōu mò　wǒ hé jiā rén kāi chē qù le hǎi biān　shàng ge zhōu mò de tiān qì fēi cháng
好，海边的人多极了。我们在海边拍了很多漂亮的照片。
hǎo　hǎi biān de rén duō jí le　wǒ men zài hǎi biān pāi le hěn duō piào liang de zhào piàn

4. 会开车的好处是不但方便，而且不会浪费时间。你可以自己开车
huì kāi chē de hǎo chu shì bú dàn fāng biàn　ér qiě bú huì làng fèi shí jiān　nǐ kě yǐ zì jǐ kāi chē
去要去的地方，比如去上班、去上学等等，不用父母开车送你去。
qù yào qù de dì fang　bǐ rú qù shàng bān　qù shàng xué děng děng　bú yòng fù mǔ kāi chē sòng nǐ qù

wǒ xǐ huan hóng sè de chē, yīn wèi hóng sè shì wǒ zuì xǐ huan de yán sè。 rú guǒ wǒ

5.我喜欢红色的车，因为红色是我最喜欢的颜色。如果我

yǒu hěn duō qián, jiù huì gěi zì jǐ mǎi yí liàng hóng sè de pǎo chē。

有很多钱，就会给自己买一辆红色的跑车。

Part Three Listening Comprehension

1. Hong Kong

2. history

3. colleagues

4. classmates

Part Four Conversation

Sample answer for reference only

zhōng xué bì yè yǐ hòu, wǒ dǎ suan shàng dà xué。 yīn wèi wǒ xiǎng zuò yī shēng, suǒ yǐ

1.中学毕业以后，我打算上大学。因为我想做医生，所以

wǒ xī wàng shàng dà xué xué yī。 wèi le zhè ge jì huà, wǒ zài gāo zhōng yào xué xí huà xué、 shēng

我希望上大学学医。为了这个计划，我在高中要学习化学、生

wù hé shù xué。

物和数学。

wǒ bú tài tóng yì nǐ de kàn fǎ。 wǒ jué de měi gè rén de xìng qù dōu bù yī yàng, bǐ

2.我不太同意你的看法。我觉得每个人的兴趣都不一样，比

rú, wǒ xiǎng zuò yī shēng, suǒ yǐ wǒ yào shàng dà xué, dàn shì rú guǒ yǒu de tóng xué xiǎng zǎo yì

如，我想做医生，所以我要上大学，但是如果有的同学想早一

diǎn gōng zuò zhuàn qián, tā men jiù bù yí dìng yào shàng dà xué。

点工作赚钱，他们就不一定要上大学。

qù nián wǒ cān jiā le xué xiào de shè huì shí jiàn huó dòng, wǒ qù yì jiā cí shàn shāng diàn zuò

3.去年我参加了学校的社会实践活动，我去一家慈善商店做

le yí gè yuè de shòu huò yuán。 suī rán zhè ge gōng zuò méi yǒu gōng zī, dàn shì zuò yì gōng ràng wǒ

了一个月的售货员。虽然这个工作没有工资，但是做义工让我

jué de hěn kuài lè。

觉得很快乐。

wǒ rèn wéi xiū xué yì nián duì jiàn kāng yǒu hǎo chu, yīn wèi wǒ men zài xué xiào xué xí le hěn

4.我认为休学一年对健康有好处，因为我们在学校学习了很

duō nián, dà jiā dōu tài lèi le, suǒ yǐ zài jiā xiū xué yì nián kě yǐ ràng zì jǐ fàng sōng

多年，大家都太累了，所以在家休学一年可以让自己放松。

xiū xué yì nián yě yǒu bú tài hǎo de dì fang, bǐ rú, rú guǒ nǐ de péng you men dōu qù

5.休学一年也有不太好的地方，比如，如果你的朋友们都去

shàng dà xué le, dà jiā dōu hěn máng, nǐ kě néng huì jué de yǒu yì diǎn bù shū fu, yīn wèi nǐ hé

上大学了，大家都很忙，你可能会觉得有一点不舒服，因为你和

tā men bù yī yàng。

他们不一样。

Unit 19 Job and Career Choices

▮ Part One Warming Up

1.1　A. 9　B. 3　C. 4　D. 8　E. 14　F. 19　G. 13

H. 6　I. 18　J. 20　K. 16　L. 7　M. 15　N. 17

O. 1　P. 12　Q. 10　R. 5　S. 11　T. 2

1.2　Sample answer for reference only

　jiào shī de gōng zuò shì jiāo kè
1. 教师的工作是教课。
　sī jī de gōng zuò shì kāi chē
2. 司机的工作是开车。
　chú shī de gōng zuò shì zuò fàn
3. 厨师的工作是做饭。
　shòu huò yuán de gōng zuò shì mài dōng xī
4. 售货员的工作是卖东西。
　yī shēng de gōng zuò shì gěi bìng rén kàn bìng
5. 医生的工作是给病人看病。
　jì zhě de gōng zuò shì gěi bào zhǐ xiě xīn wén
6. 记者的工作是给报纸写新闻。

1.3　Sample answer for reference only

　wǒ jiā jiù zài wǒ men xué xiào páng biān
1. 我家就在我们学校旁边。
　hǎo ba wǒ xiàn zài jiù qù dǎ diàn huà
2. 好吧，我现在就去打电话。
　wǒ de lǐ xiǎng jiù shì zuò yí gè yòu kuài lè yòu yǒu yòng de rén
3. 我的理想就是做一个又快乐又有用的人。
　rú guǒ néng qù měi guó shàng dà xué wǒ jiù huì fēi cháng kāi xīn
4. 如果能去美国上大学，我就会非常开心。

1.4　Sample answer for reference only

　nán chī jiù shì hěn bù hǎo chī de yì si
1. 难吃就是很不好吃的意思。
　hǎo de bù dé liǎo jiù shì fēi cháng hǎo de yì si
2. 好得不得了就是非常好的意思。
　duì jiàn kāng yǒu hài jiù shì duì shēn tǐ hěn bù hǎo de yì si
3. 对健康有害就是对身体很不好的意思。
　zēng jiā jiù shì zài dà xiǎo shù liàngshàng yuè lái yuè duō de yì si
4. 增加就是在大小、数量上越来越多的意思。

Part Two Role Play

Sample answer for reference only

1. wǒ zhǐ yǒu yí gè ài hào， nà jiù shì huà huà， wǒ hěn xiǎo de shí hou jiù xiǎng zuò yí gè
我只有一个爱好，那就是画画，我很小的时候就想做一个
huà jiā
画家。

2. wǒ méi yǒu zài guǎng gào gōng sī gōng zuò guo， dàn shì， wǒ men xué xiào yǐ qián yǒu yì běn
我没有在广告公司工作过，但是，我们学校以前有一本
xué shēng zá zhì， wǒ wèi xué shēng zá zhì huà guo hěn duō huà， yě pāi guo hěn duō zhào piàn
学生杂志，我为学生杂志画过很多画，也拍过很多照片。

3. rú guǒ gōng zuò yā lì hěn dà， wǒ huì yì biān tīng yīn yuè， yì biān huà huà
如果工作压力很大，我会一边听音乐，一边画画。

4. wǒ huì hé shuí yì qǐ gōng zuò
我会和谁一起工作？

5. wǒ de gōng zī shì duō shǎo
我的工资是多少？

Part Three Listening Comprehension

1. C　2. A　3. B　4. B

Part Four Conversation

Sample answer for reference only

1. èr shí wǔ suì yǐ hòu， wǒ xiǎng zuò yí gè lì shǐ xué jiā， wǒ zuì xǐ huan de kē mù jiù
二十五岁以后，我想做一个历史学家，我最喜欢的科目就
shì lì shǐ， wǒ xī wàng qù yīng guó zuì hǎo de dà xué xué xí lì shǐ
是历史，我希望去英国最好的大学学习历史。

2. wǒ xiǎo shí hou de lǐ xiǎng shì zuò yí gè lǚ xíng jiā， wǒ de fù mǔ dōu hěn xǐ huan lǚ
我小时候的理想是做一个旅行家，我的父母都很喜欢旅
xíng， xué xiào yí fàng jià， wǒ men jiù qù lǚ xíng， hěn xiǎo de shí hou wǒ jiù gēn tā men qù guo hěn
行，学校一放假，我们就去旅行，很小的时候我就跟他们去过很
duō dì fang
多地方。

3. wǒ rèn wéi zhuàn qián hěn zhòng yào， yīn wèi rú guǒ yǒu qián， wǒ jiù kě yǐ zì jǐ shēng
我认为赚钱很重要，因为如果有钱，我就可以自己生
huó， bú zài hé fù mǔ yì qǐ zhù， dàn shì zhuàn qián bú shì zuì zhòng yào de， shēng huó zhōng kuài lè
活，不再和父母一起住，但是赚钱不是最重要的，生活中快乐
bǐ zhuàn qián gèng zhòng yào
比赚钱更重要。

4. zài yīng guó zhǎo gōng zuò fēi cháng nán， tè bié shì nián qīng rén zhǎo gōng zuò gèng nán， xiàn zài
在英国找工作非常难，特别是年轻人找工作更难，现在
yīng guó de shī yè wèn tí yuè lái yuè dà， shè huì yīng gāi duō gěi nián qīng rén yì xiē gōng zuò jī huì
英国的失业问题越来越大，社会应该多给年轻人一些工作机会。

5. wǒ yě hěn xǐ huan qù guó wài gōng zuò， wǒ duì zhōng guó lì shǐ yǒu xìng qù， wǒ jì huà
我也很喜欢去国外工作，我对中国历史有兴趣，我计划
qù zhōng guó de xī běi dà xué xué xí zhōng guó lì shǐ
去中国的西北大学学习中国历史。

Unit 20 Internet, Mobile Technology and Social Media

■ Part One Warming Up

1.1　A.3　B.6　C.7　D.5　E.8　F.4　G.1　H.2

1.2　Sample answer for reference only

wǒ yì diǎn er yě bù xǐ huan liǎn shū
1. 我一点儿也不喜欢脸书。

jīn tiān de diàn shì jié mù yì diǎn er yě bù hǎo kàn
2. 今天的电视节目一点儿也不好看。

hěn duō shè jiāo wǎngzhàn yì diǎn er yě méi yì si
3. 很多社交网站一点儿也没意思。

shàngwǎng xué zhōng wén yì diǎn er yě bù nán
4. 上网学中文一点儿也不难。

1.3　Sample answer for reference only

wǒ měi tiān wán yí gè xiǎo shí diàn zǐ yóu xì
1. 我每天玩一个小时电子游戏。

wǒ měi gè xīng qī huā bàn tiān zài shè jiāo méi tǐ shang
2. 我每个星期花半天在社交媒体上。

wǒ měi gè xiǎo shí fā yí cì duǎn xìn
3. 我每个小时发一次短信。

wǒ měi liǎng tiān xià zài yí cì diàn yǐng
4. 我每两天下载一次电影。

1.4　Sample answer for reference only

tā měi gè xīng qī liù xià wǔ yóu yǒng yóu dào wǔ diǎn
1. 他每个星期六下午游泳游到五点。

bà ba měi tiān zài shè jiāo méi tǐ shang hé péng you liáo tiān liáo dào hěn wǎn
2. 爸爸每天在社交媒体上和朋友聊天聊到很晚。

wǒ fàng xué yǐ hòu wán diàn zǐ yóu xì wán dào mā ma xià bān huí jiā
3. 我放学以后玩电子游戏玩到妈妈下班回家。

tā zuò wán zuò yè yǐ hòu tīng yīn yuè tīng dào shuì jiào
4. 她做完作业以后听音乐听到睡觉。

■ Part Two Picture-based Task

Sample answer for reference only

zhào piàn lǐ yǒu yì jiā rén tā men zài yì qǐ wán shǒu jī tā men kàn qǐ lai hěn gāo xìng
1. 照片里有一家人，他们在一起玩手机，他们看起来很高兴。

wǒ cháng cháng yòng shǒu jī dǎ diàn huà tīng yīn yuè hé kàn diàn yǐng wǒ de shǒu jī yòu qīng
2. 我常常用手机打电话、听音乐和看电影。我的手机又轻

yòu piào liang tā shì wǒ de hǎo péng you
又漂亮，它是我的好朋友。

wǒ měi gè xīng qī wán shí duō gè xiǎo shí yóu xì wǒ yì bān měi tiān wán yí gè duō xiǎo
3.我每个星期玩十多个小时游戏。我一般每天玩一个多小
shí   xīng qī liù wǎn shang wǒ huì wán dào hěn wǎn
时，星期六晚上我会玩到很晚。

wǒ jīn tiān shàng wǔ yòng shǒu jī gěi wǒ de tóng xué dǎ le yí gè diàn huà   yīn wèi tā méi
4.我今天上午用手机给我的同学打了一个电话，因为他没
lái shàng xué   wǒ wèn tā shì bu shì bìng le
来上学，我问他是不是病了。

wǒ bù xiǎng mǎi xīn shǒu jī   yīn wèi wǒ fēi cháng xǐ huan wǒ xiàn zài de shǒu jī   wèi le
5.我不想买新手机，因为我非常喜欢我现在的手机。为了
bǎo hù huán jìng   wǒ men bù yīng gāi zǒng shì huàn shǒu jī
保护环境，我们不应该总是换手机。

■ Part Three Listening Comprehension

	advantage	disadvantage
1	• (allow the speaker to) chat with friends (after a busy day) • (make life) convenient	• waste time • (allow the speaker to) chat until late • (give the speaker) no time to sleep
2	• (allow the speaker to) read news • (allow the speaker to) learn foreign languages	• boring (content) • (boring things such as) what to eat • (boring things such as) what to wear

■ Part Four Conversation

Sample answer for reference only

wǒ fēi cháng xǐ huan wán diàn zǐ yóu xì   wǒ zuì xǐ huan wán yí gè tiào wǔ yóu xì   yīn
1.我非常喜欢玩电子游戏，我最喜欢玩一个跳舞游戏，因
wèi wǒ kě yǐ yì biān wán yóu xì   yì biān zuò yùn dòng
为我可以一边玩游戏，一边做运动。

wǒ zuó tiān wǎn shang wán le nà ge tiào wǔ yóu xì   wǒ wán le yí gè xiǎo shí   wán tiào wǔ
2.我昨天晚上玩了那个跳舞游戏，我玩了一个小时，玩跳舞
yóu xì lèi jí le
游戏累极了。

wǒ chú le yòng shè jiāo méi tǐ hé péng you liáo tiān   hái yòng shè jiāo méi tǐ kàn xīn wén   yǒu
3.我除了用社交媒体和朋友聊天，还用社交媒体看新闻。有
de shí hou   wǒ yě yòng wēi xìn gěi wǒ zài zhōng guó de péng you fā duǎn xìn
的时候，我也用微信给我在中国的朋友发短信。

wǒ měi tiān dōu shàng jǐ cì shè jiāo méi tǐ   wǒ měi tiān zài shè jiāo méi tǐ shang yí gòng huā
4.我每天都上几次社交媒体，我每天在社交媒体上一共花
yí gè duō xiǎo shí   wǒ zài shè jiāo méi tǐ shang yǒu hěn duō péng you
一个多小时，我在社交媒体上有很多朋友。

wǒ huì fā gěi wǒ shū shu   wǒ shū shu zhù zài měi guó   wǒ xiǎng gěi tā fā yí gè diàn zǐ
5.我会发给我叔叔。我叔叔住在美国，我想给他发一个电子
yóu jiàn   gào su tā wǒ xī wàng jīn nián shǔ jià qù kàn tā
邮件，告诉他我希望今年暑假去看他。

Unit 21 Weather and Environmental Issues

■ Part One Warming Up

1.1   A. duì huán jìng hǎo 对 环 境 好 (good for the environment): 2, 3, 4, 5, 8

      B. duì huán jìng bù hǎo 对 环 境 不 好 (bad for the environment): 1, 6, 7

1.2   Sample answer for reference only

1. shàng ge xīng qī wǒ xué huì le yóu yǒng
上 个 星 期 我 学 会 了 游 泳 。

2. tā shuō wán le nǐ xiǎng shuō ma
她 说 完 了 ， 你 想 说 吗 ？

3. nǐ tài cōngmíng le dá duì le
你 太 聪 明 了 ， 答 对 了 。

4. zhè běn shū zhēn méi yì si wǒ méi kàn wán
这 本 书 真 没 意 思 ， 我 没 看 完 。

1.3   1. wǒ bǎ wǎn fàn zuò le
我 把 晚 饭 做 了 。

      2. tā bǎ zuò yè xiě wán le
他 把 作 业 写 完 了 。

      3. dì di bǎ shǒu jī wán huài le
弟 弟 把 手 机 玩 坏 了 。

      4. jiě jie bǎ wǒ de yùn dòng xié chuān zāng le
姐 姐 把 我 的 运 动 鞋 穿 脏 了 。

1.4   Sample answer for reference only

1. nǎ wèi lǎo shī shì xiào zhǎng
哪 位 老 师 是 校 长 ？

2. wǒ men nǎ tiān yào jiāo zhōng wén zuò yè
我 们 哪 天 要 交 中 文 作 业 ？

3. nǎ bēi chá shì gěi mā ma de
哪 杯 茶 是 给 妈 妈 的 ？

4. chéng shì lǐ nǎ xiē hé shuǐ yǒu wū rǎn
城 市 里 哪 些 河 水 有 污 染 ？

■ Part Two Role Play

Sample answer for reference only

1. wǒ jiù shì jiā zhǎng wǒ jiào hòu làng
我 就 是 家 长 ， 我 叫 后 浪 。

2. yīn wèi wǒ men jiā yǒu shí kǒu rén rén duō lā jī jiù duō suǒ yǐ wǒ men jiā qián mian yǒu hěn duō lā jī
因 为 我 们 家 有 十 口 人 ， 人 多 垃 圾 就 多 ， 所 以 我 们 家 前 面 有 很 多 垃 圾 。

3. wǒ zài zhè er zhù le hěn cháng shí jiān yǒu shí nián le
我 在 这 儿 住 了 很 长 时 间 ， 有 十 年 了 。

qǐng wèn　　huí shōuzhōng xīn zài nǎ er
4.请问，回收中心在哪儿？
nǎ xiē lā jī kě yǐ huí shōu
5.哪些垃圾可以回收？

■ Part Three Listening Comprehension

1(a). False. He has loved the Great Wall since he was a child but only started to climb it when he was over 20 years old.

1(b). True.

2(a). False. He has put bins on the Great Wall after seeing so much rubbish on it.

2(b). True.

■ Part Four Conversation

Sample answer for reference only

wǒ duì mǎi xīn yī fu méi yǒu xìng qù　　kě shì　　wǒ de hěn duō péng you dōu fēi cháng xǐ
1.我 对 买 新 衣 服 没 有 兴 趣 ， 可 是 ， 我 的 很 多 朋 友 都 非 常 喜
huan mǎi xīn yī fu　　wǒ jué de rú guǒ dà jiā zǒng shì mǎi xīn dōng xi　　zhè ge shì jiè shang de gōng
欢 买 新 衣 服 ， 我 觉 得 如 果 大 家 总 是 买 新 东 西 ， 这 个 世 界 上 的 工
chǎng hé lā jī jiù huì yuè lái yuè duō
厂 和 垃 圾 就 会 越 来 越 多 。

wǒ yòng guò hěn duō jiù dōng xi　　wǒ qù guò yí gè jiù yī fu shāng diàn　　shāng diàn lǐ de
2.我 用 过 很 多 旧 东 西 ， 我 去 过 一 个 旧 衣 服 商 店 ， 商 店 里 的
jiù yī fu yòu hǎo kàn yòu pián yi　　wǒ zài nà ge shāng diàn lǐ gěi zì jǐ mǎi le liǎng jiàn shàng yī hé
旧 衣 服 又 好 看 又 便 宜 ， 我 在 那 个 商 店 里 给 自 己 买 了 两 件 上 衣 和
yì tiáo kù zi
一 条 裤 子 。

suī rán zuò fēi jī qù guó wài lǚ xíng hěn yǒu yì si　　dàn shì yě yǒu hěn duō huài chu
3.虽 然 坐 飞 机 去 国 外 旅 行 很 有 意 思 ， 但 是 也 有 很 多 坏 处 ，
bǐ rú fēi jī duì huán jìng de wū rǎn hěn dà　　ér qiě fēi jī lǐ de kōng qì duì shēn tǐ bù hǎo
比 如 飞 机 对 环 境 的 污 染 很 大 ， 而 且 飞 机 里 的 空 气 对 身 体 不 好 ，
děngděng
等 等 。

wǒ bù jīng cháng qí zì xíng chē shàng xué　　yīn wèi wǒ men jiā lí xué xiào hěn yuǎn　　hái
4.我 不 经 常 骑 自 行 车 上 学 ， 因 为 我 们 家 离 学 校 很 远 ； 还
yǒu　　zǎo shang lù shàng de chē hěn duō　　qí chē bú tài ān quán
有 ， 早 上 路 上 的 车 很 多 ， 骑 车 不 太 安 全 。

wèi le bǎo hù huán jìng　　wǒ dǎ suan　　dì yī　　duō yòng jiù dōng xi　　dì èr　　rú guǒ
5.为 了 保 护 环 境 ， 我 打 算 ， 第 一 ， 多 用 旧 东 西 ； 第 二 ， 如 果
yǒu jiù yī fu huò zhě jiù shū bù xiǎng yào le　　jiù sòng qù huí shōuzhōng xīn huò zhě cí shànshāng diàn
有 旧 衣 服 或 者 旧 书 不 想 要 了 ， 就 送 去 回 收 中 心 或 者 慈 善 商 店 ；
dì sān　　shǎo zuò fēi jī　　duō zǒu lù
第 三 ， 少 坐 飞 机 ， 多 走 路 。

Unit 22 Public Welfare and Volunteer Work

■ Part One Warming Up

1.1　A. 3　B. 7　C. 1　D. 6　E. 4　F. 2　G. 8　H. 5

1.2　Sample answer for reference only

　　　　qí chē shàng xué duì shēn tǐ jiàn kāng yǒu hǎo chu
1. 骑车上学对身体健康有好处。
　　　　quán qiú biàn nuǎn duì rén hé hěn duō dòng wù dōu yǒu huài chu
2. 全球变暖对人和很多动物都有坏处。
　　　　yī shēng miǎn fèi kàn bìng duì qióng rén yǒu hǎo chu
3. 医生免费看病对穷人有好处。
　　　　rén kǒu tài duō duì dì qiú huán jìng méi yǒu hǎo chu
4. 人口太多对地球环境没有好处。

1.3　Sample answer for reference only

　　　　wǒ de jiā rén xǐ huan yì biān chī wǎn fàn　　yì biān kàn diàn shì
1. 我的家人喜欢一边吃晚饭，一边看电视。
　　　　qǐng bú yào yì biān kāi chē　　yì biān dǎ diàn huà
2. 请不要一边开车，一边打电话。
　　　　yé ye　　nǎi nai men yì biān chàng gē　　yì biān kāi xīn dì tiào wǔ
3. 爷爷、奶奶们一边唱歌，一边开心地跳舞。
　　　　wǒ cháng cháng yì biān gěi hái zi men zuò fàn　　yì biān hé tā men liáo tiān
4. 我常常一边给孩子们做饭，一边和他们聊天。

1.4　Sample answer for reference only

　　　　rán ran xīng qī èr qī diǎn yǐ qián qǐ chuáng
1. 然然星期二七点以前起床。
　　　　rán ran xīng qī èr shàng wǔ de shí hou shàng kè
2. 然然星期二上午的时候上课。
　　　　rán ran xīng qī èr wǔ fàn yǐ hòu qù cí shàn shāng diàn gōng zuò
3. 然然星期二午饭以后去慈善商店工作。
　　　　rán ran xīng qī èr shuì jiào yǐ qián kàn shū
4. 然然星期二睡觉以前看书。

■ Part Two Picture-based Task

Sample answer for reference only

　　　　zhào piàn lǐ yǒu yí gè nián qīng rén hé yí gè lǎo rén　　zhè ge nián qīng rén shì yí gè yì
1. 照片里有一个年轻人和一个老人。这个年轻人是一个义
gōng　　tā zài jiāo lǎo rén yòng diàn nǎo
工，她在教老人用电脑。
　　　　　duì　　wǒ qù guò hěn duō cì lǎo rén yuàn　　wǒ měi gè xīng qī èr dōu cān jiā xué xiào shè huì shí
2. 对，我去过很多次老人院。我每个星期二都参加学校社会实
jiàn huó dòng　　wǒ hé tóng xué men yì qǐ qù lǎo rén yuàn bāng zhù nà li de yé ye　　nǎi nai men
践活动，我和同学们一起去老人院帮助那里的爷爷、奶奶们。

wǒ jué de lǎo rén men yīng gāi xué zěn me yòng diàn nǎo　　 yīn wèi diàn nǎo fēi cháng yǒu yòng

3.我觉得老人们应该学怎么用电脑，因为电脑非常有用。

lǎo rén men chú le kě yǐ xué zěn me fā duǎn xìn　　 zài wǎng shang hé jiā rén liáo tiān　　　 hái kě yǐ xué

老人们除了可以学怎么发短信、在网上和家人聊天，还可以学

zěn me wán yóu xì

怎么玩游戏。

wǒ rèn wéi cháng cháng yǒu rén hé lǎo rén men zài yì qǐ jiù huì ràng tā men kuài lè　　　 bǐ rú

4.我认为常常有人和老人们在一起就会让他们快乐，比如

gēn tā men yì qǐ tīng tā men xǐ huan de yīn yuè　　 wèn wen tā men de hái zi hé sūn zi men hǎo bu

跟他们一起听他们喜欢的音乐、问问他们的孩子和孙子们好不

hǎo　　　 hé tā men yì qǐ kàn lǎo zhào piàn　　 děng děng

好，和他们一起看老照片，等等。

rú guǒ yǒu jī huì　　 wǒ hěn xiǎng zài lǎo rén yuàn gōng zuò　　 shàng gāo zhōng yǐ hòu　　　 wǒ dǎ

5.如果有机会，我很想在老人院工作。上高中以后，我打

suan yì biān xué xí　　　 yì biān qù lǎo rén yuàn zuò yì gōng　　 hé lǎo rén men liáo tiān yǒu yì si jí le

算一边学习，一边去老人院做义工。和老人们聊天有意思极了。

■ Part Three Listening Comprehension

1(a). (at the seaside) café

1(b). 15 (yuan)

2(a). The Animal Protection Centre

2(b). (your pet) cats or dogs

■ Part Four Conversation

Sample answer for reference only

duì　　 wǒ zuò guo yì gōng　　 qù nián shǔ jià　　 wǒ zài yì jiā cí shàn shāng diàn zuò le liù gè

1.对，我做过义工。去年暑假，我在一家慈善商店做了六个

xīng qī yì gōng　　 wǒ měi gè xīng qī liù cóng zǎo shang shí diǎn gōng zuò dào xià wǔ yì diǎn

星期义工。我每个星期六从早上十点工作到下午一点。

wǒ rèn wéi shàng dà xué yīng gāi shì miǎn fèi de　　 yīn wèi měi gè rén dōu yīng gāi shàng dà xué　　 zài

2.我认为上大学应该是免费的，因为每个人都应该上大学。在

dà xué lǐ　　 nǐ bú dàn néng xué xí zì jǐ zuì xiǎng xué de kē mù　　 hái yǒu hěn duō jī huì jiāo péng you

大学里，你不但能学习自己最想学的科目，还有很多机会交朋友。

zài yī yuàn gōng zuò de hǎo chu shì kě yǐ bāng zhù bìng rén　　 suī rán zài yī yuàn gōng zuò yǒu

3.在医院工作的好处是可以帮助病人。虽然在医院工作有

de shí hou yòu lèi yòu zāng　　 dàn shì gōng zuò hěn yǒu yì si　　 yī shēng de gōng zī yě bù shǎo

的时候又累又脏，但是工作很有意思，医生的工资也不少。

fù rén chú le kě yǐ bāng zhù qióng rén zhǎo gōng zuò　　 yě néng juān qián gěi qióng rén　　 wǒ jué

4.富人除了可以帮助穷人找工作，也能捐钱给穷人。我觉

de xiàn zài fù rén yuè lái yuè fù　　 qióng rén yuè lái yuè qióng　　 fù rén yí dìng yào duō bāng zhù qióng rén

得现在富人越来越富，穷人越来越穷，富人一定要多帮助穷人。

rú guǒ juān qián　　 wǒ zuì xiǎng bǎ qián juān gěi méi yǒu jiā de rén　　 tè bié shì zài dōng tiān xià xuě de

5.如果捐钱，我最想把钱捐给没有家的人。特别是在冬天下雪的

shí hou　　 tā men yòu lěng yòu è　　 wǒ xī wàng tā men dōu yǒu nuǎn huo de dì fang chī fàn hé shuì jiào

时候，他们又冷又饿，我希望他们都有暖和的地方吃饭和睡觉。

Listening Transcript
听力文本

CHAPTER ONE My Life and My Friends

Unit 1 My Family

■ Part One Warming Up

1.1　1. 家 jiā　2. 孩子 hái zi　3. 结婚 jié hūn　4. 朋友 péng you
　　　5. 家人 jiā rén　6. 生日会 shēng rì huì　7. 岁 suì

1.2　1. 哥哥 gē ge　2. 医生 yī shēng　3. 爷爷 yé ye　4. 开生日会 kāi shēng rì huì
　　　5. 弟弟 dì di　6. 过春节 guò chūn jié　7. 过圣诞节 guò shèng dàn jié　8. 姐姐 jiě jie
　　　9. 老师 lǎo shī　10. 看朋友 kàn péng you　11. 妹妹 mèi mei　12. 奶奶 nǎi nai

---

1.3　1. 你的生日是几月几日？ nǐ de shēng rì shì jǐ yuè jǐ rì
　　　2. 你想在哪儿开生日会？ nǐ xiǎng zài nǎ er kāi shēng rì huì
　　　3. 去年生日，你做了什么？ qù nián shēng rì, nǐ zuò le shén me
　　　4. 你喜欢过生日吗？为什么？ nǐ xǐ huan guò shēng rì ma, wèi shén me

1.4　1. 你的生日是几月几日？我的生日是十月二十六日。 nǐ de shēng rì shì jǐ yuè jǐ rì, wǒ de shēng rì shì shí yuè èr shí liù rì
　　　2. 你想在哪儿开生日会？ nǐ xiǎng zài nǎ er kāi shēng rì huì
　　　3. 去年生日，你做了什么？ qù nián shēng rì, nǐ zuò le shén me
　　　4. 你喜欢过生日吗？为什么？ nǐ xǐ huan guò shēng rì ma, wèi shén me

1.6 Example: <ruby>小<rt>xiǎo</rt></ruby><ruby>明<rt>míng</rt></ruby><ruby>昨<rt>zuó</rt></ruby><ruby>天<rt>tiān</rt></ruby><ruby>参<rt>cān</rt></ruby><ruby>加<rt>jiā</rt></ruby><ruby>了<rt>le</rt></ruby><ruby>朋<rt>péng</rt></ruby><ruby>友<rt>you</rt></ruby><ruby>的<rt>de</rt></ruby><ruby>生<rt>shēng</rt></ruby><ruby>日<rt>rì</rt></ruby><ruby>会<rt>huì</rt></ruby>。 Ask when.

小明什么时候参加了朋友的生日会？

1. 小红的生日是四月十日。 Ask what date.

2. 小红在英国出生。 Ask where.

3. 妈妈和爸爸下个月去看奶奶。 Ask when.

4. 飞飞跟哥哥一起去游泳。 Ask with whom.

■ Part Two Role Play

2.1 1. 你多大了？

2. 你觉得你的新家怎么样？

3. 你的房间里有什么？

4. 你什么时候来看我？

5. (Pause and answer) 我喜欢买东西。

■ Part Three Listening Comprehension

1. 马老师，您好！我来北京已经一个星期了，住在我的中国朋友李小山家。

2. 李小山的爸爸妈妈离婚了，他和妈妈一起住，没有兄弟姐妹。

3. 上个周末，我们吃了北京烤鸭，北京烤鸭比英国的烤鸭好吃。

4. 晚上我们去看了京剧，我对京剧没有兴趣，因为音乐太吵了。

■ Part Four Conversation

4.1 1. 说说你自己，好吗？

2. 你们家有几口人？

3. 你喜欢宠物吗？为什么？

4. 去年夏天，你和家人去了哪儿？

5. 这个周末，你想和家人一起做什么？

Unit 2 My Hobbies

■ Part One Warming Up

1.1
1. 跳舞 *tiào wǔ*
2. 做饭 *zuò fàn*
3. 跑步 *pǎo bù*
4. 上网 *shàngwǎng*
5. 钓鱼 *diào yú*
6. 游泳 *yóu yǒng*
7. 遛狗 *liù gǒu*
8. 唱歌 *chàng gē*
9. 滑冰 *huá bīng*

1.2
1. 打电话 *dǎ diàn huà*
2. 看书 *kàn shū*
3. 打篮球 *dǎ lán qiú*
4. 玩儿滑板 *wán er huá bǎn*
5. 看电影 *kàn diàn yǐng*
6. 打乒乓球 *dǎ pīng pāng qiú*
7. 玩儿电脑游戏 *wán er diàn nǎo yóu xì*
8. 看电视 *kàn diàn shì*
9. 打网球 *dǎ wǎng qiú*
10. 看朋友 *kàn péng you*

1.4
1. 除了星期一有中文课 *chú le xīng qī yī yǒu zhōng wén kè*
2. 妹妹除了有英文书 *mèi mei chú le yǒu yīng wén shū*
3. 除了牛肉炒面 *chú le niú ròu chǎo miàn*
4. 除了喜欢看电影 *chú le xǐ huan kàn diàn yǐng*
5. 除了北京 *chú le běi jīng*
6. 今天除了有风 *jīn tiān chú le yǒu fēng*

■ Part Two Picture-based Task

2.1
1. 描述这张照片。/ 照片里有什么？ *miáo shù zhè zhāng zhào piàn。/ zhào piàn lǐ yǒu shén me*
2. 你喜欢运动吗？ *nǐ xǐ huan yùn dòng ma*
3. 上个星期你做了什么运动？ *shàng ge xīng qī nǐ zuò le shén me yùn dòng*
4. 你想学什么运动？ *nǐ xiǎng xué shén me yùn dòng*
5. 你想和谁一起做这个运动？ *nǐ xiǎng hé shuí yì qǐ zuò zhè ge yùn dòng*

Part Three Listening Comprehension

因为我喜欢学中文，所以我常常看中文电影。最近，我看了一个中文电影，电影叫《我的父亲母亲》。这个电影很有名，我非常喜欢。我觉得电影很有意思，女演员也很漂亮。以后我想看更多中文电影。

Part Four Conversation

4.1　1. 你的爱好是什么？
　　　2. 你喜欢看哪国的电影？为什么？
　　　3. 说说你最近看过的一个电影。
　　　4. 你觉得中国音乐怎么样？
　　　5. 你最想听谁的音乐会？

Unit 3 My Friends

Part One Warming Up

1.1　1. 嘴　　　2. 头发　　　3. 眼睛
　　　4. 耳朵　　　5. 脚　　　6. 手

1.2　1. 黑头发　　　2. 蓝眼睛
　　　3. 大耳朵　　　4. 高个子

1.5　1. 我们班来了一个新同学，他个子很高，也很聪明。
　　　2. 我的男朋友比我大一岁，但是他个子没有我高。
　　　3. 我喜欢一边和朋友聊天一边听音乐。
　　　4. 在我的生日会上，有很多我的朋友，也有我的家人。
　　　5. 我的朋友是北京人，他又帅又友好。
　　　6. 我的同学有一双大手和大脚，但是她的嘴很小，耳朵也很小。

■ Part Two Role Play

2.1   1. shuōshuo nǐ zuì hǎo de péng you
说说你最好的朋友。

        2. nǐ men shì shén me shí hou rèn shi de
你们是什么时候认识的？

        3. nǐ chángcháng hé nǐ zuì hǎo de péng you yì qǐ zuò shén me
你常常和你最好的朋友一起做什么？

        4.(Pause and answer) wǒ yě yǒu yí gè zuì hǎo de péng you
我也有一个最好的朋友。

        5.(Pause and answer) yīn wèi péng you néng gěi wǒ men kuài lè
因为朋友能给我们快乐。

■ Part Three Listening Comprehension

1. shàngzhōng xué de shí hou wǒ yǒu guò yí gè hǎo péng you tā shì cóng xī ān lái de
上中学的时候，我有过一个好朋友，他是从西安来的。

2. fàng xué yǐ hòu wǒ men chángcháng zài yì qǐ liáo tiān hé tīng yīn yuè
放学以后，我们常常在一起聊天和听音乐。

3. zhōng xué bì yè yǐ hòu tā qù měi guó shàng dà xué le
中学毕业以后，他去美国上大学了。

4. tā zài měi guó yào jié hūn le wǒ duì jié hūn méi yǒu xìng qù yīn wèi wǒ bù xiǎng jié hūn
他在美国要结婚了，我对结婚没有兴趣，因为我不想结婚。

■ Part Four Conversation

4.1   1. shuōshuo nǐ de yí gè péng you
说说你的一个朋友。

        2. nǐ cān jiā guò tā tā de shēng rì huì ma
你参加过他／她的生日会吗？

        3. tā jiā zài nǎ er
她家在哪儿？

        4. zài tā de shēng rì huì shang nǐ men chī le shén me
在她的生日会上，你们吃了什么？

        5. nǐ de shēng rì shì jǐ yuè jǐ rì
你的生日是几月几日？

Unit 4 My Leisure Time

■ Part One Warming Up

1.1   1. diào yú 钓鱼   2. kā fēi 咖啡   3. sài chē 赛车   4. huá xuě 滑雪

        5. wán huá bǎn 玩滑板   6. guǒ zhī 果汁   7. cān guān bó wù guǎn 参观博物馆

        8. miàn bāo 面包   9. zài chāo shì mǎi dōng xi 在超市买东西

        10. chǎo miàn tiáo 炒面条   11. jiǎo zi 饺子   12. pá shān 爬山   13. jī dàn chǎo fàn 鸡蛋炒饭

        14. qí zì xíng chē 骑自行车   15. liù gǒu 遛狗   16. dàn gāo 蛋糕

1.2　　1.去饭馆吃饭　　2.回家　　3.起床　　4.打工

5.上网　　6.上学　　7.睡觉　　8.健身

Part Two Picture-based Task

2.1　　1.描述这张照片。／照片里有什么？

2.你在家帮爸爸妈妈去超市买东西吗？为什么？

3.你最近去了哪儿买东西？

4.你什么时候会和家人一起吃饭？

5.这个周末，我们班要去看中国电影，你想去吗？

Part Three Listening Comprehension

1.我叫张强。我每天早上跟家人一起吃早饭。我们都喜欢吃面包和水果，但是喝的东西不一样，我爸爸喜欢喝茶，我妈妈喜欢喝咖啡，我喜欢喝果汁。

2.晚饭我们有时候在饭馆吃，有时候叫外卖，但是更多的时候是在家自己做饭，做饭是我们家每个人的爱好。

Part Four Conversation

4.1　　1.有空的时候，你看书吗？

2.你和你的朋友们周末都做什么？

3.你觉得学生周末打工好不好？

4.你周末打过工吗？

5.这个周末你想做什么？

Unit 5 My House

■ Part One Warming Up

1.1
1. jiāo qū 郊区
2. shì zhōng xīn 市中心
3. gāo lóu 高楼
4. shān qū 山区
5. nóng cūn 农村
6. xiǎo zhèn 小镇
7. hǎi biān 海边
8. chéng shì 城市

1.2
1. kè tīng 客厅
2. shū fáng 书房
3. wò shì 卧室
4. diàn shì 电视
5. mén 门
6. cè suǒ 厕所
7. yǐ zi 椅子
8. chú fáng 厨房
9. xǐ yī jī 洗衣机
10. zhuō zi 桌子
11. yù shì 浴室
12. dēng 灯
13. shū jià 书架
14. chuáng 床
15. shā fā 沙发
16. bīng xiāng 冰箱

1.3
1. nǐ zài nǎ er? wǒ zài yù shì xǐ shǒu 你在哪儿？我在浴室洗手。
2. bà ba zài nǎ er 爸爸在哪儿？
3. mā ma zài nǎ er 妈妈在哪儿？
4. jiě jie zài nǎ er 姐姐在哪儿？
5. gē ge zài nǎ er 哥哥在哪儿？
6. mèi mei zài nǎ er 妹妹在哪儿？

1.4
1. suī rán wǒ ài yùn dòng 虽然我爱运动
2. suī rán wǒ méi yǒu jiě jie 虽然我没有姐姐
3. suī rán wǒ de péng you xiǎng qǐng wǒ chī fàn 虽然我的朋友想请我吃饭
4. suī rán zhōng wén kè hěn yǒu yì si 虽然中文课很有意思
5. hǎi biān suī rán fēng hěn dà 海边虽然风很大
6. wǒ men jiā suī rán yǒu liù gè wò shì 我们家虽然有六个卧室

Part Two Role Play

2.1
1. zhè ge fáng zi zài nǎ er
   这个房子在哪儿？
2. zhè ge fáng zi yǒu jǐ gè wò shì
   这个房子有几个卧室？
3. wǒ shén me shí hòu kě yǐ qù kàn kan zhè ge fáng zi
   我什么时候可以去看看这个房子？
4. nǐ xǐ huan zhè ge fáng zi ma wèi shén me
   你喜欢这个房子吗？为什么？
5. (Pause and answer) wǒ jué de zhè ge fáng zi hěn guì
   我觉得这个房子很贵。

Part Three Listening Comprehension

1. wǒ jiào dà hǎi shì shàng hǎi rén zhù zài shàng hǎi shì zhōng xīn de yí gè xiǎo qū
   我叫大海，是上海人，住在上海市中心的一个小区。
2. wǒ jiā yǒu liǎng gè wò shì kè tīng yě shì fàn tīng chú fáng hěn xiǎo zhǐ yǒu yí gè yù shì
   我家有两个卧室，客厅也是饭厅，厨房很小，只有一个浴室。
3. suī rán wǒ jiā bú dà dàn shì wǒ men xiǎo qū de huán jìng bú cuò yòu fāng biàn yòu ān quán
   虽然我家不大，但是我们小区的环境不错，又方便又安全。
4. xiǎo qū yǒu dà mén měi tiān zǎo shang liù diǎn bàn kāi mén wǎn shang shí yì diǎn guān mén
   小区有大门，每天早上六点半开门，晚上十一点关门。

Part Four Conversation

4.1
1. shuōshuo nǐ men jiā hǎo ma
   说说你们家，好吗？
2. nǐ xǐ huan zhù zài dà chéng shì ma wèi shén me
   你喜欢住在大城市吗？为什么？
3. nǐ qù guò nǐ péng you de jiā ma
   你去过你朋友的家吗？
4. shuí chángcháng lái nǐ jiā
   谁常常来你家？
5. èr shí wǔ suì yǐ hòu nǐ xiǎng zhù zài nǎ er
   二十五岁以后，你想住在哪儿？

Unit 6 Weather, Landscape and Geography

Part One Warming Up

1.1
1. hěn lěng 很冷
2. hěn rè 很热
3. qíng tiān 晴天
4. duō yún 多云
5. yǒu fēng 有风
6. xià yǔ 下雨
7. xià xuě 下雪
8. yǒu wù 有雾

1.3
1. yuè rì běi jīng de tiān qì zěn me yàng
   3月1日北京的天气怎么样？
   yuè rì běi jīng shì qíng tiān yǒu xiǎo fēng qì wēn zuì dī dù zuì gāo dù
   3月1日北京是晴天，有小风，气温最低1度，最高6度。

2.3 月 1 日上海的天气怎么样？

3.3 月 1 日香港的天气怎么样？

4.3 月 1 日哈尔滨的天气怎么样？

1.4 1.在中国的北方

2.春天虽然晴天很多

3.夏天不太舒服

4.秋天是最好的季节

5.冬天冷极了

1.5 1.不管天气好还是不好，我都要去爬山。

2.不管天晴还是下雨

3.不管天热还是天冷

4.不管刮风还是下雪

■ Part Two Picture-based Task

2.1 1.描述这张照片。/ 照片里有什么？

2.你喜欢和谁一起去海边？

3.去年夏天你去了哪儿？

4.这个周末如果下雨，你想做什么？

5.你最喜欢什么季节？为什么？

■ Part Three Listening Comprehension

中国南方有一个大城市，它叫广州。不管春天、夏天、秋天，还是冬天，广州都有很多漂亮的花。周末早上，要是天气好，你就会看到很多广州人跟家人或者朋友一起去公园看花，然后去饭馆吃点心。

Part Four Conversation

4.1　1. 在英国，一年有几个季节？
zài yīng guó　　yì nián yǒu jǐ gè jì jié

　　　2. 春天公园里有什么？
chūn tiān gōngyuán lǐ yǒu shén me

　　　3. 去年圣诞节，天气怎么样？
qù nián shèng dàn jié　tiān qì zěn me yàng

　　　4. 如果天气好，你想做什么？
rú guǒ tiān qì hǎo　nǐ xiǎng zuò shén me

　　　5. 你有问题吗？
nǐ yǒu wèn tí ma

Unit 7 My Town/ City

Part One Warming Up

1.1　1. 地铁站　　　　2. 超市　　　　3. 电影院
dì tiě zhàn　　　chāo shì　　　diàn yǐng yuàn

　　　4. 动物园　　　　5. 飞机场　　　　6. 公共汽车站
dòng wù yuán　　fēi jī chǎng　　gōnggòng qì chē zhàn

　　　7. 火车站　　　　8. 教堂　　　　9. 停车场
huǒ chē zhàn　　jiào táng　　　tíng chē chǎng

　　　10. 学校　　　　11. 医院　　　　12. 银行
xué xiào　　　　yī yuàn　　　　yín háng

　　　13. 邮局
yóu jú

1.2　1. 我要去医院看病。
wǒ yào qù yī yuàn kàn bìng

　　　2. 我要去超市买东西。
wǒ yào qù chāo shì mǎi dōng xi

　　　3. 我要去动物园看大熊猫。
wǒ yào qù dòng wù yuán kàn dà xióng māo

　　　4. 我要去邮局寄信。
wǒ yào qù yóu jú jì xìn

　　　5. 我要去停车场停车。
wǒ yào qù tíng chē chǎng tíng chē

1.4　1. 你家在哪儿？　To the east of London.
nǐ jiā zài nǎ er

　　　2. 火车站在哪儿？　Opposite my house.
huǒ chē zhàn zài nǎ er

　　　3. 学校在哪儿？　To the left of the railway station.
xué xiào zài nǎ er

　　　4. 图书馆在哪儿？　Inside the school.
tú shū guǎn zài nǎ er

■ Part Two Role Play

2.1　　1. 请问，伦敦市中心有什么？
　　　　2. 伦敦的商店几点开门？
　　　　3. 英国的博物馆怎么样？
　　　　4.(Pause and answer) 我昨天去了公园。
　　　　5.(Pause and answer) 我很想在伦敦吃中餐。

■ Part Three Listening Comprehension

　　　　1. 中国的城市里，西安是最古老的城市之一，所以我非常喜欢西安。
　　　　2. 我住的饭店在市中心，旁边是一个博物馆，我去参观了两次。
　　　　3. 西安人喜欢吃面条、饺子和牛肉，他们吃米饭没有上海人多。
　　　　4. 在西安坐地铁最方便，用手机 APP 买票很容易。

■ Part Four Conversation

4.1　　1. 伦敦有什么？
　　　　2. 你上次去伦敦是什么时候？
　　　　3. 住在大城市有什么好处？
　　　　4. 住在大城市有什么坏处？
　　　　5. 你最想去哪个城市旅游？

Unit 8 Festivals

■ Part One Warming Up

1.1　　1. 一月一日是新年。
　　　　2. 农历一月一日是春节。
　　　　3. 复活节在三月或四月。

4.农历五月五日是端午节。

5.农历八月十五日是中秋节。

6.十二月二十五日是圣诞节。

1.2　1.吃团圆饭　2.放鞭炮　3.吃月饼　4.红包

5.饺子　6.龙舟比赛　7.火鸡　8.舞龙

9.舞狮　10.圣诞老人　11.看月亮　12.吃粽子

Part Two Picture-based Task

2.1　1.描述这张照片。/ 照片里有什么？

2.我过春节的时候和家人一起吃团圆饭。你呢？

3.去年圣诞节，谁给了你礼物？

4.家人应该常常在一起吃饭吗？为什么？

5.明年你希望怎么过生日？

Part Three Listening Comprehension

1.对于孩子们来说，春节除了看舞狮、舞龙、吃团圆饭、放鞭炮这些开心的活动以外，最让他们高兴的就是能够收到红包。

2.妹妹说，她要用红包钱做一些好事。她打算买一些故事书，送给没有父母的小朋友，还要给老人院的陈奶奶买票，和她一起看京剧。

Part Four Conversation

4.1　1.你知道哪些中国节日？

2.你喜欢吃中餐吗？

3.你觉得哪个英国的节日最有意思？

4.去年过生日，你做了什么？

5.明年春节的时候，你希望你们学校有什么活动？

Unit 9 Transport

■ Part One Warming Up

1.1 1. fēi jī 飞机　　2. huǒ chē 火车　　3. dì tiě 地铁　　4. zǒu lù 走路

5. gōnggòng qì chē 公共汽车　　6. lǚ yóu chē （bā shì） 旅游车（巴士）　　7. chuán 船

8. chū zū chē 出租车　　9. zì xíng chē 自行车　　10. piào 票

1.2 1. nà ge lǎo yé ye zěn me qù gōngyuán 那个老爷爷怎么去公园？ nà ge lǎo yé ye zuò gōnggòng qì chē qù gōngyuán 那个老爷爷坐公共汽车去公园。

2. nà ge nán hái zěn me shàng xué 那个男孩怎么上学？

3. nà ge yī shēng zěn me shàng bān 那个医生怎么上班？

4. nà ge nǚ hái zěn me qù huǒ chē zhàn 那个女孩怎么去火车站？

1.3 1. nǐ jiā lí xué xiào yuǎn ma 你家离学校远吗？ wǒ jiā lí xué xiào bù yuǎn 我家离学校不远。

2. nǐ men xué xiào lí huǒ chē zhàn jìn ma 你们学校离火车站近吗？

3. huǒ chē zhàn lí shì zhōng xīn jìn ma 火车站离市中心近吗？

4. shì zhōng xīn lí hǎi biān yuǎn ma 市中心离海边远吗？

1.4 1. yī shēngshuō wǒ méi yǒu bìng 医生说我没有病

2. gōngyuán lí wǒ jiā hěn jìn 公园离我家很近

3. tā shì fǎ guó rén 他是法国人

4. mèi mei xiǎng zì jǐ zuò zuò yè 妹妹想自己做作业

5. jīn tiān tiān qì hěn rè 今天天气很热

6. wǒ yòngshǒu jī kàn xīn wén 我用手机看新闻

Part Two Role Play

2.1
1. 你想去哪儿？
   nǐ xiǎng qù nǎ er

2. 你为什么想去那儿？
   nǐ wèi shén me xiǎng qù nà er

3. 你怎么去那儿？
   nǐ zěn me qù nà er

4. 你最喜欢坐什么车上学？
   nǐ zuì xǐ huan zuò shén me chē shàng xué

5. (Pause and answer) 火车站离运动中心不远。
   huǒ chē zhàn lí yùn dòng zhōng xīn bù yuǎn

Part Three Listening Comprehension

1. Peter：小东，欢迎下个月来伦敦！我会先去飞机场接你，然后我们一起坐火车回我家。
   xiǎo dōng　huān yíng xià ge yuè lái lún dūn　wǒ huì xiān qù fēi jī chǎng jiē nǐ　rán hòu wǒ men yì qǐ zuò huǒ chē huí wǒ jiā

2. 小东：伦敦有高铁吗？高铁就是火车，很快的火车。
   xiǎo dōng　lún dūn yǒu gāo tiě ma　gāo tiě jiù shì huǒ chē　hěn kuài de huǒ chē

3. Peter：伦敦没有高铁，只有地铁。很多英国人不喜欢新的东西。
   lún dūn méi yǒu gāo tiě　zhǐ yǒu dì tiě　hěn duō yīng guó rén bù xǐ huan xīn de dōng xi

4. 小东：我觉得英国不大，去很多地方都很近，交通不用太快。
   xiǎo dōng　wǒ jué de yīng guó bú dà　qù hěn duō dì fāng dōu hěn jìn　jiāo tōng bú yòng tài kuài

5. Peter：在伦敦，很多人骑自行车上班，对身体和环境都好。
   zài lún dūn　hěn duō rén qí zì xíng chē shàng bān　duì shēn tǐ hé huán jìng dōu hǎo

Part Four Conversation

4.1
1. 你住的地方有什么公共交通工具？
   nǐ zhù de dì fang yǒu shén me gōng gòng jiāo tōng gōng jù

2. 你们家离火车站近吗？
   nǐ men jiā lí huǒ chē zhàn jìn ma

3. 你上一次坐火车是什么时候？
   nǐ shàng yí cì zuò huǒ chē shì shén me shí hòu

4. 你喜欢骑自行车吗？
   nǐ xǐ huan qí zì xíng chē ma

5. 你想学开车吗？
   nǐ xiǎng xué kāi chē ma

Unit 10 Hotels

Part One Warming Up

1.1
1. 服务台
   fú wù tái
2. 订房间
   dìng fáng jiān
3. 度假
   dù jià
4. 双人房
   shuāng rén fáng
5. 现金
   xiàn jīn
6. 游泳池
   yóu yǒng chí
7. 单人房
   dān rén fáng
8. 免费
   miǎn fèi
9. 干净
   gān jìng
10. 酒店
   jiǔ diàn

1.2　1.　yǒu miǎn fèi de　　ma
　　　　有 免费 的 WiFi 吗？
　　　2.　wǒ men bú yòng xiàn jīn　　nín yǒu xìn yòng kǎ ma
　　　　我们 不 用 现金，您 有 信用卡 吗？
　　　3.　cān tīng de zǎo cān jǐ diǎn kāi shǐ
　　　　餐厅 的 早餐 几 点 开始？
　　　4.　qǐng gěi wǒ dìng yí gè dān rén fáng
　　　　请 给 我 订 一 个 单人房。
　　　5.　shuāng rén fáng yí gè wǎn shang duō shǎo qián
　　　　双人房 一 个 晚上 多少钱？
　　　6.　kě yǐ kàn hǎi de fáng jiān měi wǎn yào sì bǎi wǔ shí yuán
　　　　可以 看 海 的 房间 每晚 要 四百五十元。
　　　7.　wǒ de dēng huài le
　　　　我 的 灯 坏 了。

1.3　1.　yóu yǒng chí zài nǎ er
　　　　游泳池 在 哪儿？
　　　2.　jiàn shēn fáng jǐ diǎn kāi mén　　jǐ diǎn guān mén
　　　　健身房 几 点 开门？几 点 关门？
　　　3.　zǎo fàn cóng jǐ diǎn kāi shǐ
　　　　早饭 从 几 点 开始？
　　　4.　wǎn fàn ne
　　　　晚饭 呢？

■ Part Two Picture-based Task

2.1　1.　miáo shù zhè zhāng zhào piàn　　zhào piàn lǐ yǒu shén me
　　　　描述 这 张 照片。/ 照片 里 有 什么？
　　　2.　nǐ zuì xǐ huan de fàn diàn zài nǎ er
　　　　你 最 喜欢 的 饭店 在 哪儿？
　　　3.　nà ge fàn diàn lí shì zhōng xīn yǒu duō yuǎn
　　　　那 个 饭店 离 市中心 有 多远？
　　　4.　nǐ shàng yí cì qù yóu yǒng chí shì shén me shí hou
　　　　你 上 一 次 去 游泳池 是 什么 时候？
　　　5.　nǐ dǎ suan zài fàn diàn gōng zuò ma　　wèi shén me
　　　　你 打算 在 饭店 工作 吗？为 什么？

■ Part Three Listening Comprehension

　　　zhè shì yì jiā xīn kāi de jiǔ diàn　　chú le jiāo tōng fāng biàn yǐ wài　　jiǔ diàn de yóu yǒng chí
1.这 是 一 家 新 开 的 酒店，除 了 交通 方便 以外，酒店 的 游泳池
hé jiàn shēn fáng yě měi tiān miǎn fèi kāi fàng
和 健身房 也 每 天 免费 开放。
　　　zhè jiā jiǔ diàn de fáng jiān hěn dà　　tā men hěn huān yíng wǒ hé liǎng gè hái zi yì qǐ zhù
2.这 家 酒店 的 房间 很 大，他们 很 欢迎 我 和 两 个 孩子 一起 住，
tā men de cān tīng yǒu zuì xīn xiān de yú hé qīng cài
他们 的 餐厅 有 最 新鲜 的 鱼 和 青菜。
　　　jiǔ diàn zài yì tiáo xiǎo hé de páng biān　　huán jìng hǎo　　wǎn shang ān jìng jí le　　wǎn fàn yǐ
3.酒店 在 一 条 小河 的 旁边，环境 好，晚上 安静 极 了。晚饭 以
hòu　　wǒ men qù pāi le hěn duō zhào piàn
后，我们 去 拍 了 很多 照片。

Part Four Conversation

4.1　1. shuōshuo nǐ zhù guo de yí gè jiǔ diàn
说 说 你 住 过 的 一 个 酒 店。

　　　2. nǐ zhī dào zěn me shàngwǎng dìng jiǔ diàn ma
你 知 道 怎 么 上 网 订 酒 店 吗？

　　　3. nǐ jué de shén me shí hou jiǔ diàn zuì guì
你 觉 得 什 么 时 候 酒 店 最 贵？

　　　4. jiǔ diàn yǒu mei yǒu yóu yǒng chí zhòng yào ma
酒 店 有 没 有 游 泳 池 重 要 吗？

　　　5. rú guǒ qù dù jià nǐ xī wàng zhù zài nǎ er
如 果 去 度 假， 你 希 望 住 在 哪 儿？

Unit 11 Events

Part One Warming Up

1.1　1. yīn yuè jié
音 乐 节
2. diàn yǐng jié
电 影 节
3. yì shù jié
艺 术 节

　　　4. ào lín pǐ kè yùn dòng huì
奥 林 匹 克 运 动 会
5. mén piào
门 票

1.2　1. yùn dòngchǎng
运 动 场
2. yīn yuè jié
音 乐 节
3. diàn yǐng mí
电 影 迷

　　　4. zú qiú chǎng
足 球 场
5. diàn yǐng jié
电 影 节
6. gē mí
歌 迷

　　　7. wǎng qiú chǎng
网 球 场

1.5　1. wǒ men shì zuò huǒ chē qù lún dūn de
我 们 是 坐 火 车 去 伦 敦 的。

　　　2. zhè ge shēng rì lǐ wù shì dì di gěi wǒ de
这 个 生 日 礼 物 是 弟 弟 给 我 的。

　　　3. zhè ge shǒu jī shì qù nián mǎi de
这 个 手 机 是 去 年 买 的。

　　　4. nà ge xīn tóng xué shì cóngxiānggǎng lái de
那 个 新 同 学 是 从 香 港 来 的。

Part Two Role Play

2.1　1. qǐngshuōshuo zhè ge rén
请 说 说 这 个 人。

　　　2. nǐ de shǒu jī shì shén me shí hou mǎi de
你 的 手 机 是 什 么 时 候 买 的？

　　　3. nǐ jīn tiān yòngshǒu jī dǎ guo jǐ cì diàn huà
你 今 天 用 手 机 打 过 几 次 电 话？

　　　4. (Pause and answer) wǒ jiào wáng lán
我 叫 王 蓝。

　　　5. (Pause and answer) hǎo de
好 的。

■ Part Three Listening Comprehension

měi nián   shì jiè shang hěn duō dì fāng dōu yǒu gè zhǒng gè yàng de yì shù jié   lǚ yóu jié
1.每 年， 世 界 上 很 多 地 方 都 有 各 种 各 样 的 艺 术 节、 旅 游 节

hé yùn dòng huì děngděng   rè nao jí le
和 运 动 会 等 等， 热 闹 极 了。

yīng guó zài xià tiān yǒu hěn duō yīn yuè jié   yì bān dōu shì zài xiāng cūn cǎo dì shang jǔ xíng
2.英 国 在 夏 天 有 很 多 音 乐 节， 一 般 都 是 在 乡 村 草 地 上 举 行

de   ér zuì yǒu míng de diàn yǐng jié zài měi guó
的； 而 最 有 名 的 电 影 节 在 美 国。

hěn duō rén dōu duì měi sì nián jǔ bàn yí cì de ào lín pǐ kè yùn dòng huì hé shì jiè bēi zú
3.很 多 人 都 对 每 四 年 举 办 一 次 的 奥 林 匹 克 运 动 会 和 世 界 杯 足

qiú bǐ sài yǒu xìng qù   bǐ sài de mén piào dōu bù pián yi
球 比 赛 有 兴 趣， 比 赛 的 门 票 都 不 便 宜。

zhōng guó yě yǒu hěn duō yīn yuè mí   diàn yǐng mí hé zú qiú mí   hěn duō rén dōu huì hěn zǎo
4.中 国 也 有 很 多 音 乐 迷、 电 影 迷 和 足 球 迷， 很 多 人 都 会 很 早

jiù dìng hǎo piào   qù guó wài cān jiā zhè xiē huó dòng
就 订 好 票， 去 国 外 参 加 这 些 活 动。

■ Part Four Conversation

nǐ chángcháng cān jiā tǐ yù bǐ sài ma
4.1　1.你 常 常 参 加 体 育 比 赛 吗？

nǐ zuì xǐ huan kàn shén me bǐ sài
2.你 最 喜 欢 看 什 么 比 赛？

shuōshuo nǐ tīng guo de yí gè yīn yuè huì
3.说 说 你 听 过 的 一 个 音 乐 会？

nǐ jué de diàn yǐng piào guì ma
4.你 觉 得 电 影 票 贵 吗？

nǐ xī wàng ào lín pǐ kè yùn dòng huì zài nǎ er jǔ xíng
5.你 希 望 奥 林 匹 克 运 动 会 在 哪 儿 举 行？

Unit 12 Holidays

■ Part One Warming Up

fēi jī piào   qián bāo   shǒu jī
1.1　1.飞 机 票   2.钱 包   3.手 机

zhàoxiàng jī   hù zhào   xìn yòng kǎ
4.照 相 机   5.护 照   6.信 用 卡

shǒu biǎo   dì tú
7.手 表   8.地 图

nǐ qù guo hǎi biān ma
1.2　1.你 去 过 海 边 吗？

nǐ kàn guo dà xióng māo ma
2.你 看 过 大 熊 猫 吗？

nǐ huá guo xuě ma
3.你 滑 过 雪 吗？

nǐ pá guo chángchéng ma
4.你 爬 过 长 城 吗？

Part Two Picture-based Task

2.1　1.描述这张照片。/ 照片里有什么？

2.你喜欢坐飞机，还是坐火车？

3.你最近什么时候坐过火车？

4.你认为飞机票贵不贵？

5.你想坐飞机去哪儿？

Part Three Listening Comprehension

这几年，中国人越来越有钱，所以出国度假的人也越来越多。中国的一家旅游杂志说，中国人在假期里最爱做的三件事是：买东西、拍照片和参观名胜古迹。他们不但喜欢去北美洲和澳大利亚，而且很多人更喜欢去欧洲。

Part Four Conversation

4.1　1.你喜欢去度假吗？

2.很多人喜欢去国外度假，你觉得呢？

3.最近你去了哪儿度假？

4.你喜欢跟家人一起度假，还是和朋友？

5.今年暑假，你希望去哪儿度假？

Unit 13 My School Day

■ Part One Warming Up

1.1
1. xiào fú 校服
2. xiào chē 校车
3. shǔ jià 暑假
4. zuò yè 作业
5. kē mù 科目
6. hán jià 寒假
7. xiào zhǎng 校长
8. dì yī jié kè 第一节课

1.2
1. xiǎo hóng zǎo shang qī diǎn zuò shén me 小红早上七点做什么？
2. xiǎo hóng zǎo shang qī diǎn bàn zuò shén me 小红早上七点半做什么？
3. xiǎo hóng zǎo shang bā diǎn zuò shén me 小红早上八点做什么？
4. xiǎo hóng zǎo shang jiǔ diǎn zuò shén me 小红早上九点做什么？
5. xiǎo hóng zhōng wǔ shí èr diǎn bàn zuò shén me 小红中午十二点半做什么？
6. xiǎo hóng xià wǔ sān diǎn sì shí wǔ fēn zuò shén me 小红下午三点四十五分做什么？
7. xiǎo hóng wǎn shang liù diǎn shí wǔ fēn zuò shén me 小红晚上六点十五分做什么？
8. xiǎo hóng wǎn shang jiǔ diǎn bàn zuò shén me 小红晚上九点半做什么？

1.4
1. cóng wǒ jiā dào xué xiào zǒu lù yào bàn gè xiǎo shí 从我家到学校走路要半个小时。
2. cóng wǒ jiā dào lún dūn zuò huǒ chē yào liǎng gè xiǎo shí 从我家到伦敦坐火车要两个小时。
3. cóng xué xiào dào yùn dòng zhōng xīn qí chē yào èr shí fēn zhōng 从学校到运动中心骑车要二十分钟。
4. cóng yīng guó dào zhōng guó zuò fēi jī yào shí gè xiǎo shí 从英国到中国坐飞机要十个小时。

1.5
1. cóng wǒ jiā dào xué xiào hěn yuǎn 从我家到学校很远。
2. zhōng wén zuò yè hěn róng yì 中文作业很容易。
3. wǒ men de xiào zhǎng hěn yán lì 我们的校长很严厉。
4. wǒ men de xiào fú hěn nán kàn 我们的校服很难看。

Part Two Role Play

2.1   1. 你每天早上怎么上学？

         2. 你几点起床？

         3. 你早饭吃什么？

         4. 你觉得我们学校怎么样？

         5. (Pause and answer) 我很喜欢你们的校服。

Part Three Listening Comprehension

         1. 我们的学校环境美丽，离市中心不远，坐火车只要半个小时。

         2. 我们学校有五百多个学生和一百多位老师。

         3. 学生们早上九点上课，下午三点半放学；放学后，学校里还有很多课外活动。

         4. 每个星期五下午，学校的运动场上都有足球比赛。

Part Four Conversation

4.1   1. 请说说你们学校，好吗？

         2. 你喜欢你们的学校吗？为什么？

         3. 今天早饭你吃了什么？

         4. 英国的校服和中国的校服有什么不一样？

         5. 今天放学以后，你想做什么？

Unit 14 In the Classroom

Part One Warming Up

1.1   1. 星期一上午十一点有什么课？

         2. 星期二中午十二点五十分是什么课？

         3. 星期三的中文课在几点？

         4. 星期几有地理课？

         5. 星期五下午两点四十分有课吗？

1.2
1. wǒ zǎo shang jiǔ diǎn shàng kè, zhōng wǔ shí èr diǎn xià kè
我早上九点上课，中午十二点下课。
2. tā zài shì zhōng xīn chē zhàn shàng chē, zài tǐ yù guǎn xià chē
他在市中心车站上车，在体育馆下车。
3. nǐ bà ba jǐ diǎn shàng bān? jǐ diǎn xià bān?
你爸爸几点上班？几点下班？
4. tóng xué men dì yī tiān xià wǔ shàng shān, dì èr tiān shàng wǔ xià shān
同学们第一天下午上山，第二天上午下山。

1.3
1. hǎo 好
2. yǒu hǎo 友好
3. nán 难
4. róng yì 容易
5. duì 对
6. yán lì 严厉
7. xǐ huan 喜欢
8. míng bái 明白

1.4
1. měi shù kè hěn yǒu yì si. měi shù kǎo shì hěn nán
美术课很有意思。美术考试很难。
2. wǒ xǐ huan shàng kē xué kè. wǒ bú tài xǐ huan kē xué lǎo shī
我喜欢上科学课。我不太喜欢科学老师。
3. wǒ ài xué zhōng wén. wǒ bú ài xiě hàn zì
我爱学中文。我不爱写汉字。
4. jīn tiān wǒ men méi yǒu yīng wén zuò yè. wǒ men yǒu hěn duō shù xué zuò yè
今天我们没有英文作业。我们有很多数学作业。

Part Two Picture-based Task

2.1
1. miáo shù zhè zhāng zhào piàn. / zhào piàn lǐ yǒu shén me
描述这张照片。/ 照片里有什么？
2. hěn duō rén xué zhōng wén, nǐ jué de zěn me yàng
很多人学中文，你觉得怎么样？
3. nǐ xīng qī jǐ yǒu zhōng wén kè
你星期几有中文课？
4. shàng ge xīng qī nǐ zuò le shén me zhōng wén zuò yè
上个星期你做了什么中文作业？
5. nǐ xiǎng qù zhōng guó xué zhōng wén ma? wèi shén me
你想去中国学中文吗？为什么？

Part Three Listening Comprehension

1. wǒ jué de yīng wén kè hé zhōng wén kè dōu fēi cháng yǒu qù, zuò yè yě bù duō
我觉得英文课和中文课都非常有趣，作业也不多。
2. wǒ men de shù xué lǎo shī hěn qīn qiè, bú guò tā de kè wǒ tīng bù dǒng
我们的数学老师很亲切，不过他的课我听不懂。
3. wǒ bú tài xǐ huan shàng dì lǐ kè, chú le lǎo shī tài yán lì, kǎo shì yě nán jí le
我不太喜欢上地理课，除了老师太严厉，考试也难极了。
4. kē xué shì zuì zhòng yào de kē mù, wǒ xī wàng měi tiān dōu yǒu kē xué kè
科学是最重要的科目，我希望每天都有科学课。

Part Four Conversation

4.1
1. nǐ zài xué xiào xué nǎ xiē kē mù
你在学校学哪些科目？
2. xué shén me zuì zhòng yào? wèi shén me
学什么最重要？为什么？

nǐ zuó tiān shàng le shén me kè
3.你昨天上了什么课？

shuōshuo nǐ zuì xǐ huan de yí wèi lǎo shī
4.说说你最喜欢的一位老师。

rú guǒ shàng dà xué   nǐ xī wàng xué shén me
5.如果上大学，你希望学什么？

Unit 15 My School

■ Part One Warming Up

1.1
1.bàn gōng shì 办公室
2.tú shū guǎn 图书馆
3.yùn dòngchǎng 运动场
4.shí táng 食堂
5.tǐ yù guǎn 体育馆
6.zú qiú chǎng 足球场
7.lǐ táng 礼堂
8.jiào shì 教室

1.3
1.wèi le xué hǎo zhōng wén   wǒ xiǎng cān jiā zhōng guó xià lìng yíng
为了学好中文，我想参加中国夏令营。

2.wèi le hé nǚ péng you zài yì qǐ   tā méi yǒu hé jiā rén yì qǐ qù dù jià
为了和女朋友在一起，他没有和家人一起去度假。

3.tā xīng qī liù zuò jiān zhí gōng zuò shì wèi le zhuàn qián
她星期六做兼职工作是为了赚钱。

4.wèi le jiàn kāng   wǒ men yào shǎo kāi chē   duō zǒu lù
为了健康，我们要少开车，多走路。

■ Part Two Role Play

2.1
1.nǐ huā le duō cháng shí jiān zuò huǒ chē lái xué xiào
你花了多长时间坐火车来学校？

2.nǐ jué de wǒ men de tǐ yù guǎn zěn me yàng
你觉得我们的体育馆怎么样？

3.wèi le jiàn kāng   nǐ chángcháng zuò shén me
为了健康，你常常做什么？

4.(Pause and answer) wǒ men xué xiào yǒu sān gè yùn dòngchǎng
我们学校有三个运动场。

5.(Pause and answer) wǒ men xué xiào yǒu bā bǎi wǔ shí gè xué sheng
我们学校有八百五十个学生。

■ Part Three Listening Comprehension

1.wǒ zài yīng guó shàng xué yǐ jīng sān gè duō yuè le   wǒ men de xué xiào shén me dōu hǎo
我在英国上学已经三个多月了，我们的学校什么都好，
zhǐ shì yīng guó xué xiào de fàn méi yǒu zhōng guó xué xiào de hǎo chī
只是英国学校的饭没有中国学校的好吃。

2.mā ma   nín ràng wǒ zǎo shang duō chī qīng cài   kě shì yīng guó de zǎo fàn méi yǒu qīng
妈妈，您让我早上多吃青菜，可是英国的早饭没有青
cài   tā men chángcháng chī miàn bāo   jī dàn hé ròu
菜，他们常常吃面包、鸡蛋和肉。

3.xiū xī de shí hòu   xué xiào gěi wǒ men chī dàn gāo   hē qì shuǐ   dōu shì bú jiàn kāng de
休息的时候，学校给我们吃蛋糕，喝汽水，都是不健康的

dōng xi wǒ jué de zì jǐ yuè lái yuè pàng le
东西，我觉得自己越来越胖了。

wèi le jiǎn féi wǒ dǎ suan cóng míng tiān kāi shǐ měi tiān qù jiàn shēn fáng pǎo bù měi gè
4.为了减肥，我打算从明天开始每天去健身房跑步，每个
xīng qī wǔ chī yú zhōu mò chī sù
星期五吃鱼，周末吃素。

■ Part Four Conversation

nǐ zài xué xiào yǒu shén me yā lì
4.1　1.你在学校有什么压力？

nǐ men de xiào zhǎng zhī dào nǐ yǒu yā lì ma
2.你们的校长知道你有压力吗？

rú guǒ yǒu yā lì nǐ huì zhǎo shuí yì qǐ tán tan
3.如果有压力，你会找谁一起谈谈？

kǎo shì de hǎo chu shì shén me huài chu shì shén me
4.考试的好处是什么？坏处是什么？

wèi le ràng zì jǐ kuài lè nǐ zuò guo shén me
5.为了让自己快乐，你做过什么？

Unit 16 Extra-curricular Activities

■ Part One Warming Up

xué dǎ tài jí quán tán gāng qín qù jiàn shēn fáng
1.1　1.学打太极拳　2.弹钢琴　3.去健身房

chàng jīng jù cān jiā zú qiú duì bǐ sài shàng shū fǎ kè
4.唱京剧　5.参加足球队比赛　6.上书法课

liàn tǐ cāo cān jiā xué xiào yuè duì huó dòng
7.练体操　8.参加学校乐队活动

wǒ péng you de yùn dòng xié hěn shū fu wǒ de yùn dòng xié yě hěn shū fu
1.2　1.我朋友的运动鞋很舒服，我的运动鞋也很舒服。

chàng jīng jù hěn nán tán gāng qín yě hěn nán
2.唱京剧很难，弹钢琴也很难。

lǎo shī de shū fǎ hěn piào liang nà ge huà jiā de shū fǎ yě hěn piào liang
3.老师的书法很漂亮，那个画家的书法也很漂亮。

wǒ dì di xǐ huan dǎ tài jí quán wǒ yě xǐ huan dǎ tài jí quán
4.我弟弟喜欢打太极拳，我也喜欢打太极拳。

■ Part Two Picture-based Task

miáo shù zhè zhāng zhào piàn zhào piàn lǐ yǒu shén me
2.1　1.描述这张照片。/ 照片里有什么？

nǐ xǐ huan zuò fàn ma wèi shén me
2.你喜欢做饭吗？为什么？

nǐ zuì jìn shén me shí hou jiào guo zhōng cān wài mài
3.你最近什么时候叫过中餐外卖？

nǐ ài chī nǎ xiē zhōng guó cài
4.你爱吃哪些中国菜？

nǐ zuì xiǎng hé shuí yì qǐ chī zhōng cān
5.你最想和谁一起吃中餐？

■ Part Three Listening Comprehension

去年暑假我参加了一个中国夏令营。在中国的三个星期里，我们不仅参观了很多有名的地方，而且试了又好吃又新鲜的中国菜。在长城上，我认识了一个有趣的中国朋友，他爬过十多次长城了，他说长城的历史和长城一样长。

■ Part Four Conversation

4.1

1. 放学以后，你一般都参加哪些课外活动？

2. 参加课外活动的好处是什么？

3. 上个周末，你做了什么？

4. 做运动和学习，哪个更重要？

5. 如果能参加奥运会，你想参加什么比赛？

Unit 17 Gap Year and Work Experience

■ Part One Warming Up

1.1
1. 咖啡厅 (kā fēi tīng)
2. 书店 (shū diàn)
3. 媒体公司 (méi tǐ gōng sī)
4. 医院 (yī yuàn)
5. 幼儿园 (yòu ér yuán)
6. 警察局 (jǐng chá jú)
7. 展览馆 (zhǎn lǎn guǎn)
8. 购物中心 (gòu wù zhōng xīn)

1.3
1. 我想这个周末请她去看电影。(wǒ xiǎng zhè ge zhōu mò qǐng tā qù kàn diàn yǐng)
2. 我们今天去吃意大利海鲜，他请客。(wǒ men jīn tiān qù chī yì dà lì hǎi xiān, tā qǐng kè)
3. 妈妈请我参观她的办公室。(mā ma qǐng wǒ cān guān tā de bàn gōng shì)
4. 爸爸昨天请病假没去上班。(bà ba zuó tiān qǐng bìng jià méi qù shàng bān)

■ Part Two Role Play

2.1
1. 你是几年级的学生？(nǐ shì jǐ nián jí de xué sheng)
2. 你为什么想在咖啡厅工作？(nǐ wèi shén me xiǎng zài kā fēi tīng gōng zuò)
3. 你的爱好是什么？(nǐ de ài hào shì shén me)
4. 你想在星期几工作？(nǐ xiǎng zài xīng qī jǐ gōng zuò)
5. (Pause and answer) 你这个周末可以开始工作。(nǐ zhè ge zhōu mò kě yǐ kāi shǐ gōng zuò)

■ Part Three Listening Comprehension

1. 我周末去实习做护士，帮助生病的老人，我希望他们都能和我爷爷一样健康。(wǒ zhōu mò qù shí xí zuò hù shi, bāng zhù shēng bìng de lǎo rén, wǒ xī wàng tā men dōu néng hé wǒ yé ye yí yàng jiàn kāng)

2. 我的爱好是做饭，我们的小镇有一个面包店，我常常去那儿学做面包。(wǒ de ài hào shì zuò fàn, wǒ men de xiǎo zhèn yǒu yí gè miàn bāo diàn, wǒ cháng cháng qù nà er xué zuò miàn bāo)

3. 每天下午，我都去大学旁边的图书馆，一边为他们工作，一边看书。(měi tiān xià wǔ, wǒ dōu qù dà xué páng biān de tú shū guǎn, yì biān wèi tā men gōng zuò, yì biān kàn shū)

4. 我在一家美国咖啡馆做服务员，那里的生意不错，中午有很多广告公司的客人。(wǒ zài yì jiā měi guó kā fēi guǎn zuò fú wù yuán, nà li de shēng yi bú cuò, zhōng wǔ yǒu hěn duō guǎng gào gōng sī de kè rén)

wǒ zài wǎng shang gōng zuò   yí gè zhōng guó guǎng gào gōng sī qǐng wǒ bāng tā men xiě yīng wén
5.我在网上工作，一个中国广告公司请我帮他们写英文
de kā fēi guǎng gào
的咖啡广告。

wǒ jiā páng biān yǒu yí gè jiào   qiū yuè   de zhōng cān diàn   wǒ qí zì xíng chē wèi tā
6.我家旁边有一个叫"秋月"的中餐店，我骑自行车为他
men sòng wài mài
们送外卖。

■ Part Four Conversation

nǐ cān jiā guò xué xiào de shè huì shí jiàn huó dòng ma
4.1   1.你参加过学校的社会实践活动吗？
zhōng xué sheng cān jiā shè huì shí jiàn huó dòng de hǎo chu shì shén me
2.中学生参加社会实践活动的好处是什么？
zhōng xué sheng zuò shén me jiān zhí néngzhuàn hěn duō qián
3.中学生做什么兼职能赚很多钱？
nǐ huì yòng zuò jiān zhí zhuàn de qián mǎi shén me
4.你会用做兼职赚的钱买什么？
nǐ zuì xiǎng qù nǎ er zuò shí xí shēng
5.你最想去哪儿做实习生？

Unit 18 Life after Secondary School

■ Part One Warming Up

qù yà zhōu lǚ xíng   zài cān tīng dǎ gōng   shàng dà xué
1.1   1.去亚洲旅行   2.在餐厅打工   3.上大学
zài gōngchǎng shí xí   zuò yì gōng   zhǎogōng zuò
4.在工厂实习   5.做义工   6.找工作
xiū xué yī nián   zì jǐ kāi gōng sī zuò shēng yi
7.休学一年   8.自己开公司做生意

tā zài kàn shén me
1.2   1.他在看什么？
xiǎo gǒu zài wán shén me
2.小狗在玩什么？
zhè ge nǚ hái zài xiǎngshén me
3.这个女孩在想什么？
tā men zài zuò shén me
4.他们在做什么？

cóng shí yí suì dào shí bā suì   wǒ zài xiǎo zhènzhōng xué shàng xué
1.3   1.从十一岁到十八岁，我在小镇中学上学。
cóng shí jiǔ suì dào èr shí suì   wǒ zài fēi zhōu zuò yì gōng
2.从十九岁到二十岁，我在非洲做义工。
cóng   nián dào   nián   wǒ zài lún dūn dà xué xué xí
3.从2017年到2020年，我在伦敦大学学习。
cóng qù nián dào xiàn zài   wǒ zài tái wān diàn nǎo gōng sī zuò gōngchéng shī
4.从去年到现在，我在台湾电脑公司做工程师。

1.4　1. yīn yuè huì jiù yào kāi shǐ le
音乐会就要开始了。

2. wǒ de tóng xué yǐ jīng kāi shǐ zài fàn diàn gōng zuò le
我的同学已经开始在饭店工作了。

3. shuì le yì tiān wǒ hái shì jué de lèi jí le
睡了一天，我还是觉得累极了。

4. tā kuài yào èr shí suì le zǎo jiù kě yǐ hē jiǔ le
他快要二十岁了，早就可以喝酒了。

Part Two Picture-based Task

2.1　1. miáo shù zhè zhāng zhào piàn zhào piàn lǐ yǒu shén me
描述这张照片。/ 照片里有什么？

2. nǐ xiǎng xué kāi chē ma wèi shén me
你想学开车吗？为什么？

3. zuì jìn nǐ hé jiā rén kāi chē qù le nǎ er
最近你和家人开车去了哪儿？

4. huì kāi chē de hǎo chu shì shén me
会开车的好处是什么？

5. nǐ xǐ huan shén me yán sè de chē
你喜欢什么颜色的车？

Part Three Listening Comprehension

wǒ shì lún dūn rén wǒ zhèng zài xiāng gǎng de yì jiā zhōng guó yín háng shí xí wǒ de zhōng
我是伦敦人。我正在香港的一家中国银行实习。我的中
guó péng you xiǎo wěi qù nián cān jiā le gāo kǎo tā kǎo de fēi cháng hǎo xiàn zài zài běi jīng dà xué
国朋友小伟去年参加了高考，他考得非常好，现在在北京大学
xué lì shǐ wǒ men bàn gōng shì de zhōng guó tóng shì gào su wǒ wǒ kě yǐ shēn qǐng běi jīng dà xué
学历史。我们办公室的中国同事告诉我，我可以申请北京大学
de zhōng wén kè chéng rú guǒ wǒ de shēn qǐng néng chéng gōng wǒ jiù kě yǐ hé xiǎo wěi zài běi jīng dà
的中文课程。如果我的申请能成功，我就可以和小伟在北京大
xué zuò tóng xué
学做同学。

Part Four Conversation

4.1　1. zhōng xué bì yè yǐ hòu nǐ dǎ suan zuò shén me
中学毕业以后，你打算做什么？

2. wǒ jué de měi gè xué sheng dōu yīng gāi shàng dà xué nǐ tóng yì ma
我觉得每个学生都应该上大学，你同意吗？

3. nǐ zuò guo shén me gōng zuò
你做过什么工作？

4. xiū xué yì nián de hǎo chu shì shén me
休学一年的好处是什么？

5. xiū xué yì nián yǒu méi yǒu huài chu
休学一年有没有坏处？

Part One Warming Up

1.1
1. kē xué jiā 科学家
2. zuò jiā 作家
3. yì shù jiā 艺术家
4. huà jiā 画家
5. jiào shī 教师
6. gōngchéng shī 工程师
7. lǜ shī 律师
8. chú shī 厨师
9. yǎn yuán 演员
10. yùn dòngyuán 运动员
11. fú wù yuán 服务员
12. shòu huò yuán 售货员
13. yī shēng 医生
14. yá yī 牙医
15. hù shi 护士
16. jì zhě 记者
17. jǐng chá 警察
18. gōngchǎnggōng rén 工厂工人
19. sī jī 司机
20. jiā tíng zhǔ fù 家庭主妇

1.2
1. shuí de gōng zuò shì jiāo kè 谁的工作是教课？
2. shuí de gōng zuò shì kāi chē 谁的工作是开车？
3. shuí de gōng zuò shì zuò fàn 谁的工作是做饭？
4. shuí de gōng zuò shì mài dōng xi 谁的工作是卖东西？
5. shuí de gōng zuò shì gěi bìng rén kàn bìng 谁的工作是给病人看病？
6. shuí de gōng zuò shì gěi bào zhǐ xiě xīn wén 谁的工作是给报纸写新闻？

Part Two Role Play

2.1
1. qǐng nǐ shuōshuo nǐ zì jǐ hǎo ma 请你说说你自己，好吗？
2. nǐ yǒu shén me guǎng gào gōng sī de gōng zuò jīng yàn 你有什么广告公司的工作经验？
3. rú guǒ gōng zuò yā lì hěn dà nǐ huì zěn me zuò 如果工作压力很大，你会怎么做？
4. (Pause and answer) nǐ huì hé wǒ yì qǐ gōng zuò 你会和我一起工作。
5. (Pause and answer) nǐ de gōng zī yì kāi shǐ bù hěn gāo dàn shì huì yuè lái yuè gāo 你的工资一开始不很高，但是会越来越高。

Part Three Listening Comprehension

1. zhōng guó yǒu yí wèi fēi cháng yǒu míng de nǚ zuò jiā yě shì fān yì jiā tā jiào yáng jiàng 中国有一位非常有名的女作家，也是翻译家，她叫杨绛。
jié hūn yǐ hòu yáng jiàng hé tā de zhàng fu qù le yīng guó niú jīn shàng dà xué rán hòu yòu yì qǐ 结婚以后，杨绛和她的丈夫去了英国牛津上大学，然后又一起
huí zhōng guó gōng zuò 回中国工作。

2. 2004 年，九十三岁的杨绛写了一本书，书的名字是《我们仨》，"仨"就是三口人的意思。在书里，杨绛写了她和丈夫六十多年的结婚生活，还有他们做英语老师的女儿。

Part Four Conversation

4.1　1. 二十五岁以后，你想做什么工作？

2. 你小时候的工作理想是什么？

3. 你认为赚钱重要吗？

4. 在英国找工作难不难？

5. 我很喜欢去外国工作，你呢？

Unit 20 Internet, Mobile Technology and Social Media

■ Part One Warming Up

1.1

1. bó kè
博客

2. shè jiāo méi tǐ
社交媒体

3. diàn nǎo
电脑

4. diàn zǐ shū
电子书

5. duǎn xìn
短信

6. xià zài
下载

7. shǒu jī
手机

8. diàn zǐ yóu jiàn
电子邮件

1.2

1. wǒ fēi cháng bù xǐ huan liǎn shū
我非常不喜欢脸书。

2. jīn tiān de diàn shì jié mù tài bù hǎo kàn le
今天的电视节目太不好看了。

3. hěn duō shè jiāo wǎng zhàn dōu hěn méi yì si
很多社交网站都很没意思。

4. shàng wǎng xué zhōng wén róng yì jí le
上网学中文容易极了。

1.3

1. nǐ měi tiān wán duō cháng shí jiān diàn zǐ yóu xì
你每天玩多长时间电子游戏？

2. nǐ měi gè xīng qī huā duō cháng shí jiān zài shè jiāo méi tǐ shang
你每个星期花多长时间在社交媒体上？

3. nǐ duō cháng shí jiān fā yí cì duǎn xìn
你多长时间发一次短信？

4. nǐ duō cháng shí jiān xià zài yí cì diàn yǐng
你多长时间下载一次电影？

■ Part Two Picture-based Task

2.1

1. miáo shù zhè zhāng zhào piàn zhào piàn lǐ yǒu shén me
描述这张照片。/ 照片里有什么？

2. nǐ cháng cháng yòng shǒu jī zuò shén me
你常常用手机做什么？

3. nǐ měi gè xīng qī yòng shǒu jī wán duō cháng shí jiān yóu xì
你每个星期用手机玩多长时间游戏？

4. nǐ jīn tiān yòng shǒu jī gěi shuí dǎ le diàn huà
你今天用手机给谁打了电话？

5. nǐ xiǎng mǎi xīn shǒu jī ma wèi shén me
你想买新手机吗？ 为什么？

■ Part Three Listening Comprehension

1. 我白天很忙，晚上喜欢在社交媒体上和朋友聊天，社交媒体让生活很方便；当然，社交媒体的坏处是浪费时间，让我聊到很晚，没有时间睡觉。

2. 我除了在社交媒体上看新闻，还在社交媒体上学外语；不过，有的朋友常常在社交媒体上告诉大家要吃什么、要穿什么，一点儿也没意思。

■ Part Four Conversation

4.1　1. 你喜欢玩电子游戏吗？

2. 你上一次玩电子游戏是什么时候？

3. 你用社交媒体做什么？

4. 你每天都上社交媒体吗？

5. 如果让你给一个人发电子邮件，你会发给谁？

Unit 21 Weather and Environmental Issues

■ Part One Warming Up

1.1　1. 多开车

2. 骑自行车上学

3. 种树

4. 在花园用雨水浇花

5. 少用电

6. 二十四小时开空调

7. 经常换新手机

8. 在咖啡厅用自己的杯子喝咖啡

1.3　1. 我做了晚饭。(pause) 我把晚饭做了。

2. 他写完了作业。(pause) 他把作业写完了。

3. 弟弟玩坏了手机。(pause) 弟弟把手机玩坏了。

4. 姐姐穿脏了我的运动鞋。(pause) 姐姐把我的运动鞋穿脏了。

1.4
1. 这位老师是校长。哪位？
2. 我们明天要交中文作业。哪天？
3. 那杯茶是给妈妈的。哪杯？
4. 城市里所有的河水都有污染。哪些？

■ Part Two Role Play

2.1
1. 请问，哪位是家长？
2. 为什么你们家前面有很多垃圾？
3. 你在这儿住了多长时间？
4. (Pause and answer) 回收中心在你家后边。
5. (Pause and answer) 空瓶子和旧报纸都可以回收。

■ Part Three Listening Comprehension

1. 这位英国人是地理学家，他从小就喜欢中国的长城。从二十多岁开始，他就经常去爬长城，他还写过几本关于长城的书。

2. 看到长城上有太多垃圾，他就在长城上放了很多垃圾桶。为了保护长城的环境，他跟很多义工和家人一起，每年都去长城捡垃圾。

■ Part Four Conversation

4.1
1. 你喜欢买新衣服吗？
2. 你用过什么旧东西？
3. 坐飞机去国外旅行有什么坏处？
4. 你经常骑自行车上学吗？
5. 为了保护环境，你打算做些什么？

Unit 22 Public Welfare and Volunteer Work

■ Part One Warming Up

1.1
1. lǎo rén yuàn
   老人院
2. juān qián
   捐钱
3. zuò yì gōng
   做义工
4. bǎo hù dòng wù
   保护动物
5. gè rén jiǎn lì
   个人简历
6. bāng zhù qióng rén
   帮助穷人
7. cí shàn shāng diàn
   慈善商店
8. jīng yàn
   经验

1.2
1. qí chē shàng xué duì shén me yǒu hǎo chu
   骑车上学对什么有好处？
2. quán qiú biàn nuǎn duì shuí yǒu huài chu
   全球变暖对谁有坏处？
3. yī shēng miǎn fèi kàn bìng duì shuí yǒu hǎo chu
   医生免费看病对谁有好处？
4. rén kǒu tài duō duì shén me méi yǒu hǎo chu
   人口太多对什么没有好处？

1.4
1. rán ran xīng qī èr qī diǎn yǐ qián zuò shén me
   然然星期二七点以前做什么？
2. rán ran xīng qī èr shàng wǔ de shí hou zuò shén me
   然然星期二上午的时候做什么？
3. rán ran xīng qī èr wǔ fàn yǐ hòu zuò shén me
   然然星期二午饭以后做什么？
4. rán ran xīng qī èr shuì jiào yǐ qián zuò shén me
   然然星期二睡觉以前做什么？

■ Part Two Picture-based Task

2.1
1. miáo shù zhè zhāng zhào piàn   zhào piàn lǐ yǒu shén me
   描述这张照片。/ 照片里有什么？
2. nǐ qù guò lǎo rén yuàn ba
   你去过老人院吧？
3. nǐ jué de lǎo rén men yīng gāi xué zěn me yòng diàn nǎo ma
   你觉得老人们应该学怎么用电脑吗？
4. zěn me ràng lǎo rén men kuài lè
   怎么让老人们快乐？
5. rú guǒ yǒu jī huì   nǐ xiǎng zài lǎo rén yuàn gōng zuò ma
   如果有机会，你想在老人院工作吗？

■ Part Three Listening Comprehension

1. huān yíng zhè ge xīng qī liù lái hǎi biān kā fēi tīng cān jiā dòng wù cí shàn wǎn huì   jié mù yǒu
   欢迎这个星期六来海边咖啡厅参加动物慈善晚会，节目有
   chàng gē   tiào wǔ hé chǒng wù sài pǎo   mén piào měi zhāng shí wǔ yuán   shí jiān shì wǎn shang qī diǎn
   唱歌、跳舞和宠物赛跑，门票每张十五元，时间是晚上七点
   shí wǔ fēn
   十五分。

suǒ yǒu de qián dōu huì juān gěi dòng wù bǎo hù zhōng xīn　　yào shi nǐ yǒu chǒng wù māo huò zhě

2.所有的钱都会捐给动物保护中心。要是你有宠物猫或者

chǒng wù gǒu　　qǐng nǐ dài tā men yì qǐ lái ba　　zhè ge zhōu mò yí dìng huì yòu rè nao yòu kuài lè

宠物狗，请你带它们一起来吧！这个周末一定会又热闹又快乐！

■ Part Four Conversation

4.1

nǐ zuò guo yì gōng ba

1.你做过义工吧？

nǐ rèn wéi shàng dà xué yīng gāi miǎn fèi ma

2.你认为上大学应该免费吗？

zài yī yuàn gōng zuò de hǎo chu shì shén me

3.在医院工作的好处是什么？

fù rén kě yǐ bāng zhù qióng rén zuò shén me

4.富人可以帮助穷人做什么？

rú guǒ juān qián　　nǐ zuì xiǎng bǎ qián juān gěi shuí

5.如果捐钱，你最想把钱捐给谁？

Key Question Words
疑问词总表

	中文 CHINESE	拼音 PINYIN	英文 ENGLISH	位置 LOCATION
1	怎么样	zěn me yang	how about (asking for opinion)	Unit 1
2	什么	shén me	what	Unit 2/7
3	说说……	shuō shuo	talk about... (asking for details)	Unit 3
4	吧	ba	(particle for suggestion/question confirmation)	Unit 4/22
5	好吗	hǎo ma	okay?	Unit 4
6	好不好	hǎo bù hǎo	okay or not	Unit 4
7	吗	ma	(particle for question)	Unit 4
8	哪儿 / 哪里	nǎ er / nǎ lǐ	where	Unit 5
9	为什么	wèi shén me	why	Unit 6
10	呢	ne	how about, what about	Unit 8
11	怎么	zěn me	how	Unit 9
12	有多远	yǒu duō yuǎn	how far	Unit 10
13	几次 / 几遍	jǐ cì / jǐ biàn	how many times	Unit 11
14	A 还是 B	A hái shì B	A or B (choice type question)	Unit 12
15	要多长时间	yào duō cháng shí jiān	how long does it take	Unit 13
16	几月几日	jǐ yuè jǐ rì	what is the date	Unit 14
17	星期几	xīng qī jǐ	on what day of the week	Unit 14
18	几点	jǐ diǎn	what time	Unit 14
19	几	jǐ	how many (re. less than ten)	Unit 15
20	多少	duō shǎo	how many (re. more than ten)	Unit 15
21	多少钱	duō shǎo qián	how much (re. asking about price)	Unit 15
22	哪些	nǎ xiē	which ones	Unit 16/21
23	什么时候	shén me shí hou	when	Unit 17
24	在 + verb + 什么	zài + verb + shén me	(a question structure to ask about action in progress)	Unit 18
25	谁	shuí	who	Unit 19
26	谁的	shuí de	whose	Unit 19
27	多长时间	duō cháng shí jiān	how long does it take	Unit 20
28	多长时间……一次	duō cháng shí jiān...yí cì	how often	Unit 20
29	哪	nǎ	which	Unit 21
30	哪个	nǎ ge	which one	Unit 21

Key Grammar List
语法总表

	中文 CHINESE	拼音 PINYIN	英文 ENGLISH	位置 LOCATION
1	要，想，会，打算，计划，希望，快要	yào, xiǎng, huì, dǎ suàn, jì huà, xī wàng, kuài yào	used in future events and/or a future time expression	Unit 1
2	了	le	used in past events and/or a past time expression	Unit 1/18
3	除了……也 / 还……	chú le... yě / hái...	apart from... also...	Unit 2
4	因为……所以……	yīnwèi... suǒyǐ...	because... therefore...	Unit 2
5	adjective and adjective-verb			Unit 3
6	又……又……	yòu... yòu...	both... and...	Unit 3
7	也	yě	also	Unit 3
8	但是 / 可是 / 不过	dàn shì / kě shì / bù guò	but	Unit 3/13
9	有……也有……	yǒu... yě yǒu...	there is/are... there is/are also...	Unit 3
10	是……的	shì... de	emphasising a certain part of a sentence; indicating a past action	Unit 3/11
11	吧 / 好吗 / 好不好 / 你想……吗?	ba / hǎo ma / hǎo bu hǎo / nǐ xiǎng... ma ?	making suggestions	Unit 4
12	先……再……然后……	xiān... zài... rán hòu...	express sequences, eg. first... then... after that...	Unit 4
13	得	de	adverbial marker	Unit 4
14	verb + 会了 / 完了	verb + huì le / wán le	indicating the successful result of an action	Unit 4
15	在	zài	at, in, on	Unit 5
16	住在	zhù zài	live in	Unit 5
17	虽然……但是……	suī rán... dàn shì...	although...but...	Unit 5
18	describing the temperature			Unit 6
19	不管……还是……都……	bù guǎn... hái shi... dōu...	regardless...	Unit 6
20	要是 / 如果……就……	yào shi / rú guǒ... jiù...	if...	Unit 6/18
21	边 / 面	biān / miàn	used in describing locations	Unit 7
22	而	ér	whereas; but	Unit 7
23	每……都……	měi... dōu...	every...	Unit 8
24	坐，骑，开，走	zuò, qí, kāi, zǒu	used in expressing means of transport	Unit 9
25	A（地点）+ 离 + B（地点）+ 很近 / 很远 / 不太远	A（dì diǎn）+ lí + B（dì diǎn） + hěn jìn /hěn yuǎn / bù tài yuǎn	A (place) is close/far/not too far from B (place)	Unit 9
26	不用	bù yòng	no need, unnecessary	Unit 9
27	A 对 B 好 / 不好	A duì B hǎo / bù hǎo	A is good/not good for B	Unit 9
28	最 + adjective/verb	zuì + adjective/verb	the most	Unti 10
29	新 + noun	xīn + noun	new	Unit 10

	中文 CHINESE	拼音 PINYIN	英文 ENGLISH	位置 LOCATION
30	新 + verb + 的 + noun	xīn + verb + de + noun	newly	Unit 10
31	一……就……	yī... jiù...	as soon as/once...	Unit 11
32	每	měi	used in expressing frequency	Unit 11
33	过	guò	used in past experience	Unit 12
34	越来越 + adjective/verb	yuè lái yuè + adjective/verb	more and more...	Unit 12
35	A 比 B + adjective	A bǐ B + adjective	expressing a comparative, eg. A is more... than B	Unit 12
36	不但 / 不仅 …… 而且……	bù dàn / bù jǐn... ér qiě...	not only... but also...	Unit 12/16
37	从 A (place) 到 B (place) + 要 + length of time	cóng A (place) dào B (place) + yào + length of time	it takes... to travel from A to B	Unit 13
38	adjective + 极了	adjective + jí le	extremely/terribly	Unit 13
39	multiple meanings of 上	multiple meanings of shàng	go to; attend; board; climb	Unit 14
40	multiple meanings of 下	multiple meanings of xià	finish; get off; go down	Unit 14
41	不太	bù tài	not very, not quite	Unit 14
42	花	huā	flower; floral; multi-patterned; spend	Unit 15
43	为了……	wèi le...	in order to...; for the purpose of...	Unit 15
44	多 + verb	duō + verb	do... more	Unit 15
45	少 + verb	shǎo + verb	do... less	Unit 15
46	A 没有 B + adjective	A méi yǒu B + adjective	expressing a negative comparison, eg. A is not as... as B	Unit 15
47	A 和 / 跟 B 一样	A hé / gēn B yí yàng	A is the same as B	Unit 16
48	比如…… 等等	bǐ rú... děng děng	to give a list of example "such as... and so on"	Unit 16
49	请	qǐng	please; invite	Unit 17
50	能 , 可以 , 会	néng, kě yǐ, huì	can, may, be able to	Unit 17
51	为 / 给 + somebody + do something	wèi / gěi + somebody + do something	do something for somebody	Unit 17
52	正在 + verb	zhèng zài + verb	indicating an action in progress	Unit 18
53	从 …… 到 ……	cóng... dào...	from... to...	Unit 18
54	common usages of 了			Unit 18
55	就	jiù	used in front of a verb to add emphasis	Unit 19
56	A 就是 B 的意思	A jiù shì B de yì si	the meaning of A is B	Unit 19
57	一点儿也不 / 没	yī diǎnr yě bù / méi	not at all	Unit 20
58	describing length of time in an action			Unit 20
59	到	dào	continuation of time until a point	Unit 20
60	verb + adjective	verb + adjective	indicating the result of an action	Unit 21
61	subject + 把 + object + verb + 了	subject + bǎ + object + verb + le	emphasising how a person or a thing is being acted upon	Unit 21
62	A 对 B 有好处 / 坏处	A duì B yǒu hǎo chu / huài chu	A is good/bad for B	Unit 22
63	A 对 B 没有好处 / 坏处	A duì B méi yǒu hǎo chu / huài chu	A is not good/not harmful for B	Unit 22
64	一边…… 一边……	yì biān... yì biān...	used to express two actions happening at the same time	Unit 22
65	……以前 / 以后 / 的时候	... yǐ qián / yǐ hòu / de shí hou	before/after/during...	Unit 22

Glossary
词汇总表

			My Family	
1	爸爸	bà ba	dad
2	妈妈	mā ma	mum
3	哥哥	gē ge	elder brother
4	姐姐	jiě jie	elder sister
5	弟弟	dì di	younger brother
6	妹妹	mèi mei	younger sister
7	爷爷	yé ye	granddad
8	奶奶	nǎi nai	grandma
9	家人	jiā rén	family (member)
10	朋友	péng you	friend
11	宠物	chǒng wù	pet
12	岁	suì	years old
13	出生	chū shēng	to be born
14	过生日	guò shēng rì	to celebrate a birthday
15	开生日会	kāi shēng rì huì	to hold a birthday party
16	结婚	jié hūn	to get married
17	离婚	lí hūn	to be divorced
18	爱	ài	love
19	看	kàn	to look at; to see; to watch; to visit (a person)
20	房间	fáng jiān	room

My Hobbies

1	爱好	ài hào	hobby
2	最喜欢	zuì xǐ huan	like ... best
3	上网	shàng wǎng	go online
4	打网球	dǎ wǎng qiú	play tennis
5	打篮球	dǎ lán qiú	play basketball
6	打乒乓球	dǎ pīng pāng qiú	play table tennis
7	打电话	dǎ diàn huà	make a telephone call
8	踢足球	tī zú qiú	play football
9	跑步	pǎo bù	jog
10	玩电脑游戏	wán diàn nǎo yóu xì	play computer games
11	玩 (儿) 滑板	wán (er) huá bǎn	skateboard
12	滑冰	huá bīng	ice skate
13	游泳	yóu yǒng	swim
14	看书	kàn shū	read
15	看电视	kàn diàn shì	watch TV
16	看电影	kàn diàn yǐng	watch films
17	看朋友	kàn péng you	visit friends
18	唱歌	chàng gē	sing
19	做运动	zuò yùn dòng	do exercises
20	比赛	bǐ sài	competition

My Friends

1	大	dà	big
2	小	xiǎo	small
3	长	cháng	long (for length)
4	短	duǎn	short (for length)
5	高	gāo	tall (for height)
6	矮	ǎi	short (for height)
7	胖	pàng	fat
8	瘦	shòu	thin
9	黑色	hēi sè	black
10	白色	bái sè	white
11	蓝色	lán sè	blue
12	棕色	zōng sè	brown
13	金黄色	jīn huáng sè	blonde
14	漂亮	piào liang	pretty
15	帅	shuài	handsome
16	难看	nán kàn	ugly
17	聪明	cōng míng	clever
18	笨	bèn	stupid
19	友好	yǒu hǎo	friendly
20	亲切	qīn qiè	kind

My Leisure Time

1	钓鱼	diào yú	fishing
2	赛车	sài chē	motor racing
3	遛狗	liù gǒu	walk the dog
4	滑雪	huá xuě	ski
5	爬山	pá shān	climb mountains
6	健身	jiàn shēn	do exercise
7	回家	huí jiā	return home
8	叫外卖	jiào wài mài	order a takeaway
9	吃饭	chī fàn	have a meal
10	做饭	zuò fàn	cook a meal
11	炒饭	chǎo fàn	fried rice
12	面包	miàn bāo	bread
13	面条	miàn tiáo	noodles
14	鸡蛋	jī dàn	egg
15	蛋糕	dàn gāo	cake
16	水果	shuǐ guǒ	fruit
17	果汁	guǒ zhī	fruit juice
18	茶	chá	tea
19	周末	zhōu mò	weekend
20	有空	yǒu kòng	having free time

My House

1	城市	chéng shì	city
2	市中心	shì zhōng xīn	city center
3	郊区	jiāo qū	suburb
4	小镇	xiǎo zhèn	small town
5	农村	nóng cūn	countryside
6	海边	hǎi biān	seaside
7	山区	shān qū	mountain area
8	客厅	kè tīng	living room
9	饭厅	fàn tīng	dining room
10	厨房	chú fáng	kitchen
11	书房	shū fáng	study
12	卧室	wò shì	bedroom
13	浴室	yù shì	bathroom
14	门	mén	door
15	灯	dēng	light
16	床	chuáng	bed
17	桌子	zhuō zi	table
18	椅子	yǐ zi	chair
19	书架	shū jià	bookshelf
20	沙发	shā fā	sofa

Weather, Landscape and Geography

1	冷	lěng	cold
2	热	rè	hot
3	不冷（也）不热	bù lěng (yě) bú rè	neither cold nor hot
4	晴天	qíng tiān	sunny day
5	多云	duō yún	cloudy
6	有雨 / 下雨	yǒu yǔ / xià yǔ	rainy / to rain
7	有雪 / 下雪	yǒu xuě / xià xuě	snowy / to snow
8	有风 / 刮风	yǒu fēng / guā fēng	windy
9	有雾	yǒu wù	foggy
10	天气	tiān qì	weather
11	气温	qì wēn	air temperature
12	零上 / 零下	líng shàng / líng xià	above zero / below zero
13	度	dù	degree
14	春天	chūn tiān	spring
15	夏天	xià tiān	summer
16	秋天	qiū tiān	autumn
17	冬天	dōng tiān	winter
18	季节	jì jié	season
19	北方	běi fāng	north (region)
20	南方	nán fāng	south (region)

My Town / City

1	市中心	shì zhōng xīn	city centre
2	商店	shāng diàn	shop
3	超市	chāo shì	supermarket
4	银行	yín háng	bank
5	邮局	yóu jú	post office
6	医院	yī yuàn	hospital
7	教堂	jiào táng	church
8	博物馆	bó wù guǎn	museum
9	动物园	dòng wù yuán	zoo
10	公园	gōng yuán	park
11	公共汽车站	gōng gòng qì chē zhàn	bus stop
12	火车站	huǒ chē zhàn	railway station
13	地铁站	dì tiě zhàn	underground station
14	飞机场	fēi jī chǎng	airport
15	停车场	tíng chē chǎng	carpark
16	伦敦	lún dūn	London
17	北京	běi jīng	Beijing
18	上海	shàng hǎi	Shanghai
19	西安	xī ān	Xi'an
20	香港	xiāng gǎng	Hong Kong

Festivals

1	节日	jié rì	festival
2	新年	xīn nián	New Year
3	春节	chūn jié	Chinese New Year
4	端午节	duān wǔ jié	Dragon Boat Festival
5	中秋节	zhōng qiū jié	Mid-Autumn Festival
6	复活节	fù huó jié	Easter
7	圣诞节	shèng dàn jié	Christmas
8	团圆饭	tuán yuán fàn	family reunion dinner
9	中餐	zhōng cān	Chinese meal
10	饺子	jiǎo zi	Chinese dumpling
11	粽子	zòng zi	rice dumpling (related to the Dragon Boat Festival)
12	月饼	yuè bing	mooncake (related to the Mid-Autumn Festival)
13	看月亮	kàn yuè liang	moon watching
14	舞龙	wǔ lóng	dragon dance
15	舞狮	wǔ shī	lion dance
16	红包	hóng bāo	red envelope (Chinese celebratory custom)
17	放鞭炮	fàng biān pào	set off firecrackers
18	龙舟比赛	lóng zhōu bǐ sài	dragon boat race
19	礼物	lǐ wù	gift
20	庆祝会	qìng zhù huì	celebratory party

Transport

1	公共交通工具	gōng gòng jiāo tōng gōng jù	public transport
2	公共汽车	gōng gòng qì chē	bus
3	火车	huǒ chē	train
4	出租车	chū zū chē	taxi
5	自行车	zì xíng chē	bicycle
6	旅游车	lǚ yóu chē	tourist coach
7	飞机	fēi jī	plane
8	地铁	dì tiě	underground
9	高铁	gāo tiě	high-speed train
10	船	chuán	ferry, boat, ship
11	走路	zǒu lù	walk
12	坐	zuò	sit
13	骑	qí	ride
14	开	kāi	drive
15	票	piào	ticket
16	离……很远	lí…hěn yuǎn	far from...
17	离……很近	lí…hěn jìn	close to...
18	只有	zhǐ yǒu	only
19	不用	bú yòng	no need
20	吃药	chī yào	take medicine

Hotels

1	饭店	fàn diàn	hotel, restaurant
2	酒店	jiǔ diàn	hotel, restaurant
3	订房间	dìng fáng jiān	book a room
4	单人房	dān rén fáng	single room
5	双人房	shuāng rén fáng	double room
6	免费	miǎn fèi	free of charge
7	现金	xiàn jīn	cash
8	信用卡	xìn yòng kǎ	credit card
9	餐厅	cān tīng	restaurant; dining hall; canteen
10	健身房	jiàn shēn fáng	gym
11	游泳池	yóu yǒng chí	swimming pool
12	服务台	fú wù tái	service desk; reception desk
13	欢迎	huān yíng	welcome
14	开门	kāi mén	open; open the door
15	关门	guān mén	close; close the door
16	干净	gān jìng	clean
17	安静	ān jìng	quiet
18	方便	fāng biàn	convenient
19	便宜	pián yi	cheap
20	贵	guì	expensive

Events

1	节	jié	festival
2	音乐节	yīn yuè jié	music festival
3	电影节	diàn yǐng jié	film festival
4	艺术节	yì shù jié	art festival
5	旅游节	lǚ yóu jié	tourism festival
6	世界杯	shì jiè bēi	World Cup
7	奥林匹克运动会 / 奥运会	ào lín pǐ kè yùn dòng huì / ào yùn huì	the Olympic Games
8	运动会	yùn dòng huì	sports event; sports day
9	运动场	yùn dòng chǎng	sports field
10	足球场	zú qiú chǎng	football field
11	网球场	wǎng qiú chǎng	tennis court
12	球迷	qiú mí	sports fan (for ball games)
13	影迷 / 电影迷	yǐng mí / diàn yǐng mí	film fan
14	歌迷	gē mí	music fan (for singers)
15	活动	huó dòng	activity
16	参加	cān jiā	participate
17	告诉	gào su	tell
18	乡村	xiāng cūn	rural village
19	草地	cǎo dì	grassy field, turf
20	门票	mén piào	entrance ticket

Holidays

1	假期	jià qī	holiday
2	度假	dù jià	spend a holiday
3	暑假	shǔ jià	summer holiday
4	旅游	lǚ yóu	travel, tourism
5	飞机票	fēi jī piào	air ticket
6	钱包	qián bāo	wallet
7	护照	hù zhào	passport
8	信用卡	xìn yòng kǎ	credit card
9	地图	dì tú	map
10	参观	cān guān	visit
11	手表	shǒu biǎo	wristwatch
12	照相机	zhào xiàng jī	camera
13	拍照片	pāi zhào piàn	take a photo
14	国外	guó wài	abroad
15	亚洲	yà zhōu	Asia
16	欧洲	ōu zhōu	Europe
17	北美洲	běi měi zhōu	North America
18	北京烤鸭	běi jīng kǎo yā	Peking roast duck
19	大熊猫	dà xióng māo	giant panda
20	长城	cháng chéng	the Great Wall

My School Day

1	起床	qǐ chuáng	get up
2	吃早饭	chī zǎo fàn	have breakfast
3	穿校服	chuān xiào fú	wear uniform
4	坐校车	zuò xiào chē	take the school bus
5	上学	shàng xué	go to school
6	上课	shàng kè	go to lessons
7	吃午饭	chī wǔ fàn	have lunch
8	下课	xià kè	finish lessons
9	放学	fàng xué	finish school
10	参加课外活动	cān jiā kè wài huó dòng	participate in extra-curricular activities
11	做作业	zuò zuò yè	do homework
12	吃晚饭	chī wǎn fàn	have dinner
13	睡觉	shuì jiào	go to bed
14	暑假	shǔ jià	summer holiday
15	寒假	hán jià	winter holiday
16	学生	xué sheng	student
17	老师	lǎo shī	teacher
18	校长	xiào zhǎng	headteacher
19	科目	kē mù	subject
20	节	jié	(measure word for school lessons)

In the Classroom

1	中文 / 汉语	zhōng wén / hàn yǔ	Chinese
2	法文	fǎ wén	French
3	西班牙文	xī bān yá wén	Spanish
4	英文	yīng wén	English
5	数学	shù xué	mathematics
6	科学	kē xué	science
7	化学	huà xué	chemistry
8	物理	wù lǐ	physics
9	生物	shēng wù	biology
10	历史	lì shǐ	history
11	地理	dì lǐ	geography
12	美术	měi shù	art
13	电脑	diàn nǎo	computing, computer
14	考试	kǎo shì	exam
15	友好	yǒu hǎo	friendly
16	严厉	yán lì	strict
17	容易	róng yì	easy
18	难	nán	difficult
19	有趣	yǒu qù	fun, interesting
20	明白 / 懂	míng bai / dǒng	understand

My School

1	教室	jiào shì	classroom
2	办公室	bàn gōng shì	office
3	图书馆	tú shū guǎn	library
4	体育馆	tǐ yù guǎn	stadium
5	运动场	yùn dòng chǎng	sports field
6	足球场	zú qiú chǎng	football pitch
7	健身房	jiàn shēn fáng	gym
8	礼堂	lǐ táng	assembly hall
9	食堂	shí táng	canteen
10	餐厅	cān tīng	canteen, restaurant
11	饭厅	fàn tīng	canteen, dining room
12	卫生间	wèi shēng jiān	bathroom
13	洗手间	xǐ shǒu jiān	restroom
14	厕所	cè suǒ	toilet
15	压力	yā lì	pressure
16	快乐	kuài lè	happy
17	好处	hǎo chu	advantage, benefit
18	坏处	huài chu	disadvantage, harm
19	谈谈	tán tan	talk about; talk
20	让	ràng	let, allow

Extra-curricular Activities

1	课外活动	kè wài huó dòng	extra-curricular activities
2	参加足球队比赛	cān jiā zú qiú duì bǐ sài	participate in football team games
3	学打太极拳	xué dǎ tài jí quán	learn Tai Chi
4	去健身房	qù jiàn shēn fáng	go to the gym
5	练体操	liàn tǐ cāo	practise gymnastics
6	骑马	qí mǎ	horse riding
7	参观博物馆	cān guān bó wù guǎn	visit the museum
8	上书法课	shàng shū fǎ kè	attend a calligraphy class
9	学画画	xué huà huà	learn to draw
10	参加学校乐队活动	cān jiā xué xiào yuè duì huó dòng	participate in school band activities
11	参加合唱团	cān jiā hé chàng tuán	join the choir
12	玩儿乐队	wán er yuè duì	play in a band
13	弹钢琴	tán gāng qín	play the piano
14	唱歌	chàng gē	sing
15	唱京剧	chàng jīng jù	sing Beijing opera
16	做中餐	zuò zhōng cān	cook Chinese food
17	学外语	xué wài yǔ	learn foreign languages
18	室外	shì wài	outdoor
19	中餐外卖	zhōng cān wài mài	Chinese takeaway
20	夏令营	xià lìng yíng	summer camp

Gap Year and Work Experience

1	学校社会实践	xué xiào shè huì shí jiàn	school work experience
2	书店	shū diàn	bookstore
3	咖啡馆 / 咖啡厅 / 咖啡店	kā fēi guǎn / kā fēi tīng / kā fēi diàn	café; coffee shop
4	中餐店	zhōng cān diàn	Chinese restaurant
5	快餐店	kuài cān diàn	fast food restaurant
6	超市	chāo shì	supermarket
7	展览馆	zhǎn lǎn guǎn	exhibition hall
8	幼儿园	yòu ér yuán	nursery
9	警察局	jǐng chá jú	police station
10	媒体公司	méi tǐ gōng sī	media company
11	广告公司	guǎng gào gōng sī	advertising company
12	实习	shí xí	do work experience; do an apprenticeship; do an internship
13	实习生	shí xí shēng	trainee; apprentice; intern
14	做服务员	zuò fú wù yuán	be a waiter
15	做护士	zuò hù shi	be a nurse
16	不舒服	bù shū fu	unwell; uncomfortable
17	生病	shēng bìng	get ill
18	送外卖	sòng wài mài	deliver takeaway
19	送报纸	sòng bào zhǐ	deliver newspapers
20	赚钱	zhuàn qián	earn money

Life after Secondary School

1	中学毕业以后	zhōng xué bì yè yǐ hòu	after graduating from secondary school
2	去亚洲旅行	qù yà zhōu lǚ xíng	travel to Asia
3	在餐厅打工	zài cān tīng dǎ gōng	work in a restaurant
4	上大学	shàng dà xué	go to university
5	在工厂实习	zài gōng chǎng shí xí	do work experience in a factory
6	找工作	zhǎo gōng zuò	find a job
7	休学一年	xiū xué yì nián	take a gap year
8	自己开公司	zì jǐ kāi gōng sī	start your own company
9	做生意	zuò shēng yi	do business
10	学开车	xué kāi chē	learn to drive
11	高考	gāo kǎo	National College Entrance Examination
12	同学	tóng xué	classmate
13	同事	tóng shì	colleague
14	申请	shēn qǐng	apply; application
15	成功	chéng gōng	success; successful
16	颜色	yán sè	colour
17	正在 + verb	zhèng zài	(a sentence structure to indicate an action in progress)
18	从……到……	cóng... dào...	from... to...
19	快要 / 就要……了	kuài yào / jiù yào... le	(a sentence structure to indicate events or actions that will take place very soon)
20	……极了	... jí le	extremely...

Job and Career Choices

1	科学家	kē xué jiā	scientist
2	作家	zuò jiā	writer
3	艺术家	yì shù jiā	artist (general)
4	画家	huà jiā	artist (painter)
5	教师	jiào shī	teacher
6	工程师	gōng chéng shī	engineer
7	律师	lǜ shī	lawyer
8	厨师	chú shī	chef
9	演员	yǎn yuán	actor
10	运动员	yùn dòng yuán	sportsperson
11	服务员	fú wù yuán	waiter
12	售货员	shòu huò yuán	shop assistant
13	医生	yī shēng	doctor
14	牙医	yá yī	dentist
15	护士	hù shi	nurse
16	记者	jì zhě	journalist
17	警察	jǐng chá	policeman
18	工厂工人	gōng chǎng gōng rén	factory worker
19	司机	sī jī	driver
20	家庭主妇	jiā tíng zhǔ fù	housewife

Internet, Mobile Technology and Social Media

1	科技	kē jì	technology
2	社交媒体	shè jiāo méi tǐ	social media
3	手机	shǒu jī	mobile phone
4	电脑	diàn nǎo	computer
5	电子游戏	diàn zǐ yóu xì	computer games
6	电子邮件	diàn zǐ yóu jiàn	email
7	电子书	diàn zǐ shū	e-book
8	脸书	liǎn shū	Facebook
9	微信	wēi xìn	WeChat
10	短信	duǎn xìn	text message
11	博客	bó kè	blog
12	网站	wǎng zhàn	website
13	上网	shàng wǎng	go online
14	下载	xià zài	download
15	聊天	liáo tiān	chat
16	打电话	dǎ diàn huà	make a phone call
17	看新闻	kàn xīn wén	read/watch the news
18	学外语	xué wài yǔ	learn foreign languages
19	发	fā	send (e.g. send text, send email)
20	浪费时间	làng fèi shí jiān	waste time

Weather and Environmental Issues

1	少开车	shǎo kāi chē	drive less
2	少用电	shǎo yòng diàn	use less electricity
3	多骑自行车	duō qí zì xíng chē	cycle more
4	多种树	duō zhòng shù	plant more trees
5	二十四小时开空调	èr shí sì xiǎo shí kāi kōng tiáo	24 hours with air conditioning on
6	经常换手机	jīng cháng huàn shǒu jī	frequently change mobile phones
7	在花园用雨水浇花	zài huā yuán yòng yǔ shuǐ jiāo huā	water flowers in the garden with rain water
8	在咖啡店用自己的杯子喝咖啡	zài kā fēi diàn yòng zì jǐ de bēi zi hē kā fēi	drink coffee with your own cup in a coffee shop
9	干净	gān jìng	clean
10	脏水	zāng shuǐ	dirty water
11	河水	hé shuǐ	river water
12	污染	wū rǎn	pollution
13	垃圾	lā jī	rubbish
14	垃圾桶	lā jī tǒng	rubbish bin
15	捡垃圾	jiǎn lā jī	pick up rubbish
16	回收	huí shōu	recycle
17	保护环境 / 环保	bǎo hù huán jìng / huán bǎo	protect the environment / environmental protection
18	空瓶子	kōng píng zi	empty bottle
19	旧报纸	jiù bào zhǐ	old newspaper
20	旧东西	jiù dōng xi	old things

Public Welfare and Volunteer Work

1	做义工	zuò yì gōng	be a volunteer
2	慈善商店	cí shàn shāng diàn	charity shop
3	老人院	lǎo rén yuàn	elderly people's home
4	富人	fù rén	the rich
5	帮助穷人	bāng zhù qióng rén	help the poor
6	病人	bìng rén	patient
7	人口	rén kǒu	population
8	保护动物	bǎo hù dòng wù	animal protection
9	保护中心	bǎo hù zhōng xīn	protection centre
10	捐钱	juān qián	donate money
11	经验	jīng yàn	experience
12	个人简历	gè rén jiǎn lì	resume
13	抽烟	chōu yān	smoke
14	喝酒	hē jiǔ	drink alcohol
15	健康	jiàn kāng	health; healthy
16	全球变暖	quán qiú biàn nuǎn	global warming
17	机会	jī huì	opportunity
18	晚会	wǎn huì	evening party
19	热闹	rè nao	lively
20	应该	yīng gāi	should

12-Minutes Preparation Tips

Before the speaking exam, you will be given 12 minutes to prepare your Role Play (Task 1) and Picture-based Task (Task 2). You will be supervised during this time and you should write your notes on one side of a form/sheet given to you. No dictionaries, phones or writing on stimuli are allowed.

•Number the questions
If the bullet points on the Role Play or Picture-based Task cards are not numbers, write each number on your notes to avoid confusion or mistakes.

•Read the questions carefully and focus on your answers
Look at the topics and prompts and work out how the questions will be asked, and then focus on your answers. It may not always be the case that you know how to say all the words on the task sheet in Chinese but it really doesn't matter — as long as you can apply what you do know to address the question as well as you can.

•Don't write full sentences but only the key words/phrases
For example, a time expression or a verb with 了 to remind yourself to answer a question relating to a past event, 想 or 打算 with an action referring to a future plan; a few adjectives for your opinions, 因为 to lead your justification.

•Write in pinyin to make it easier, if preferred

•Mark the questions that you need to listen to carefully when asked in Chinese
This technique will allow you to take full advantage of Chinese questions during the exam — the question words are not normally placed at the beginning of the questions as many European languages do. The word order in questions are usually exactly the same as how you answer them. So remind yourself to listen to the question carefully, take note of the word order and identify the question word. It will then help you to give your answer in the sentence in the same word order by replacing the question word with the answer phrases that you have prepared.

•Prepare for the unprepared questions
The same above technique applies to those unprepared questions by really focusing on the question words. For example, say a place to replace for 哪儿, a person for 谁, a time for 什么时候, etc. whilst keeping the rest of the sentence in the same structure as the question. You may try to predict those unprepared questions under the topic or context by writing down some short possible responses.

•Write "ASK" as you will have to ask a question or questions
Once again, the word order for questions in Chinese are usually exactly the same as how you answer them. Proofread your questions carefully.

•Emergency phrases
Better still, write down one or two emergency phrases such as:
对不起！ (duì bù qǐ — Sorry and excuse me!)
你说什么？ (nǐ shuō shén me — What did you say?)
请再说一次。(qǐng zài shuō yí cì — Please repeat.)